The Light of the Soul

The
Light of the Soul

Theories of Ideas in Leibniz,
Malebranche, and Descartes

Nicholas Jolley

CLARENDON PRESS · OXFORD
1990

Oxford University Press, Walton Street, Oxford OX2 6DP
Oxford New York Toronto
Delhi Bombay Calcutta Madras Karachi
Petaling Jaya Singapore Hong Kong Tokyo
Nairobi Dar es Salaam Cape Town
Melbourne Auckland
and associated companies in
Berlin Ibadan

Oxford is a trade mark of Oxford University Press

Published in the United States
by Oxford University Press, New York

British Library Cataloguing in Publication Data
Jolley, Nicholas
The light of the soul: theories of ideas in Leibniz,
Malebranche, and Descartes.
1. Knowledge. Ideas
I. Title
121
ISBN 0–19–824443–6

Library of Congress Cataloging in Publication Data
Jolley, Nicholas.
The light of the soul: theories of ideas in Leibniz, Malebranche,
and Descartes / Nicholas Jolley.
Bibliography. Includes index.
1. Idea (Philosophy)—History—17th century. 2. Leibniz,
Gottfried Wilhelm, Freiherr von, 1646–1716—Contributions in theory
of ideas. 3. Malebranche, Nicholas, 1638–1715—Contributions in
theory of ideas. 4. Descartes, René, 1596–1650—Contributions in
theory of ideas. I. Title
B822.J65 1989 121'.4—dc20 89–35608
ISBN 0–19–824443–6

Set by Hope Services (Abingdon) Ltd
Printed in Great Britain by
Biddles Ltd, Guildford & King's Lynn

Acknowledgements

IN the course of writing this book I have been helped by a number of friends and colleagues. Michael Mendelson discussed various issues with me, and in particular gave me the benefit of his knowledge of the Augustinian tradition. I am deeply grateful to Henry Allison, Mark Kulstad, and Ezio Vailati for reading all or parts of an earlier draft, and for making valuable comments. It is a pleasure to thank the British Leibniz Association and the British Society for the History of Philosophy for giving me the opportunity to present my ideas for this book to two enjoyable conferences; I am grateful to members of the audience on both occasions.

Some of the material in Chapters 5, 8, and 9 was first published in the *Philosophical Review*, 97 (1988). I am grateful to the editors for permission to reprint.

Finally, I should like to thank Angela Blackburn and her colleagues at the Oxford University Press for their invaluable assistance at every stage.

A Note on the Translations

ALL quotations from French and Latin works appearing in the body of the text are given in translation. I have generally followed the cited translations; any significant modifications are indicated in the footnotes. All translations other than those cited are my own.

Contents

	Abbreviations	ix
1	Introduction	1
2	Descartes: The Theory of Ideas	12
3	Descartes: Innate Ideas	32
4	Malebranche: The Theory of Ideas	55
5	Malebranche: Vision in God	81
6	Malebranche: Vision in God and Occasionalism	99
7	Malebranche: Ideas and Self-Knowledge	114
8	Leibniz: Ideas and Illumination	132
9	Leibniz: The Defence of Innate Ideas	153
10	Leibniz: Innate Ideas, Reflection, and Self-Knowledge	173
11	Some Further Developments	189
	Bibliography	203
	Index	207

Abbreviations

A   German Academy of Sciences (ed.), *G. W. Leibniz: Sämtliche Schriften und Briefe* (Darmstadt, 1923–). References are to series and volume.

AT   C. Adam and P. Tannery (eds.), *Œuvres de Descartes* (12 vols., Paris, 1897–1913; repr. Paris, 1964–76).

CB   J. Cottingham (trans.), *Descartes' Conversation with Burman* (Oxford, 1976).

CSM   J. Cottingham, R. Stoothoff, and D. Murdoch (trans.), *The Philosophical Writings of Descartes* (2 vols., Cambridge, 1985).

D   W. Doney (trans.), *Nicolas Malebranche: Entretiens sur la Métaphysique/Dialogues on Metaphysics* (New York, 1980).

Dutens   L. L. Dutens (ed.), *G. G. Leibnitii Opera Omnia* (6 vols., Geneva, 1768).

Essay   P. H. Nidditch (ed.), *John Locke: An Essay Concerning Human Understanding* (Oxford, 1975). References are to book, chapter and section.

G   C. I. Gerhardt (ed.), *Die philosophischen Schriften von G. W. Leibniz* (7 vols., Berlin, 1875–90).

Gr   G. Grua (ed.), *G. W. Leibniz: Textes inédits* (2 vols., Paris, 1948).

K   A. Kenny (trans.), *Descartes: Philosophical Letters* (Oxford, 1970).

L   L. E. Loemker (ed.), *G. W. Leibniz: Philosophical Papers and Letters* (2nd edn., Dordrecht, 1969).

NE   *New Essays on Human Understanding* (*Nouveaux essais sur l'entendement humain*). References are to series VI, volume vi of the Academy edition and to the Remnant and Bennett translation. The pagination of Remnant and Bennett is identical with that of the Academy text; one page number thus serves for both.

OCM   A. Robinet (ed.), *Œuvres complètes de Malebranche* (20 vols., Paris, 1958–67).

P   G. H. R. Parkinson (trans. and ed.), *Leibniz: Philosophical Writings* (London, 1973).

R   A. Robinet (ed.), *Malebranche et Leibniz: Relations personnelles* (Paris, 1955).

RB   P. Remnant and J. Bennett (trans. and eds.), *G. W. Leibniz: New Essays on Human Understanding* (Cambridge, 1981).

RB (1982)   P. Remnant and J. Bennett (trans. and eds.), *G. W. Leibniz:*
             New Essays on Human Understanding (Cambridge, 1982),
             abridged edition.
SAT   T. M. Lennon and P. J. Olscamp (trans.), *Nicolas Malebranche:*
             The Search after Truth (Columbus, Ohio, 1980).

I

Introduction

THERE is a story about seventeenth-century philosophy which goes roughly as follows. Descartes broke with the scholastic tradition by advancing an austere new mechanistic theory of the physical world; according to this theory, bodies intrinsically possess only geometrical properties. Descartes thus stripped the world of many properties which were formerly classified as unambiguously physical. Some of the properties which were left over from the new scientific picture of the world could be safely discarded; the powers, natures, and faculties beloved of the scholastics are obvious examples. But there were many other properties, such as secondary qualities, which could not be treated in this cavalier fashion; they had to be located somewhere, and Descartes invented a new concept of mind in order to accommodate them. Indeed, almost every genuine property which could not be counted as physical by the austere standards of seventeenth-century science was now reclassified as mental. Such a drastic procedure of classification might be expected to produce a thoroughly heterogeneous group of items, and this expectation is fulfilled; the Cartesian mind collects such seemingly disparate entities as concepts, thoughts, mental images, sense-perceptions, and sensations.[1]

At the end of the seventeenth century the Cartesian conception of mind was taken over in its essentials by Locke. The most obvious sign of Locke's fundamental acceptance of the new theory is to be found in his terminology. Descartes had adopted the word 'idea' to denote all the items which he had reclassified as mental, and Locke simply followed Descartes in this umbrella usage.[2] Of course, no one would deny that there are important differences between

---

[1] Some aspects of this account of 17th cent. philosophy are found in R. Rorty, *Philosophy and the Mirror of Nature* (Princeton, 1979). Cf. M. D. Wilson, 'Skepticism without Indubitability', *Journal of Philosophy*, 81 (1984), 537–44.

[2] For standard criticisms of Locke's use of the term 'idea' see G. J. Warnock, *Berkeley* (Harmondsworth, 1953), 64; G. Berkeley, *Philosophical Writings*, ed. D. M. Armstrong (New York and London, 1965), 8.

Locke and Descartes. For Descartes, the paradigm ideas are
intellectual items; they are entities such as thoughts of God and
triangles. On Descartes's view the mind is essentially pure intellect,
and sense-perceptions are explained as confused modes of thinking
which arise from the mind's union with the body. For Locke, by
contrast, it is the data of sensation and reflection which are basic;
intellectual ideas are explained as the result of performing various
operations (such as abstraction) on the raw materials which
sensation and reflection provide. In spite of these differences
between Locke and Descartes, it is widely agreed that they
subscribe to the same basic picture of mind; for both philosophers,
the mental collects almost everything which is not physical by
seventeenth-century standards. Thus Richard Rorty can write not
merely of a Cartesian–Lockean use of the term 'idea' but of a notion
of mind that is common to Descartes and Locke.[3]

According to the story I am sketching, then, the revolutionary
Cartesian conception of the mental enjoyed great and almost
immediate success. Indeed, it was the dominant theory throughout the seventeenth century; it was largely unquestioned and
unchallenged except by materialists such as Hobbes and unrepentant
scholastics and other conservatives. In any case, whatever its
birthpangs, it emerges triumphant at the end of the seventeenth
century. The essentials of the theory were thoroughly absorbed by
Locke, and as a result of Locke's prestige, it entered into the
philosophical mainstream of the Enlightenment. Indeed, the new
theory of mind was broadly accepted throughout the eighteenth
century until the time of Reid and Kant.

This picture of seventeenth-century philosophy is, I believe,
grossly distorted and oversimplified. Its defenders may be right that
the Cartesian–Lockean view won out in the seventeenth century,
but what they fail to notice is that it did so only after a struggle. In
reality the Cartesian–Lockean view encountered a powerful current
of opposition. This opposition was not confined to materialists on
the left and scholastics on the right; it emerged even within the
ranks of those who were broadly sympathetic to Descartes's
enterprise. Here the most important figure is Malebranche, a
philosopher who is often classified as a Cartesian. Although he has
aroused some interest in recent years, it is still true to say that he

[3] R. Rorty, pp. 6, 28.

remains a largely unknown and misunderstood figure; today, he is mainly confined to footnotes where his name is linked with a garbled version of the doctrine of occasionalism. Yet in his own day Malebranche was almost universally regarded as a philosopher of the front rank, challenging comparison with Descartes, Leibniz, and Spinoza.[4] Leibniz himself, for instance, held Malebranche in high esteem; he had no hesitation in placing him above Locke in philosophical importance. Writing to a correspondent about Locke, he remarked that 'Plato, Aristotle, Descartes, Hobbes in places, and Malebranche wrote much more profoundly.'[5] Perhaps we can help to bring out the importance of Malebranche by means of an imaginary example. Suppose that some future generation were to write a history of twentieth-century philosophy from which Wittgenstein was almost totally excluded; perhaps his name appeared only in footnotes in conjunction with a misleading reference to something mysteriously called 'the private language argument'. Whatever other merits it might have, such a work would not be a very good history of twentieth-century philosophy. To omit Malebranche from our picture of seventeenth-century philosophy is to run the risk of comparable distortion.

What was the nature of Malebranche's opposition to the Cartesian or Cartesian–Lockean view of the mind? In the first place and most importantly, Malebranche protests against the fundamental Cartesian tendency to classify everything non-physical as mental. Malebranche does not dispute the Cartesian thesis that the mental and the physical are exclusive categories; what he denies is that they are exhaustive. Now it has been claimed that Descartes himself tends on occasion to express dissatisfaction with the limitations imposed by his official dualism.[6] Descartes sometimes seems to suggest that there is a need for a third category of entities; when discussing the faculties of sensation and imagination, he writes as if they are 'hybrids' of thought and extension which fall into a separate and irreducible category of their own. There is thus a

[4] Cf. L. E. Loeb, *From Descartes to Hume: Continental Metaphysics and the Development of Modern Philosophy* (Ithaca and London, 1981), 191.

[5] 'Longe profundiore, Plato, Aristoteles, Cartesius, Hobbius alicubi et Malebranchius dedere': Leibniz to Bierling, undated draft of the letter of 24 Oct. 1709 (G vii. 485); Leibniz Briefwechsel 67, fo. 51ᵛ, Niedersächsische Landesbibliothek, Hanover.

[6] See J. Cottingham, *Descartes* (Oxford, 1986), 127–32. Cf. also R. C. Richardson, 'The "Scandal" of Cartesian Interactionism', *Mind*, 91 (1982), 20–37.

strain of 'trialism' in Descartes's philosophy.[7] Malebranche may also be called a 'trialist', but his 'trialism' is not of this kind. Malebranche holds that there is a 'third realm' of entities which are not reducible to either the mental or the physical; reverting to the Augustinian tradition in philosophy, Malebranche calls these items 'ideas'. As we shall see, Malebranche expresses his doctrine in unashamedly theological terms, and we must always keep this in mind in our positive characterization of his ontology. But there can be no question about how to characterize the negative part of his thesis; Malebranche's ideas are neither mental nor physical entities.

Secondly, Malebranche quarrels with a subsidiary element in the Cartesian–Lockean picture of mind which we have not yet brought up. In both Descartes and Locke there is a tendency to imply that intentionality is a defining mark of the mental. At the very least it is fair to say that Locke and Descartes play down the apparent difference between mental phenomena which are intentional and those which are not. Richard Rorty, for instance, complains of the Cartesian–Lockean tendency to conflate pains and beliefs, in spite of the fact that pains, unlike beliefs, do not seem to be about anything.[8] This tendency is of course implicit in the Cartesian–Lockean umbrella use of the term 'idea'. By contrast, Malebranche firmly resists the temptation to treat intentionality as a characteristic of all mental phenomena. Within the sphere of mental acts, Malebranche recognizes a class of items which have no objects of any kind; such items are called *sentiments*. In this category, as we shall see, Malebranche places sensations such as pains and all perceptions of secondary qualities. Thus Malebranche challenges the Cartesian theory of mind in two ways; he rejects its claims about both the scope and the nature of the mental.

Malebranche's attack on the Cartesian theory of the mind was so important that it deserved a serious response, and such a response was indeed forthcoming. The philosopher who is best known for his opposition to Malebranche is of course Antoine Arnauld; in *Des vraies et des fausses idées* (*On True and False Ideas*) he defended Cartesian orthodoxy in an uncompromising, and somewhat uncomprehending, fashion. Yet in many ways Malebranche's most formidable opponent was a philosopher who was not closely identified with the Cartesians: Leibniz. Somewhat

---

[7] The term is used by Cottingham, p. 127.
[8] R. Rorty, p. 27.

curiously in view of his Jansenist sympathies, Arnauld was not much attracted to the Augustinian elements in Malebranche's philosophy. Leibniz, by contrast, is drawn to this side of Malebranche's philosophy, and he appreciates the strength of his position; he concedes that there is a prima-facie case for recognizing the existence of irreducibly abstract entities. Yet Leibniz is also subject to the pull of other philosophical forces. As Benson Mates has recently emphasized, there are important nominalist tendencies in Leibniz's philosophy.[9] Despite his attraction to Plato and Augustine Leibniz cannot ultimately countenance the existence of abstract entities. Thus Leibniz is in a strong position to defend a broadly Cartesian thesis on ideas while remaining sympathetic to the thrust of Malebranche's case. Unlike Arnauld, Leibniz sees that a successful answer to Malebranche requires a reductionist strategy; in other words, he must show how logical items can be reduced to the mental. But Leibniz does not just take issue with Malebranche's 'trialism'; he also challenges the other element in Malebranche's resistance to the Cartesian theory of mind. By means of his famous doctrine of expression, Leibniz tends to reinstate the Cartesian–Lockean position on the intentional character of all mental phenomena.

In this study we shall focus on Descartes, Malebranche, and Leibniz as major participants in a dialogue on the nature of ideas, and ultimately, on the nature of the mind. The decision to focus on these three figures may require some justification; some readers may be surprised that Malebranche, rather than Spinoza, is treated as a central figure. By virtue of his pantheistic metaphysics Spinoza was of course a powerful adversary for Leibniz and other seventeenth-century philosophers, but it is arguable that in his epistemology he was decidedly less influential than Malebranche.[10] Thus no distortion is involved in assigning Spinoza a position on the margins of our study. By isolating the views of Descartes, Malebranche, and Leibniz for special attention it is possible to tell a historically important story which is also philosophically coherent. Indeed, the story exhibits a degree of dialectical development. For

[9] B. Mates, *Philosophy of Leibniz: Metaphysics and Language* (Oxford, 1986), esp. p. 246. I am much indebted to Mates's persuasive discussion of the nominalistic tendencies of Leibniz's metaphysics.

[10] It may also be remarked that Spinoza's theory of ideas is unclear with respect to the major lines of division discussed in this study. See e.g. J. Bennett, *Study of Spinoza's Ethics* (Cambridge, 1984), 50–4.

Malebranche reacts against the Cartesian theory of ideas on the grounds that it conflates logic and psychology. Leibniz in turn responds to Malebranche by seeking to integrate his nominalist intuitions in a broadly Cartesian framework.

It is scarcely an exaggeration to say that Malebranche mounted a counter-revolution against the Cartesian theory of mind. But in one respect this characterization is a little misleading. It would be a mistake to convey the impression that Malebranche sees himself as wholly turning his back on Descartes. Although of course Malebranche can be openly critical of Descartes, he is also capable of portraying himself as Descartes's true heir. Here we encounter a situation which is not unfamiliar in the history of philosophy, and which was to recur in the quarrels of Hegelians and Marxists. The death of a great and original philosopher such as Descartes tends to produce a number of rival claimants for the succession. Malebranche, Leibniz, and Arnauld all embraced different theories of ideas, but each was capable on occasion of claiming that he spoke with the authority of Descartes.

Such claims to the succession were not wholly implausible, for Descartes himself spoke with an ambiguous voice on the nature of ideas. As Robert McRae has written, there are:

three main conceptions of 'idea' fundamentally opposed to one another, which can be found among Descartes' successors and all of which find expression in the writings of Descartes himself. The three conceptions are (a) that an idea is an object (Malebranche, Locke, Berkeley); (b) that an idea is an act (Spinoza, Arnauld); (c) that an idea is a disposition (Leibniz).[11]

There are points at which McRae's analysis might be challenged. For one thing, in spite of their similar definitions of 'idea', the differences between Malebranche and Locke are so great that it is doubtful whether it is helpful to assimilate them as proponents of the 'object' theory of ideas. Certainly Locke did not develop, as Malebranche did, a consistent theory of ideas as non-mental, abstract entities. Moreover, it is less clear than McRae implies that Descartes in fact articulated a theory of ideas as mental dispositions; there are hints of such a theory in Descartes, but they remain little more than hints. Yet in spite of these cavils, McRae is surely right in his core thesis; Descartes's successors advanced different theories of

---

[11] R. McRae, ' "Idea" as a Philosophical Term in the Seventeenth Century', *Journal of the History of Ideas*, 26 (1965), 175.

ideas, and they did so on the basis of what they found in Descartes himself.

As is so often the case in seventeenth-century philosophy, the debate does not remain at a purely philosophical level, or at what we today would regard as a purely philosophical level; rather, it has an important theological dimension. Each of the parties to the debate over ideas seeks to ally his philosophical position with a major doctrine of Christian theology. In each case the theological doctrines serve as slogans or rallying-cries by means of which philosophers can gain adherents to their cause. It is tempting to suggest that in the seventeenth century philosophical claims needed, not just to be argued for, but also to be legitimated by appealing to Christian dogmas. However that may be, the debate over the nature of ideas was presented as a conflict between two competing theological models of the mind's powers and of its relationship to God. One model represents the mind as cognitively powerless without divine assistance; the other model represents it as to a large degree cognitively self-sufficient. As we shall see, some important qualifications must be made, but we can say in general terms that Malebranche is on one side, Leibniz and Descartes are on the other.

Malebranche has philosophical arguments for his theory of ideas, but he also supports his theory by appealing to the Christian doctrine that God (specifically, the Word) is the light of the soul. As St John puts it at the opening of his Gospel, God is the true light which illumines everyone who comes into the world ('*Lux vera quae illuminat omnem hominem venientem in hunc mundum*').[12] Malebranche of course was not the first philosopher to give St John's text an epistemological interpretation; on the contrary, he is self-consciously following in the tradition of Augustine and Christian Platonism. Indeed, Malebranche sees himself as reverting to the Augustinian doctrine of divine illumination; if the mind is to achieve knowledge it must be enlightened by the light of God's ideas. We shall see that Malebranche seeks to carry the doctrine of divine illumination to lengths which Augustine himself had not envisaged.[13]

The opening of St John's Gospel is not the only part of Christian teaching which seems to leave its mark on Malebranche's philosophy.

---

[12] John 1: 9. See Malebranche, *Search after Truth*, III.2.6 (*OCM*, i. 440; *SAT* 231).

[13] On Malebranche's relationship to the Augustinian tradition see C. J. McCracken, *Malebranche and British Philosophy* (Oxford, 1983), 54–8.

It is not, I think, fanciful to see a remarkable isomorphism between Malebranche's epistemological models and the Christian—especially Pauline—theology of sin and grace. According to Pauline theology, our souls are immersed in sin unless they are acted upon by divine grace; according to Malebranche's philosophy, our minds are immersed in sensations of no cognitive value unless they are illuminated by the light of God's ideas. Malebranche's epistemology is, as it were, Pauline theology transposed into a philosophical key; sensations take the place of sin, and the light of ideas takes the place of divine grace. Such a parallel becomes less fanciful when we remember that there is a famous precedent in the mainstream of seventeenth-century philosophy. Various writers have noticed that Descartes's theory of error in the 'Fourth Meditation' is a philosophical variation on a traditional solution to the theological problem of evil.[14]

Historically, it would not of course be surprising if Malebranche's epistemology were influenced by models drawn from Pauline theology. For Malebranche, as we have seen, was an Augustinian, and it is well known that Augustine's own theology of grace is thoroughly Pauline. Indeed, Malebranche might have been happy to acknowledge the parallel and the influence. None the less, the Pauline theology of grace remains in the background of his philosophy; it is the doctrine of St John's Gospel which he tends to parade. Moreover, to emphasize the parallel with St Paul is possibly misleading, for it might suggest that Malebranche was an innovator in exploiting the philosophical potential of theological doctrines. But Malebranche would have been the first to admit that he was not original in this respect; he would have pointed to the tradition of Augustine and Christian Platonism. Malebranche's originality lies in exploiting this tradition for the twin purposes of criticizing and extending Cartesian philosophy.

The Book of Genesis, rather than St John's Gospel, furnishes the key text for Leibniz and Descartes; they invoke the doctrine that man (i.e. the human mind) is made in the image of God. Edward Craig has shown that the influence of this doctrine was pervasive in seventeenth-century philosophy,[15] but obviously, as it stands, the doctrine is extremely indeterminate; some definite

---

[14] See B. Williams, *Descartes: The Project of Pure Enquiry* (Hassocks, 1978), 169; M. Wilson, *Descartes* (London, 1978), 150.

[15] E. Craig, *Mind of God and the Works of Man* (Oxford, 1988).

philosophical content must be introduced to fix the shape of the likeness.[16] The choice of content varies from philosopher to philosopher. In the case of Descartes, Craig denies that it is a thesis about knowledge which fixes the shape of the likeness; it is rather a thesis about the nature of the will and its freedom.[17] But this is an unduly restrictive reading of Descartes. In fact, the Genesis text is intimately bound up with Descartes's whole campaign against scholasticism. Much that is most revolutionary in Descartes's philosophy of mind and knowledge is captured in his insistence on the doctrine that the mind is made in the image of God. As we shall see, the doctrine is even implicit in Descartes's choice of the term 'idea'.

The 'image of God' doctrine permeates much of Descartes's philosophy but it does not dominate it; contrary influences are at work, such as the creation of the eternal truths. In Leibniz's philosophy, by contrast, the Genesis doctrine achieves an almost complete ascendancy; it is pushed further perhaps than ever before. Previous writers, such as Galileo, had argued that human knowledge resembles divine knowledge intensively if not extensively; God knows infinitely more truths than we do, but at least in mathematics we are capable of knowing truths with the same certainty and immediacy as he does.[18] Leibniz gives a radically new twist to this thesis. By virtue of his metaphysics he is in a position to claim that human knowledge resembles divine knowledge in its extensive aspect; since every mind expresses the whole universe according to its point of view, there is a real sense in which it is omniscient.[19] Such omniscience is of course unlike divine omniscience in that it is, for the most part, extremely confused; but Leibniz need not deny that, in the case of a priori truths, human knowledge can be close to godlike in its quality.[20]

That God is the light of the soul and that man is made in the image of God are doctrines explicitly asserted in Scripture. Thus, as Christian philosophers, the parties to the debate could not simply reject the doctrine which their opponents invoked as rallying-cries.

---

[16] Ibid. 13–14.
[17] Ibid. 24. Craig overlooks the fact that on Descartes's account the will plays a crucial role in belief, and is thus involved in epistemological issues.
[18] Ibid. 18–20.
[19] *Discourse on Metaphysics*, 9 (G iv. 434; L, p. 308); 'A Specimen of Discoveries', G vii. 311; P, p. 77.
[20] See e.g. *Principles of Nature and of Grace*, 15 (G vi. 605; L, p. 640).

This of course did not really tie their hands. It would seem that there was an obvious strategy available to them; accept the doctrine invoked by their opponents, but deny that it had any philosophical implications. There was perhaps reason to fear that such a strategy might have boomeranged, and in fact the philosophers under study tend not to take this line. Rather, we find that Malebranche and Leibniz at least try to accommodate their opponents' theological doctrines within their own philosophical systems.

Vague as the theological doctrines are, they go with some philosophical positions better than others. Consequently, Malebranche and Leibniz are not very convincing in their attempts at accommodation. Malebranche tries to find room for the doctrine that the human mind is made in the image of God, but the doctrine does not really belong in his philosophical system. For *pace* Craig, Malebranche's position is not that there is a similarity of structure between the human mind and the mind of God;[21] it is rather that the cognitive impotence of the human mind can be remedied only by divine assistance; it must be illuminated by the light of God's ideas. Similarly, Leibniz strives valiantly to do justice to the doctrine of divine illumination. Indeed, there are passages in the *Discourse on Metaphysics* which could have been written by Malebranche himself; Leibniz, like Malebranche, quotes the opening of St John's Gospel and claims to find it philosophically significant. But divine illumination is out of place in Leibniz's system, for it has no real work to do within the nominalist framework of his metaphysics.

Theories of ideas are thus bound up with competing philosophical and theological views of the mind and of its relationship to God. Not surprisingly, then, the topic of ideas leads off into other central areas of seventeenth-century philosophy. Thus the focus of the present book is much broader than it might at first appear. Some of these connections with other issues are of course obvious. Views on the nature of ideas determine, or at least constrain, views on the topic of innate ideas; we shall thus approach the debate on this issue between Leibniz, Malebranche, and Descartes by way of their competing conceptions of ideas. The debate over innate ideas is historically tied to a debate over self-knowledge; here too we shall see how philosophical positions are constrained by theories of the nature of ideas.

[21] Craig, p. 66.

Other connections, however, are a good deal less obvious; indeed, they may even surprise us. Malebranche, as we shall see, has an illuminating diagnosis of some of the deepest problems in Descartes's philosophy. It is to a fundamental mistake about the nature of ideas that Malebranche traces Descartes's difficulties with the charge of circularity; the conflation of logic and psychology left him unable to conquer scepticism. It is to the same fundamental mistake about the nature of ideas that Malebranche traces Descartes's bizarre teaching concerning the creation of the eternal truths. The desire to avoid Cartesian voluntarism and to defeat scepticism in a way that Descartes could not is one of the major motives for Malebranche's whole theory of ideas. Thus the debate over ideas takes us to the very heart of seventeenth-century philosophy.

In their eagerness to reject Aristotle and his legacy, seventeenth-century philosophers sometimes convey the impression that they are engaged in a total rejection of the philosophical past. But, as many people have observed, this impression is misleading. Philosophers in the period were not really turning their back on the tradition as a whole; rather, they were casting down Aristotle in order to raise up Plato. The presence of Platonic elements in Descartes has often been noticed; his conception of the body as the mind's prison is an obvious example. But in his theory of the objects of knowledge Descartes was not a Platonist; other philosophers— Leibniz to some extent and Malebranche in particular—were far more sympathetic to the Platonic tradition in this area. This book is a study of a seventeenth-century debate over how far philosophers should be prepared to travel on the road to Platonism.

2

Descartes
The Theory of Ideas

IN the 'Third Replies' Descartes explains to Hobbes why he had chosen the word 'idea' as the central term in his theory of knowledge:

I used the word 'idea' because it was the standard philosophical term used to refer to the forms of perception belonging to the divine mind, even though we recognize that God does not possess any corporeal imagination. And besides, there was not any more appropriate term at my disposal.[1]

In this passage Descartes acknowledges that his use of the term 'idea' marks a break with philosophical tradition. Commentators have of course noticed that Descartes was an innovator in this respect, and that he himself was aware of his originality. Kenny, for instance, is typical when he writes that 'Descartes was consciously giving [the word 'idea'] a new sense. Before him, philosophers used it to refer to archetypes in the divine intellect: it was a new departure to use it systematically for the contents of a human mind.'[2] But one remarkable feature of this passage has failed to receive the attention it deserves. Descartes does not claim, as we might expect, that he is using the term 'idea' *in spite of* the fact that it had been traditionally used to refer to the forms of divine perception. On the contrary, he says that he is using the term *because* of this fact. In other words, Descartes seems to be hinting that in his philosophy the human mind is taking on at least some of the properties which were formerly associated with God alone.

Descartes's remark to Hobbes suggests, I believe, a remarkably fruitful way of approaching the Cartesian revolution in the philosophy of mind and knowledge. Taking our cue from Descartes,

---

[1] 'Third Replies', AT vii. 181; CSM ii. 127–8.
[2] A. Kenny, *Descartes: A Study of his Philosophy* (New York, 1968), 96. It is worth noting that in Descartes's early philosophy the term 'idea' denotes physical states of the brain. On Descartes's early theory of ideas, see J. Rée, *Descartes* (London, 1974), ch. 5.

we can see that his break with scholasticism can indeed be aptly characterized by saying that in Descartes's philosophy the mind has become godlike. Indeed, despite his lip-service to the Genesis text, it was just this implication of the Cartesian revolution which so offended Malebranche. Later in this chapter we shall use the hint that Descartes provides us to define some of the main features of his opposition to scholasticism in the philosophy of mind. But, first of all, we must explore the more familiar features of the Cartesian revolution to which Kenny draws our attention. For to say that ideas, for Descartes, are not divine archetypes but mental or psychological entities leaves a number of questions unanswered. We shall see that in Descartes's mature writings there are at least two, and possibly three, main conceptions of 'idea'. As McRae notes, each of these conceptions was developed with greater consistency by Descartes's successors.[3]

Ideas: The Problem of Terminology

In the 'Second Replies' Descartes gives what looks like his official definition of 'idea': '*Idea*: I understand this term to mean the form of any given thought, immediate perception of which makes me aware of the thought'.[4] This definition is couched in scholastic terminology, and is thus not perspicuous to the modern reader. Perhaps it was not immediately perspicuous to a seventeenth-century reader familiar with scholasticism; for as Kenny remarks, 'the word "form" is a piece of scholastic jargon, but no scholastic theory seems to be involved'.[5] Before trying to interpret the definition, it is useful to look at several distinctions that Descartes draws while discussing ideas. As we shall see, the word 'form' and its cognates appear in two of them.

Descartes's most famous distinction with regard to ideas occurs in the 'Third Meditation'. While laying the foundations for his first proof of the existence of God, Descartes distinguishes between the 'formal' and 'objective' reality of ideas: ideas have formal (or intrinsic) reality by virtue of being modes of thought, or mental events; and they have objective reality by virtue of their object or

---

[3] R. McRae, ' "Idea" as a Philosophical Term in the Seventeenth Century', *Journal of the History of Ideas*, 26 (1965), 175.

[4] 'Second Replies', AT vii. 160; CSM ii. 113.

[5] Kenny, *Descartes*, p. 110.

representational content.[6] Here Descartes is drawing a distinction
between two irreducible aspects of all ideas. On other occasions,
however, he employs scholastic jargon in order to distinguish
between two different senses of the term 'idea'. In the 'Fourth
Replies' Descartes tells Arnauld that he has misunderstood his
position on the issue of material falsity because he has failed to
attend to the distinction between 'idea' in the formal sense and 'idea'
in the material sense:

> When M. Arnauld says 'if cold is merely an absence, there cannot be an idea
> of cold which represents it as a positive thing', it is clear that he is dealing
> solely with an idea taken in the *formal* sense. Since ideas are forms of a kind,
> and are not composed of any matter, when we think of them as representing
> something, we are taking them not *materially* but *formally*. If, however, we
> were considering them not as representing this or that but simply as
> operations of the intellect, then it could be said that we were taking them
> materially, but in that case they would have no reference to the truth or
> falsity of their objects.[7]

And in the Preface to the Reader in the *Meditations* Descartes draws
a distinction between two senses of 'idea' in different terms again.
Descartes answers an objector as follows:

> 'Idea' can be taken materially, as an operation of the intellect, in which case
> it cannot be said to be more perfect than me. Alternatively, it can be taken
> objectively, as the thing represented by that operation; and this thing, even
> if it is not regarded as existing outside the intellect, can still, in virtue of its
> essence, be more perfect than myself.[8]

Thus Descartes gives us the following three distinctions: (1) the
formal versus the objective reality of ideas; (2) 'idea' in the formal
sense versus 'idea' in the material sense; (3) 'idea' in the objective
sense versus 'idea' in the material sense.

It is difficult to imagine anything more calculated to confuse the
reader than these three distinctions. The problem is not just that in
each case Descartes is employing scholastic jargon; it is rather that
Descartes seems to employ this jargon in such a haphazard and
inconstant manner. It is as if on each occasion Descartes simply
reached for a traditional scholastic pair of opposites without any
regard to consistency. But two results seem to emerge from these
passages. First, it is clear that (2) and (3) really come to the same

---

[6] 'Third Meditation', AT vii. 40–1; CSM ii. 27–8.
[7] ''Fourth Replies', AT vii. 232; CSM ii. 162–3.
[8] Preface, *Meditations*, AT vii. 8; CSM ii. 7.

thing; in each case Descartes is distinguishing between 'idea' in the sense of mental event and 'idea' in the sense of content or object of thought. However, while he uses the word 'material' in the same sense in both cases, Descartes confuses the reader by using 'formal' in (2) to mean what he calls 'objective' in (3). Secondly, and relatedly, it seems clear that 'form' in (2) is used in a quite different sense from 'form' in (1). For in (2) 'form' means intentional object or representational content; in (1), however, the formal reality of an idea is the intrinsic reality which an idea possesses by virtue of being a mode of thought or mental event; in this sense 'form' is not synonymous with 'object', but opposed to it. So while Descartes is at least consistent in his use of 'material' and 'objective', he seems to employ the term 'form' and its cognates in two diametrically opposite senses.

In view of his inconsistency in this respect, it is unfortunate, to say the least, that the word 'form' is central to Descartes's official definition of 'idea'. The definition obviously prompts us to ask which of the two senses of 'form' is in question. As Kenny notes, a knowledge of scholasticism will not solve this problem for us, for no scholastic theory is involved. Kenny himself suggests that 'by calling ideas "forms" Descartes seems to mean simply that they are nonmaterial representations of things'.[9] But unfortunately this suggestion is ambiguous in just the respect that concerns us most. To say that an idea is a representation does not settle the question of whether it is a representing or that which is represented. There is even a further, associated ambiguity in the term 'nonmaterial'. If Kenny means that an idea is a representing, then it will be non-material in the straightforward sense that it is the mode of a thinking substance (*res cogitans*). If, on the other hand, Kenny means that an idea is the object represented, then it could be non-material, not because it is mental, but because, as a form or essence, it is an abstract, logical entity.

Kenny's own positive interpretative suggestion is thus not particularly helpful. Fortunately, however, the context of Descartes's definition comes to our aid; this seems to establish beyond reasonable doubt that the term 'form' is being used in the sense of distinction (1), not distinction (2). For, after giving his definition, Descartes goes on to talk about the objective reality of ideas,

[9] Kenny, *Descartes*, pp. 110–11.

and this would be quite inexplicable if the term 'form' had already been earmarked for the object or representational content of thought.[10] Indeed, if ideas were simply identified by definition with representational content, it would hardly make sense to go on to say that ideas *have* representational content.

Descartes's official definition of 'idea' must thus be read in the spirit of the 'Third Meditation' where ideas are modes of thought which have representational content. This interpretation receives further support from external sources; it is confirmed by the authority of Arnauld and Leibniz. In his famous controversy with Malebranche, Arnauld, like his antagonist, was greatly concerned to establish just what Descartes meant by 'idea', and it was this definition from the 'Second Replies' which Arnauld adduced as decisive evidence that, for Descartes, ideas are perceptions—i.e. mental events.[11] Indeed, Arnauld went so far as to claim somewhat implausibly that Descartes always understood the term 'idea' in this way. Similarly, Leibniz in the *Discourse on Metaphysics* and other writings contrasted those, like Arnauld, who took ideas to be forms of thought with those, like Malebranche, who took them to be objects of thought.[12] Everything that Leibniz says about forms of thought shows that he understood them in the same way as Arnauld; in other words, for Leibniz they are mental acts or events.

Despite the traps that Descartes lays for his readers, the mystery surrounding his official definition of 'idea' can be dispelled. But a mystery none the less remains. If Descartes is advancing an act or event conception of ideas, why does he call them 'forms'? And why does he also use this term for the representational content of thought? How is it that Descartes can use the term 'form' in two such very different ways? The key to the solution of this puzzle seems to lie in the fact that forms are essences. Strictly speaking, Descartes does not equivocate on the word 'form', but he gets ensnared in a terminological thicket because he wants to talk about essences in two very different contexts. Ideas are called 'forms of thought' because it is of the essence of a thought that it is a mode of a mind, or as Descartes sometimes says, an operation

---

[10] 'Second Replies', AT vii. 161; CSM ii. 113–14.

[11] A. Arnauld, *Des vraies et des fausses idées*, ch. vi, in *Œuvres de Messire Antoine Arnauld*, xxxviii (Paris, 1780; repr. Brussels, 1967), 205. Cf. S. Nadler, *Arnauld and the Cartesian Philosophy of Ideas* (Princeton, 1989), ch. v.

[12] *Discourse on Metaphysics*, 26 (G iv. 451; L, p. 320).

of the understanding.[13] But forms—i.e. essences—are also what is represented by an idea (= occurrent thought). We can illustrate this double use of 'form' by means of an example. When I have an idea (= occurrent thought) of a triangle, a certain form or essence, namely, a triangle, is the object or content of my idea; but my idea (= occurrent thought) is formally or essentially a mode of my mind. We could also do justice to Descartes's position by saying that an idea (= occurrent thought) is intrinsically a mode of mind.

Ideas: Events, Objects, and Dispositions

Arnauld may not have been right about everything but he was right in his basic intuition: ideas, for Descartes, being forms of thought, are datable mental events. Following some commentators we can also say that Descartes is officially committed to an act theory of ideas. Descartes himself says on one occasion that 'I do not claim that the idea is different from the action itself'.[14] Yet Arnauld was wrong if he supposed that Descartes was unwavering in his commitment to the act theory of ideas, for, as we have seen, Descartes himself admits that the term 'idea' is ambiguous: it can be used to refer to, not the act or event, but the object of thought. With Vere Chappell, we will say that in addition to ideas$_m$ (acts or events), there are also ideas$_o$ (objects of thought).[15]

Descartes's admission that there are ideas$_o$ raises a serious problem in the ontology of thought. It is clear that ideas$_m$ are mental or psychological items, but it is less clear that this is also true of ideas$_o$; it seems possible that they could be abstract, logical entities existing over and above mental events. Thus the question arises as to whether, when ideas are ideas$_o$, Descartes is working with the same ontology as in the 'Third Meditation'—where content is simply an aspect of thought. It would of course be a mistake to suppose that there must be a difference of ontology where ideas$_o$ are in question. From the fact that Descartes uses the term 'idea' to denote objective realities, it does not follow that these objective realities are ontologically distinct from mental events. It

---

[13] Some support for this interpretation is provided by Descartes's letter to Regius, June 1642, AT iii. 565; K, p. 133.

[14] Descartes to Mersenne, 28 Jan. 1641, AT iii. 295; K, p. 93.

[15] V. Chappell, 'The Theory of Ideas', in A. Rorty (ed.), *Essays on Descartes's Meditations* (Berkeley and Los Angeles, 1986), 177–98.

would similarly be a mistake to suppose that Spinoza's talk of minds and bodies means that he is committed to an ontology of substantial dualism.

The importance of the issue should be obvious. If ideas$_o$ are abstract entities, they can—and perhaps must—pre-exist and post-exist the appearance of minds on the scene; if, on the other hand, they are aspects of mental events, it would seem that they exist only when they are being thought of by Cartesian minds. A further issue at stake is whether two people can think of the very same object. If ideas$_o$ are abstract entities, then it would seem that there is a perfectly literal sense in which when you and I think of a triangle in general, we are thinking of the very same object (= idea$_o$); in other words, there is an abstract entity to which both our minds are related in thinking. If, however, ideas$_o$ are merely aspects of thought, then to say that you and I are thinking of the same object can be no more than a *façon de parler*. Problems like these are isomorphic with those which arise with regard to bodies in Berkeley's idealism.

Vere Chappell in his paper testifies implicitly to the exegetical difficulty of the issue by taking an ambiguous stand. At first it seems that Chappell takes up a definite position on the issue:

to what extent are an idea$_m$ and its associated idea$_o$ two distinct entities? Here again it is useful to know beforehand what the answer will be. It is that these are not distinct entities at all—not one individual thing and then a second, different one—but are rather one thing on the one hand, and an aspect or component of that same thing on the other. The idea$_m$ and the idea$_o$ only differ from one another, to use Descartes' own expression, by a 'distinction of reason'.[16]

Yet at the end of his paper Chappell seems to reverse himself: he writes that 'ideas$_o$ do seem to be abstract entities for Descartes, in a way that ideas$_m$ are not'.[17] Chappell does not spell out what he means by an 'abstract entity', but he seems to be suggesting that Descartes does after all think of ideas$_o$ as existing over and above ideas$_m$; in other words, the *esse* of ideas$_o$ is not *percipi* or even *posse percipi*. If this were in fact Descartes's view, then we would have a conception of ideas very like Malebranche's.

It seems likely that Chappell's apparent inconsistency testifies to an unresolved ambiguity in Descartes himself. There is certainly

---

[16] V. Chappell, 'The Theory of Ideas', in A. Rorty (ed.), *Essays on Descartes's Meditations* (Berkeley and Los Angeles, 1986), 178–9.   [17] Ibid. 194.

evidence in favour of Chappell's first and principal claim to the effect that ideas$_o$ are simply aspects of ideas$_m$. In the 'First Replies', for instance, Descartes tells Caterus that an idea 'is never outside the intellect';[18] as Chappell says, it is clearly an idea$_o$ which is in question here, for Descartes and Caterus are debating the nature of 'objective being'.[19] Yet when Descartes has his eye on true and immutable natures, it often seems that ideas are thought of as abstract, non-psychological entities. Now it is true that Descartes tends to say, not that ideas are true and immutable natures, but rather that they are of, or represent, true and immutable natures.[20] However, little seems to ride on this linguistic point. For Descartes may be talking about ideas$_m$, and in this case true and immutable natures, as abstract entities, could be ideas$_o$ to which our minds are related in thinking. But even if Descartes is reluctant to say that true and immutable natures are themselves ideas, the way in which he speaks of such natures often suggests that he thinks of them as abstract entities. Of course, even if Descartes does slip into this mode of thinking, his 'true and immutable natures' cannot be quite the same as Malebranche's ideas. For any account of Descartes's 'true and immutable natures' must take note of his extreme voluntarism which sets him apart from both Malebranche and Leibniz; for Descartes, even essences have been created by God, and could be other than they are. None the less, it does seem that Descartes is at least sometimes tempted by the view that in pure thought our minds are related to non-mental entities. Perhaps Descartes never achieved a fully consistent and satisfactory position on this issue. If there is such an unresolved tension in his thought, it would help to illuminate the controversy between Malebranche and Arnauld.

The act or event theory and the object theory of ideas were taken up and developed later in the century by Arnauld and Malebranche respectively. Did Descartes also anticipate Leibniz in advancing a dispositional theory of ideas? Kenny, McRae, and Chappell all believe that he did.[21] Now, as we have seen, Descartes explicitly acknowledges that the word 'idea' is ambiguous between 'idea$_m$' and 'idea$_o$', but he does not seem to acknowledge a further use of

---

[18] 'First Replies', AT vii. 102; CSM ii. 74.
[19] Chappell, p. 186.
[20] See e.g. Descartes to Mersenne, 16 June 1641, AT iii. 383; K, p. 104.
[21] Kenny, *Descartes*, pp. 100–1; McRae, p. 175; Chappell, p. 179.

'idea' to mean 'disposition'. Perhaps, however, Descartes is at times committed to there being a dispositional sense of 'idea', even if, unlike Leibniz, he never embodies it in an explicit definition. Chappell observes that Descartes uses 'idea' to mean 'disposition' only in connection with the topic of innate ideas.[22] And while Chappell may be right in the negative part of his claim, the positive thesis is harder to document than one might suppose. We must be careful to see what is at issue here. It is true, of course, that Descartes sometimes advances a dispositional theory of innate ideas; in other words, to have an innate idea is to have a disposition to form certain occurrent thoughts under certain conditions. What is less clear is whether Descartes ever identified the idea with the disposition itself.

Sometimes when Descartes states the dispositional theory of innate ideas, it is clear that the idea is not being identified with the disposition. In the 'Third Replies', for instance, Descartes tells Hobbes:

Lastly, when we say that an idea [*idea*] is innate in us, we do not mean that it is always there before us. This would mean that no idea was innate. We simply mean that we have within ourselves the faculty of summoning up the idea [*illa*].[23]

In the last sentence at least, an idea must be an occurrent thought, not a disposition. For if by 'idea' Descartes meant 'disposition', his claim would immediately become nonsense; he would be saying that we have within ourselves the disposition ('faculty') of summoning up the disposition. Here, then, to talk about innate ideas is simply an elliptical way of talking about an innate psychological disposition to have or form certain ideas (= occurrent thoughts). The same ellipsis reappears in what is probably Descartes's most famous statement of the dispositional theory of innate ideas. In the *Comments on a Certain Broadsheet* Descartes speaks of the mind forming ideas by means of the faculty innate to it.[24]

Descartes's dispositional theory of innate ideas does not entail the claim that ideas themselves are psychological dispositions; talk of innate ideas, for Descartes, can be simply a pardonable ellipsis. Yet the dispositional theory of innate ideas is obviously consistent with a dispositional theory of ideas themselves; indeed, the two theories

---

[22] Chappell, p. 179.   [23] 'Third Replies', AT vii. 189; CSM ii. 132.
[24] *Comments on a Certain Broadsheet*, AT viii/ʙ. 359; CSM i. 304.

were to be run in tandem to considerable effect by Leibniz. And though, unlike Leibniz, Descartes never seems to have explicitly advocated the dispositional theory of ideas, Kenny, McRae, and Chappell are right to this extent: there are passages which strongly suggest that, for Descartes, ideas can be dispositions. In the 'Fifth Meditation' Descartes describes how the idea of God is present in us:

Now admittedly, it is not necessary that I ever light upon any thought of God; but whenever I do choose to think of the first and supreme being, and bring forth the idea of God from the treasure house of my mind as it were, it is necessary that I attribute all perfections to him, even if I do not at that time enumerate them or attend to them individually.[25]

Descartes does not of course tell us how his metaphor is to be unpacked, but it is natural to suppose that bringing an idea out of the treasure house could be a matter of activating a disposition. It is natural to place the same interpretation on another passage where Descartes discusses the idea of God:

The idea of God is so imprinted on the human mind that there is no one who does not have in himself the faculty of knowing him; but this does not prevent many people from being able to pass their whole lives without ever distinctly representing this idea to themselves.[26]

Descartes, then, is not explicit that there is a dispositional sense of 'idea', and this interpretation is surprisingly not required by his doctrine of innate ideas. But it would be rash to claim that Descartes is never committed to such a view of ideas. It was, however, left to Leibniz to define an idea as a psychological disposition, and to incorporate this definition into his theory of innate ideas.

The results of the discussion so far may be summarized as follows. First, once we cut through the thicket of scholastic terminology, we can see that Descartes advances two, and perhaps three, distinct conceptions of ideas; these conceptions look forward to Arnauld, Malebranche, and Leibniz. Secondly, according to two of these theories, ideas are clearly psychological entities; ideas as events and ideas as dispositions are obviously properties of minds. On the remaining theory, this is less clear: there is an ambiguity in Descartes's conception of an idea$_o$ which perhaps he never succeeded in resolving. Although, as Chappell suggests, Descartes

---

[25] 'Fifth Meditation', AT vii. 67; CSM ii. 46–7.
[26] *Comments on a Certain Broadsheet*, AT iv. 187.

predominantly thinks of ideas$_o$ in psychological terms, he is perhaps also tempted by the view that they are abstract or at least non-psychological entities. If such a strand is present in Descartes's thought, then it may constitute a residue of an earlier, Augustinian theory of ideas. Whether or not this theory is really present in Descartes, perhaps in a merely vestigial form, it was to be explicitly and brilliantly revived by Malebranche.

Ideas and Representation

So far we have been assuming that all ideas$_m$ have, or at least are associated with, representational content. But we cannot allow this assumption to go unchallenged. Certainly it seems that Descartes is under some philosophical pressure to hold that intentionality is a mark of all ideas$_m$. In introducing the distinction between the formal and objective reality of ideas in the 'Third Meditation', Descartes seems to imply that it is essential to ideas to have both aspects; in other words, ideas are necessarily intentional or *of* things. Yet it is not clear that this is a position which Descartes can comfortably hold. Even in the 'Third Meditation' Descartes speaks of having an idea or sensation of heat;[27] in a letter to Hyperaspistes he writes of the mind of an infant as being wholly occupied with 'perceiving or feeling the ideas of pain, pleasure, heat, cold and other similar ideas which arise from its union and, as it were, intermingling with the body'.[28] Thus Descartes seems committed by his theory of ideas to the claim that even such things as pain and pleasure sensations have objective reality, or are, in other words, intentional. Such a claim naturally invites Richard Rorty's response: 'The obvious objection to defining the mental as the intentional is that pains are not intentional—they do not represent, they are not about anything'.[29] Thus, by his umbrella use of the term 'idea', Descartes seems to make intentionality at least a, if not the, mark of the mental. In this way he seems to leave himself wide open to the charge that he is mistakenly assimilating pains and other sensations to concepts and beliefs.

At a fundamental level it may be that this criticism is unanswerable. But Descartes does at least have the resources for some kind of

---

[27] 'Third Meditation', AT vii. 38; CSM ii. 26.
[28] Descartes to Hyperaspistes, Aug. 1641, AT iii. 424, K, p. 111.
[29] R. Rorty, *Philosophy and the Mirror of Nature* (Princeton, 1979), 22.

interim response to this objection. For in the 'Third Meditation' Descartes distinguishes between a broad and narrow sense of the term 'idea' (i.e. idea$_m$):

Some of my thoughts are as it were the images of things, and it is only in these cases that the term 'idea' is strictly appropriate—for example, when I think of a man, or a chimera, or the sky, or an angel, or God.[30]

By saying that only those thoughts which are, as it were, images of things are ideas in the strict sense, Descartes does not of course mean that all ideas are mental images; for we know that, for Descartes, the paradigm ideas are not images at all but purely intellectual conceivings. Rather, Descartes's point is that ideas in the strict sense necessarily have objective reality or representational content; thus my thought—not image—of God meets this standard. But this leaves it open to Descartes to say that having representational content is not a logically necessary condition of ideas in the broad sense. Thus Descartes can concede to Rorty that pain and heat sensations are not intentional, while still claiming that they are in a loose sense ideas.

Descartes's distinction between a broad and a narrow sense of 'idea' (i.e. idea$_m$) allows him to avoid the unwelcome conclusion that intentionality is a mark of all mental phenomena. But Descartes does not always seem to avail himself of this option. There is a tendency in Descartes's philosophy to say that sensations are representational but confusedly so: a pain in my foot, for instance, could be a confused representation of tissue-damage; this seems to be the import of Descartes's claim that sensations are confused modes of thought which arise from the mind's union and, as it were, intermingling with the body.[31] Thus Descartes seems at least tempted by a version of the strategy which, as Rorty notes, has appealed to some twentieth-century philosophers:

We can gerrymander, of course, so as to make pain the acquisition of a belief that one of one's tissues is damaged, construing pain reports as Pitcher and Armstrong construe perceptual reports. But such a tactic still leaves us with something like a dualistic intuition on our hands—the intuition that there is 'something more' to being conscious of a pain or a sensation of redness than being tempted to acquire a belief that there is tissue-damage or a red object in the vicinity.[32]

---

[30] 'Third Meditation', AT vii. 37; CSM ii. 25.
[31] See e.g. 'Sixth Meditation', AT vii. 81; CSM ii. 56.
[32] R. Rorty, pp. 22–3.

We may wonder whether Descartes is well placed to defend the claim that sensations are confused representations of physical states. Descartes holds that the correlations between brain events and *qualia* are purely arbitrary;[33] thus, there is nothing about a toothache or a sensation of redness which would allow us even in principle to 'read off' the corresponding states of our body or of surrounding bodies which are causally affecting our own. In this respect Descartes seems less well placed than Leibniz who holds that mental states 'express' physical states in a technical sense which we will examine later. Leibniz is thus in a rather strong position to defend the claim that sensations are confused representations of events in bodies.

Descartes, then, seems unclear on the issue of the intentionality of sensations. On the one hand, he has the resources to deny that all mental phenomena are intentional; on the other hand, he appears at least to flirt with the thesis that sensations are confusedly representational. In this respect he compares unfavourably not just with Leibniz but even more clearly with Malebranche. Whereas Descartes flirts with a distinction between ideas in the narrow sense and ideas in the broad sense, Malebranche firmly and consistently denies that sensations are ideas of any kind. For Malebranche, it is of the nature of ideas that they are representative entities, and Malebranche is clear that sensations (*sentiments*) are wholly lacking in representational content. Unlike both Descartes and Leibniz, Malebranche is never remotely tempted by the thesis that intentionality is a mark of the mental.

Mind and the Image of God

Descartes was aware that in his theory of ideas he was taking a traditional term and putting it to a new use. Yet, as we saw at the beginning of this chapter, it is a mistake to suppose that Descartes wished to suppress the traditional connotations of the term 'idea'. On the contrary, he told Hobbes that he chose the term precisely because it had been the standard one for the forms of divine perception. The implication seems to be that in Descartes's philosophy the mind is taking on some of the traditional attributes of God, and that Descartes wishes to draw attention to this

---

[33] See 'Sixth Meditation', AT vii. 88; CSM ii. 60.

development through his choice of terminology. In a rather similar way Spinoza noticed that the physical universe, according to the new science, had taken on the divine attribute of infinity, and he reflected this development through the famous phrase 'God or nature'.

Descartes's remark to Hobbes is no isolated occurrence; it receives support from the *Meditations*. In the 'Third Meditation' Descartes follows up his discovery that he has an innate idea of God with the remark:

> the mere fact that God created me is a very strong basis for believing that I am somehow made in his image and likeness, and that I perceive that likeness, which includes the idea of God, by the same faculty which enables me to perceive myself.[34]

In the 'Fourth Meditation' Descartes discovers that his will is infinite:

> It is only the will, or freedom of choice, which I experience within me to be so great that the idea of any greater faculty is beyond my grasp; so much so that it is above all in virtue of the faculty of will that I understand myself to bear in some way the image and likeness of God.[35]

In these passages Descartes is preparing the reader for his new doctrine of mind. By the 'Sixth Meditation' it will emerge that the mind, in Cartesian philosophy, is indeed more godlike than it was according to scholasticism. Descartes's readers were sensitive to this implication of the Cartesian revolution; Hyperaspistes complained that Descartes seemed to be attributing to the human mind a form of perception which theologians attribute to God alone.[36] Hyperaspistes was thus registering his awareness of the extent of Descartes's rejection of scholasticism. We shall see that several of Descartes's main departures from the scholastic tradition could indeed be captured by saying that the Cartesian mind has become godlike. As we shall also see, the transformation of the scholastic soul into Cartesian mind has both a metaphysical and an epistemological dimension.

On a metaphysical level, the most important element of the Cartesian revolution is that, for Descartes, the mind is a substance.

---

[34] 'Third Meditation', AT vii. 51; CSM ii. 35. Cf. *Conversation with Burman*, AT v. 156; CB [24], p. 17.
[35] 'Fourth Meditation', AT vii. 57; CSM ii. 40.
[36] Hyperaspistes to Descartes, July 1641, AT iii. 400.

In the *Meditations* Descartes prefers to use the non-technical term *res*, but in the more academic work, the *Principles of Philosophy*, Descartes is prepared to say outright that the mind is a substance. 'As for corporeal substance and mind (or created thinking substance), these can be understood to fall under this common concept [of substance]: things that need only the concurrence of God in order to exist.'[37] In other words, the mind is an entity which is causally independent of everything except God; it thus satisfies the requirements for substantiality. In particular, the existence of the mind does not depend causally on the existence of bodies, not even the body to which it is particularly attached. Now it is true of course that Descartes carefully qualifies the claim that mind and God are both substances. For God alone enjoys a wholly unrestricted degree of causal independence, and thus God alone satisfies the strict definition of substance; as Descartes puts it, the term 'substance' does not apply univocally to God and creatures.[38] Yet Descartes does not withdraw his claim that the mind is a substance, and the fact that the mind does occupy this place in the metaphysical hierarchy is sufficient to mark a real difference from scholasticism. According to scholasticism, the mind or soul is not a substance at all but is rather the substantial form of the body; it is an element of a substance, and has no natural capacity for independent existence. Thus the transformation of the scholastic substantial form into a substance is one major way in which the mind is becoming more godlike.

Epistemologically, the transformation of scholastic soul into Cartesian mind is perhaps even more striking, and even more important for our purposes. On Descartes's view, pure under-standing and volition occupy a privileged place among the properties of a human mind. Such properties are intrinsic properties of a mind in the sense that they do not arise from its union with an extraneous substance; they are also essential in that a mind could not possibly fail to have them. It may perhaps be doubted whether the will is quite on a par with pure understanding; for at times Descartes may seem to give the intellect primacy over volition. But Descartes's doctrine that assent is a function of the will entails that a mind which lacked a will would also be incapable of believing anything, and it does not seem that Descartes would wish to

---

[37] *Principles of Philosophy*, 1. 52 (AT ix/B. 25; CSM i. 210).
[38] Ibid. 51 (AT ix/B. 24, CSM i. 210).

countenance the possibility that a mind could lack a capacity for belief. But even if will is not an essential property of minds, it is certainly an intrinsic one; it is not a property which the mind simply comes to possess through interacting with something extraneous to itself. The fact that pure understanding and will are the only intrinsic general properties of minds is enough to show how much they have in common with God.

Descartes does not of course claim that the human mind is perfectly godlike. In the 'Fourth Meditation' he stresses that the intellect, though not the will, is finite;[39] Descartes can see that he does not possess all the ideas which he might possess, and which must be present in God. Since Descartes holds that we may possess ideas implicitly, without being aware that we possess them, there is no guarantee that any attempt to make an inventory of my ideas will be accurate; it is possible that I may be mistaken in supposing that I lack a given idea. Could I not, then, be mistaken in supposing that my intellect was finite? Yet Descartes would surely want to insist that even if I did possess all God's ideas, the fact that I possessed at least some of them in a dispositional form would be enough to mark a significant difference between my mind and God's. In the case of the divine mind, there can be no latency, no unactualized potentiality.[40]

Even in the case of occurrent thoughts, there is a certain disanalogy between the human intellect and the divine. In the *Principles*, a work which tends to minimize the break with scholasticism, Descartes stresses that God does not have a series of discrete intellectual acts:

Even his understanding and willing does not happen, as in our case, by means of operations that are in a certain sense distinct one from another; we must rather suppose that there is always a single identical and perfectly simple act by means of which he simultaneously understands, wills and accomplishes everything.[41]

None the less, there is a real and important sense in which the human intellect does resemble the divine intellect. One of Descartes's truly remarkable claims about the human mind is that, in respect of acts of pure understanding, there are no corresponding brain events; such acts 'need no place and depend on no material

---

[39] 'Fourth Meditation', AT vii. 57; CSM ii. 39–40.
[40] 'Third Meditation', AT vii. 47; CSM ii. 32.
[41] *Principles of Philosophy*, I 23 (AT ix. 14; CSM i. 201).

thing'.[42] As Margaret Wilson has noted, this is one of the most striking differences between Descartes's dualism and 'Cartesian dualism' today.[43] The contemporary philosophical position which passes under the name of Cartesian dualism holds only that mental states are not identical with brain states; it does not claim that there can be any mental events without correlative brain events. Descartes's thesis to the contrary may strike us, with Cottingham, as 'preposterous'.[44] What is important for our present purposes is that this property of the Cartesian mind is something which it shares with God.

Of course only a comparatively small part of the history of a Cartesian mind will be spent in pure thought. As a result of its union and intermingling with the body, the mind comes to have sense-perception and sensations. Naturally, Descartes does not claim that mental events of this kind can occur without brain activity. It is, however, not entirely clear that the subject of these sensations is, strictly speaking, the mind; as several commentators have noticed, Descartes sometimes seems to say that they should be regarded as properties of a compound substance, the complete human being.[45] Yet even if sense-perceptions and sensations are attributed to the mind itself, they are not intrinsic but interactive properties. Descartes tells Hyperaspistes that although the infant's mind is wholly occupied with sensory experiences, none the less, it 'has in itself the ideas of God, itself, and all such truths as are called self-evident, in the same way as adult humans have when they are not attending to them; it does not acquire these ideas later on, as it grows older. I have no doubt that if it were taken out of the prison of the body it would find them within itself.'[46] Indeed, Descartes seems committed to the truth of the stronger counterfactual conditional claim: if the mind were taken out of the prison of the body, it would have *only* acts of pure intellect and volition.

Descartes's view that the mind comes to experience already supplied with pure concepts marks a major departure from scholasticism. For scholasticism, as for Locke and Aristotle, the mind is a *tabula rasa*; the only way we can acquire concepts is by

---

[42] See J. Cottingham, *Descartes* (Oxford, 1986), 119.
[43] M. D. Wilson, *Descartes* (London, 1978), 180 f.
[44] Cottingham, p. 119.
[45] See e.g. R. C. Richardson, 'The "Scandal" of Cartesian Interactionism', *Mind*, 91 (1982), 20–37, esp. p. 34.
[46] Descartes to Hyperaspistes, Aug. 1641, AT iii. 424; K, p. 111.

abstracting from sense-experience. As Aquinas puts it, our intellect understands material things by abstracting from phantasms.[47] The scholastic intellect is thus ultimately dependent for its concepts on the physical world. The Cartesian intellect, by contrast, needs no source outside itself; in this respect it resembles the divine intellect. There is thus good reason why Descartes should speak of the intellectual acts of the mind as ideas.

There is also a sense, I believe, in which Descartes's theory of sense-perception makes the mind more godlike than it is on the scholastic conception. This may seem a surprising claim. As one might expect, Descartes does not try to conceal the fact that God does not perceive through the senses:

the fact that we perceive through the senses is for us a perfection of a kind; but all sense-perception involves being acted upon, and to be acted upon is to be dependent on something else. Hence it cannot in any way be supposed that God perceives by means of the senses, but only that he understands and wills.[48]

And, in the reply to Hobbes, Descartes reminds us that God does not possess any corporeal imagination.[49] In these passages indeed it seems as if Descartes is at pains to emphasize the disanalogy between the human mind and God. It may seem, then, that when Descartes speaks of sensations and sense-perceptions as ideas, he must mean simply to suppress or discard the traditional meaning of the term 'idea'. But this, I believe, is not the case. Even here there is real point to Descartes's choice of the term 'idea'.

It is well known that Descartes's theory of sense-perception marks a revolutionary break with scholastic doctrine. We shall discuss the nature of this revolution in some detail in the next chapter. Here the important point is that, for Descartes, in contrast to the scholastics, there is nothing which literally comes into the mind from outside in sense-perception. The sensation of green, for example, which I get when I look at the grass is not transmitted from the grass, for the grass itself possesses only primary, geometrical properties. Rather, the stimulation of the sense-organ and the mechanical transmission of impulses to the brain simply provide the occasion for my mind to form the appropriate sensory ideas. As we shall see in the next chapter, Descartes notoriously

[47] Aquinas, *Summa Theologica*, i, q. 85, a. 1.
[48] *Principles of Philosophy*, 1. 23 (AT viii/A. 13–14; CSM i. 201).
[49] 'Third Replies', AT vii. 181; CSM ii. 127.

tends to be unclear on the question of whether this account implies
that even sensory ideas are innate. But Descartes's uncertainty on
this issue has no tendency to call in question the completeness
of his break with the scholastic theory of perception. Consider,
for instance, Descartes's insistence in the *Principles* that sense-
perception involves the mind's being acted upon by the body. In
other words, the existence of sensory states is causally dependent on
the existence of certain physical states. Yet even though sense-
perceptions are in this sense adventitious, there is no sense in which
such perceptions are literally transmitted into the mind from
outside. Thus sensory perception is not tied to the body in the
direct way that it is for scholasticism.

We can now see why Descartes should be prepared to call even
sensations and sense-perceptions 'ideas'. It is true that such
perceptions are not intellectual, and it is perhaps hard to see how
they can all be intentional. None the less, Descartes is right that
even colour and pain sensations resemble the forms of divine
perception. Although they may have been caused by external
physical objects, they have not been literally transmitted into the
mind by those objects; in some sense, the mind gets them out of its
own storehouse. The mind of man, like the mind of God, does not
need to go outside itself. This is perhaps the basic reason why
Descartes thought that 'idea' was the most appropriate term for the
forms of human perception.

For the purposes of understanding Malebranche, we must note a
yet further sense in which the human mind is godlike. Here the
important point is not just that the mind is like God; it is that the
mind has been created by God in his own image and likeness. In
other words, the Cartesian mind has been so structured that just
through its own resources it is in principle at least capable of
attaining to a God's-eye view of the world; by abstracting from the
prejudices of the subjective viewpoint we are able to form a
conception of the world as it is in itself.[50] This is what Bernard
Williams has called the absolute conception of the world;[51] or, as
Nagel puts it, it is the view from nowhere.[52]

To abstract from the subjective viewpoint of course involves
purely intellectual understanding; thus we are in part returning to a

[50] This point is well made by Cottingham, p. 146.
[51] B. Williams, *Descartes: The Project of Pure Enquiry* (Hassocks, 1978), ch. 10.
[52] T. Nagel, *The View from Nowhere* (Oxford, 1986).

feature of the Cartesian mind which we have already examined. But we are also bringing in something new. On Cartesian principles it is at least logically possible that creatures might have pure intellects which were none the less useless for an understanding of the physical world; they might have the wrong geometry or they might even operate with an arithmetic in which two plus three equal six. But fortunately this nightmare scenario is not realized in our world; our intellects are such that they have been endowed with a set of concepts which faithfully mirror the structure of physical reality. In other words, we have innate ideas implanted by a benevolent God. It is to the doctrine of innate ideas that we must now turn.

3
Descartes
Innate Ideas

IT is well known that Descartes revived the ancient doctrine of innate ideas. It is also widely believed that this was the most influential aspect of his theory of ideas, at least among his rationalist successors. Indeed, a commitment to a doctrine of innate ideas is often taken to be a hallmark of seventeenth-century rationalism. In fact, however, Descartes's position on innate ideas was accepted as it stands by none of his rationalist successors. The 'Cartesian' Malebranche, as we shall see, rejected the doctrine of innate ideas altogether. Leibniz, it is true, defended a version of the doctrine, but he found it necessary to modify Cartesian teaching to accommodate the criticisms which not only Locke but Malebranche had advanced. At the centre of subsequent debate was the nature of ideas themselves, for obviously theories of ideas strongly constrain theories of innate ideas.

To talk of Descartes's doctrine of innate ideas is perhaps as misleading as to talk of his doctrine of ideas, for it is doubtful whether Descartes advanced a single doctrine. Descartes invokes innate ideas on a number of occasions apparently in response to a number of different questions, and it is not clear that the same concept of innateness is involved throughout. It is often supposed that Descartes needs innate ideas primarily in order to explain a priori knowledge, but this is by no means the whole truth. We shall see, for instance, that innate ideas play a major role in Descartes's anti-scholastic theory of perception. Moreover, as Loeb has argued, when Descartes does appeal to innate ideas in connection with a priori knowledge, he has special reasons of his own deriving from his strange theory of the creation of the eternal truths.[1] In this chapter we shall attempt to do justice to the range of Descartes's teaching concerning innate ideas, but we shall focus on those

[1] L. E. Loeb, *From Descartes to Hume: Continental Metaphysics and the Development of Modern Philosophy* (Ithaca and London, 1981), 68.

features of his teaching which became central in the writings of Leibniz and Malebranche.

Innate Ideas and Dispositions

In the 'Third Meditation' Descartes announces his famous threefold classification of ideas. Elsewhere Descartes confirms that each of the three classes has members, but in the 'Third Meditation' of course he is not yet in a position to assign his ideas to classes:

> Among my ideas, some appear to be innate, some to be adventitious, and others to have been invented by me. My understanding of what a thing is, what truth is, and what thought is, seems to derive simply from my own nature. But my hearing a noise, as I do now, or seeing the sun, or feeling the fire, comes from things which are located outside me, or so I have hitherto judged. Lastly, sirens, hippogriffs and the like are my own invention.[2]

This classificatory scheme is somewhat surprising. In the first place, the category of innate ideas appears to be the odd man out. To say that an idea is adventitious or factitious is to give a possible answer to a causal question; to say that an idea is innate, however, may appear to suggest a possible answer to a temporal question; it seems to say that an idea has been possessed at least since birth. Relatedly, as Kenny notes, Descartes seems to be comparing entities of different kinds under the rubric of ideas: the examples of innate ideas are capacities, whereas the examples of acquired ideas are sensations.[3] It may seem, then, that Descartes is simply mixing apples and pears.

In fact, however, this criticism is premature. Descartes's presentation of his views in the 'Third Meditation' may be misleading, but his classificatory scheme is not muddled in this way. At the risk of being dogmatic, let us say that Descartes's three categories are all addressed to the same question about the same kind of entity; in each case Descartes is giving a possible answer to a causal question about ideas$_m$. In its most basic form Descartes's theory of innate ideas is an explanatory theory about a class of occurrent thoughts; it locates the causal source of certain thoughts in a dispositional property of the mind.

This account of Descartes's position is open to an obvious objection. On our analysis, Descartes is prepared to say of

---

[2] 'Third Meditation', AT vii. 37–8; CSM ii. 26.
[3] A. Kenny, *Descartes: A Study of his Philosophy* (New York, 1968), 101.

occurrent thoughts that they are innate. But if this is Descartes's view, then it may seem that he is guilty of a category mistake; for innateness should be predicated, not of the thought of *x*, but rather of the disposition to think of *x*. This objection might be buttressed by claiming, as Kenny does, that Descartes's examples of innate ideas in the 'Third Meditation' are all capacities. In fact, it is less clear than Kenny suggests that the examples in question are not particular mental events. But as we shall see, there are cases where Descartes is prepared to apply the term 'innate' directly to the occurrent thought, meaning thereby that its causal source is a dispositional property of the mind. Yet it would be wrong to suggest that Descartes never applies the term 'innate' to the disposition itself. Sometimes indeed Descartes says in the very same breath that both the disposition and its display are innate:

So everything over and above . . . utterances and pictures which we think of as being signified by them is represented to us by means of ideas which come to us from no other source than our own faculty of thinking. Consequently these ideas, along with that faculty, are innate in us, i.e. they always exist in us potentially, for to exist within some faculty is not to exist actually, but merely potentially, since the term 'faculty' denotes nothing but a potentiality.[4]

The ideas whose causal source is the faculty of thinking are clearly occurrent thoughts. And as this passage shows, Descartes is prepared to say of them that they are innate. Yet Descartes also says that the faculty of thinking is innate in us. And when Descartes applies the term 'innate' to the faculty, he seems committed to the view that we can have an innate idea of *x* even if we never think of *x*; we have an innate idea in the sense that we have a disposition which may or may not be activated. As we noted in the last chapter, however, even here it is not necessary to suppose that the disposition is itself an idea. Indeed, if ideas were themselves dispositions, it would make no sense to say, as Descartes does, that they exist in us potentially.

In its most basic form, Descartes's theory of innate ideas is an explanatory theory about the origin of certain occurrent thoughts. But in that case Descartes seems to have a new problem on his hands; for there appears to be no guarantee that the disposition which explains the idea should be innate in the ordinary sense.

---

[4] *Comments on a Certain Broadsheet*, AT viii/B. 360–1; CSM i. 305.

Consider, for instance, the idea of God. According to the 'Third Meditation' God has placed this idea in us as 'the mark of the craftsman stamped on his work'.[5] In other words, God has implanted in us a disposition to have certain occurrent thoughts. Now Descartes suggests that this disposition is innate in the further, temporal sense of 'inborn'; God placed it in him in creating him.[6] But how does Descartes know this? It does not follow from the fact that an idea is caused by a mental disposition that it is caused by a mental disposition which is innate in the familiar, temporal sense. For all that Descartes has shown, it is possible that he received this disposition from God at some stage after birth; perhaps God judged that Descartes's mind was not ready for it until then. Here the artist's signature analogy is helpful. Typically, artists sign their work as soon as it is finished, but it is not unknown, and in any case quite possible, for an artist to affix his signature at a later date. Descartes in fact can be confronted with a dilemma. Either his concept of innateness has the familiar temporal implications, in which case his classification is not exhaustive; or it has no temporal implications, in which case there need be nothing innate about Descartes's innate ideas.

Perhaps the key to Descartes's apparent oversight is to be found in his loose talk of faculties. In the *Comments on a Certain Broadsheet* Descartes famously denies that the mind needs innate ideas which are something distinct from its own faculty of thinking.[7] Clearly, given Descartes's metaphysics, there is a sense in which the mind must possess a general faculty of thinking from its inception; the faculty of thinking is in this sense innate. But it does not follow from this that the mind possesses specific dispositions to have certain kinds of thoughts as part of its native endowment. Descartes could answer this objection by trying to show that all mental dispositions are such that they must be inborn if the mind possesses them at all. But Descartes does not in fact attempt to fill this gap in his argument. Thus Descartes may simply have conflated the general faculty of thinking with specific dispositions to have certain kinds of thoughts. As Kenny suggests, Descartes may be handicapped here by his contempt for the Aristotelian notion of potentiality; it seems that Descartes needs something like Aristotle's

---

[5] 'Third Meditation', AT vii. 51; CSM ii. 35.
[6] See n. 5 above.
[7] *Comments on a Certain Broadsheet*, AT viii/B. 357; CSM i. 303.

distinction between mere potentiality and first actuality.[8] However that may be, Descartes is much more concerned with the causal aspect of innateness than with its temporal aspect.

So far then, we have seen that Descartes is committed to the following two claims. First, to say that an idea is innate is to commit oneself to the existence of a corresponding mental disposition. Secondly, this disposition has causal properties; in other words, it has the power to cause certain occurrent thoughts. There is also a third feature of Descartes's conception of innateness which we have not yet noted. The dispositional properties are basic; Descartes makes no attempt to ground them in non-dispositional properties of the mind. This will be a major issue in the subsequent debate involving Leibniz and Malebranche. We shall also see later in this chapter that while Descartes is no reductionist about dispositions, he does sometimes seem to suggest an alternative to the dispositional account of innateness.

Our account of Descartes's core theory of innateness naturally invites two questions. We have said that innate ideas, for Descartes, are basically thoughts which are caused by mental dispositions, but nothing has been said about the role of the stimulus. Yet surely Descartes must allow that some stimulus is necessary to activate the mental disposition, and it would seem that this stimulus must play a causal role in the occurrence of the thought. Descartes does not of course ignore the stimulus altogether, but what he does say is rather surprising. In the *Comments on a Certain Broadsheet* Descartes discusses the problem in answer to Regius's objection to the claim that the idea of God is innate:

In article *fourteen* he goes on to assert that even the idea of God which is within us derives its being not from our faculty of thinking, in which the idea is innate, 'but from divine revelation, or verbal instruction, or observation of things'. It is easier to recognize the error in this assertion if we consider that something can be said to derive its being from something else for two different reasons: either the other thing is its proximate and primary cause, without which it cannot exist, or it is a remote and merely accidental cause, which gives the primary cause occasion to produce its effect at one moment rather than another. Thus workers are the primary and proximate causes of their work, whereas those who give them the orders to do the work, or promise to pay for it, are accidental and remote causes, for the workers might not do the work without instructions. There is, however, no doubt, that verbal instruction or observation of things is

    [8] Kenny, *Descartes*, p. 103.

óften a remote cause which induces us to give some attention to the idea which we can have of God, and to bring it directly before our mind. But no one can say that this is the proximate and efficient cause of the idea, except someone who thinks that all we can ever understand about God is what he is called, namely 'God', or what corporeal form painters use to represent him.[9]

In this passage Descartes leaves no doubt that it is the disposition which, so to speak, wears the causal trousers. The disposition is a proximate and primary cause, whereas the stimulus is a remote and accidental cause. Thus Descartes downgrades the role of a stimulus to a remarkable degree, and he does so in a surprising way; it certainly seems odd to claim that the stimulus which activates a disposition is merely a remote cause. It is far more natural to say that the stimulus is a part-cause of the event to be explained; we should be inclined to say, for instance, that the dropping of the glass, together with its fragility, jointly explain its breakage. Indeed, some philosophers would deny that the disposition plays any causal role on the ground that dispositions are not genuine properties.[10]

Some readers may believe that we can defend Descartes's position by drawing on his theory of perception. Consider Descartes's claim that 'the observation of things or verbal instruction' can be remote causes which activate our mental disposition. Suppose that someone comes to have a thought of God as a result of listening to a parable told by an elementary schoolteacher. Descartes will regard the physical process here as a complex, temporally extended series of events; sound waves stimulate the sense-organs (in this case, the ears) which in turn send messages to the brain. Now in a process of this kind there is clearly a sense in which we can regard the initial stimulus as a remote cause with respect to later events in the sequence; similarly, we can regard the initial push given to the first domino as a remote cause with respect to the collapse of subsequent dominoes. We might even go beyond the purely physical processes of perception and say that the teacher's utterances are the remote cause with respect to the mental event to be explained—the occurrent thought of God. But, on reflection, this will not really make Descartes's thesis more plausible. For we do not want to say that there is no part of the physical process which is a proximate cause of the occurrent thought of God; the events in the brain, for

---

[9] *Comments on a Certain Broadsheet.* AT viii/B. 360; CSM i. 305.
[10] See e.g. G. Ryle, *Concept of Mind* (London, 1949), ch. 5.

instance, may well be a suitable candidate. And by the same token, we do not want to inflate the mental disposition to the status of proximate and primary cause.

The second question which needs to be addressed concerns the role of God. As is well known and as we have already seen, Descartes claims in the 'Third Meditation' that his innate idea of God was implanted by God himself in creating him. It may seem, then, that any innate idea which is divinely implanted must really be caused by God. Yet Descartes is reluctant to say that God is the causal source of innate ideas. Indeed, in the 'Second Replies' Descartes denies that innate ideas have any external source:

Secondly, when you say that we can find simply within ourselves a sufficient basis for forming the idea of God, your claim in no way differs from my own view. I expressly said at the end of the Third Meditation that 'this idea is innate in me'—in other words, that it comes to me from no other source than myself. I concede also that 'we could form this idea even supposing that we did not know that the supreme being exists'; but I do not agree that we could form the idea 'even supposing that the supreme being did not exist'. On the contrary, I pointed out that the whole force of the argument lies in the fact that it would be impossible for me to have the power of forming this idea unless I were created by God.[11]

So Descartes does not take back what he had said about divine implantation in the 'Third Meditation', but he does deny that his idea of God has any other source than his own mind.

What, then, exactly is the role of God? It may seem that, for Descartes, God must be the remote cause of any occurrent thought of himself. For the innate disposition is the proximate cause of the thought, and the disposition is said to be divinely implanted; and it is natural to suppose that talk of divine implanting should be given a causal interpretation. But on reflection we can see that Descartes would be very unlikely to concede that God is a remote cause. In the first place, Descartes has reserved this concept for the stimulus which activates the disposition. But God does not activate a disposition; rather, he implants it, and this is clearly a very different matter. Thus, God can hardly be said to be a remote cause in Descartes's peculiar sense of the term. But, further, God can hardly be said to be a remote cause in the more familiar sense; it is not as if God's causal activity is exercised at some earlier point in the temporal sequence, for God is outside time altogether. Thus if the

---

[11] 'Second Replies', AT vii. 133; CSM ii. 96.

divine implanting of mental dispositions is to be understood causally at all, it is causal activity of a very special kind.

Innate Ideas and the Theory of Perception

Descartes's views on proximate and remote causes are curious, but they do have interesting consequences for the theory of perception. Taken in conjunction with other assumptions, they provide the materials for an argument to the effect that all sensory ideas are innate. Let us assume that Descartes subscribes to a stimulus-disposition model of perception; in other words, when I perceive a table, there is a physical process involving my sense-organs and the brain which activates my mental disposition to form the appropriate sensory ideas (= occurrent perceptions). Let us suppose also that Descartes would accept the following definition:

Innate = df. proximately caused by a mental disposition.

On this basis, then, we get an argument for the innateness of all sensory ideas. All sensory ideas are proximately caused by a mental disposition; so, by the definition of innateness, all sensory ideas are innate.

An objection to this reconstruction is that innateness is defined solely in causal terms; the definition thus fails to capture the temporal dimension of innateness. As we have seen, it is not clear that this objection is sound; none the less, we can easily revise our definition to accommodate it:

Innate = df. proximately caused by an inborn mental disposition.

The first premiss of our argument will of course have to be revised accordingly. Our definition may now appear to be circular, but this is not really the case, for the *definiendum* is a term of art whereas the word 'inborn' which appears in the *definiens* has its ordinary, non-technical meaning.

It is also possible to see how, in terms of his distinction between remote and proximate causes, Descartes could mount an argument for the conclusion that no sensory ideas are adventitious. Suppose that Descartes accepts the following definition:

Adventitious = df. proximately caused by external physical objects.

If we assume that no idea can be both adventitious in this sense and proximately caused by a mental disposition, we get the following argument:

(1) All sensory ideas are proximately caused by mental dispositions.

(2) No adventitious ideas are proximately caused by mental dispositions.

(3) Therefore, no sensory ideas are adventitious.

That Descartes would subscribe to both these arguments is strongly suggested by the *Comments on a Certain Broadsheet*. In that work, Descartes explicitly asserts that all sensory ideas are innate, and he implies that no sensory ideas are adventitious.

There are of course deeper pressures in Descartes's philosophy which drive him to hold that all sensory ideas are innate. As Robert Adams has shown in an illuminating article, Descartes's radical innatism is fuelled by his revolutionary account of perception. Descartes's position is in fact a curious one. On the one hand, he is advancing an anti-scholastic theory of perception; but on the other hand, he has not yet emancipated himself from Aristotelian views of the nature of causality. Indeed, it is not too much to say that the whole theory of causality is unstable in Descartes's writings. The categories of innate and adventitious are possible answers to causal questions about ideas, but the real question of course is: what is causality? The different formulations of his causal principle which Descartes offers at various points suggest that he was unclear on this crucial issue. Descartes's break with the scholastic theory of perception is not in doubt, but his failure to make a comparably clean break with scholastic teaching concerning causality produces tensions in his statements about sensory ideas. In other words, it is Descartes's unclarity about causality which explains how he can sometimes say that all sensory ideas are innate and at other times say that they are all adventitious.

On the traditional Aristotelian theory, causality is regarded as a process of contagion; in causal transactions, one thing comes to be infected with the properties of another. As Adams has shown, this general theory of causality has a straightforward application to the specific case of perception:

Perception was interpreted as a transaction in which a form (the sensible form) is transmitted from the perceived object to the perceiver. Typically a medium (light, in the case of vision) is required, through which the form can pass on its way from the object to the perceiver. On reaching the sense organ (in the case of vision, the eye) the form transmitted from the object informs the organ, and is eventually received in the mind. This is a greatly simplified statement of the Aristotelian theory of perception. For our present purpose the most important point to grasp about it is that one and the same form, originally present in the object, is present also in the medium, the sense organ, and the mind. There is something (the sensible form) which literally comes into the mind from the object.[12]

Descartes sometimes formulates his causal principle in a way which suggests he accepts the Aristotelian view of causality in general; he tells Hyperaspistes, for instance, that 'there can be nothing in the effect which is not pre-existent in the cause'.[13] Taken at face value, this does indeed suggest that the effect comes to be infected with the properties of the cause. Now, Descartes denies the Aristotelian view that in perception something literally comes into the mind from outside. Thus his remark to Hyperaspistes, taken in conjunction with his anti-Aristotelian view of perception, clearly implies that there are no adventitious ideas.

The strong Aristotelian requirement for causality, however, is not the basis of Descartes's argument in the *Comments on a Certain Broadsheet*. Here Descartes seems to take it for granted that, on the 'contagion' view of causality, no sensory ideas are caused by external physical objects. Instead, Descartes's crucial argument for the innateness of all sensory ideas turns on a weaker claim; he appeals, implicitly at least, to a causal-likeness principle. This may be regarded as a corollary of the Aristotelian thesis:

Nothing reaches our mind from external objects through the sense organs except certain corporeal motions . . . But neither the motions themselves nor the figures arising from them are conceived by us exactly as they occur in the sense organs, as I have explained at length in my *Optics*. Hence it follows that the very ideas of the motions themselves and of the figures are innate in us. The ideas of pain, colours, sounds and the like must be all the more innate if, on the occasions of certain corporeal motions, our mind is to be capable of representing them to itself, for there is no similarity between these ideas and the corporeal motions.[14]

Descartes's argument is very compressed, and depends on assumptions which he does not spell out. For our purposes, however, the

[12] R. M. Adams, 'Where Do our Ideas Come from?', in S. Stich (ed.), *Innate Ideas* (Berkeley and Los Angeles, 1975), 73.

[13] Descartes to Hyperaspistes, Aug. 1641, AT iii. 428; K, p. 114.

[14] *Comments on a Certain Broadsheet*, AT viii/B. 359; CSM i. 304.

important point is that Descartes is arguing that sensory ideas cannot be adventitious (and must, therefore, be innate) because there is no similarity between such ideas and corporeal motions. He is thus committed here to a causal-likeness principle.

If, however, we give up both the strong Aristotelian requirement and the causal-likeness principle, the way is open to the admission of adventitious ideas. Indeed, by weakening the assumptions concerning causality in this way, Descartes could perhaps admit that there are ideas which are both innate and adventitious, or partly innate and partly adventitious. In another context Descartes seems to countenance the possibility of such 'hybrid' ideas; in conversation with Burman, for instance, he implies that the idea of the Trinity is partly innate and partly factitious.[15] Now in the *Meditations* Descartes seems to insist on neither the strong Aristotelian requirement nor the causal-likeness principle. The causal principle which he proposes in this work states only that there must be at least as much reality in the cause as in the effect; it does not require that if the effect is F, the cause must also be F.[16] Such a principle does indeed seem to weaken the requirements for causality at least to the point where adventitious ideas are possible. Consistently with this version of his causal principle, Descartes argues in the 'Sixth Meditation' that our sensory ideas are caused by external physical objects.[17] Indeed, Descartes's whole recovery of the physical world in the 'Sixth Meditation' is very much tied in with the causation of sensory ideas.

In spite of the weakening moves in the *Meditations* and elsewhere, it is fair to say that Descartes does no serious rethinking of causality in general. It is true that in the *Comments on a Certain Broadsheet* Descartes gestures in the direction of occasionalism; our mind is said to be capable of representing sensory ideas to itself on the occasion of corporeal motions. But the hint remains only a hint; for, unlike Malebranche, Descartes does not develop the idea of psycho-physical laws which are not strictly causal. And Malebranche's occasionalism, as we shall see, has no truck with innate ideas; for, on Descartes's version, innatism ascribes genuine causal properties to mental dispositions, and this is something which occasionalism denies. Moreover, for all the brilliance of

---

[15] *Conversation with Burman*, AT v. 165; CB [49], p. 31.
[16] 'Third Meditation', AT vii. 40, CSM ii. 28.
[17] 'Sixth Meditation', AT vii. 79–80; CSM ii. 55.

Malebranche's insights, even occasionalism stops short of the conceptual revolution which Hume achieved. What is striking in Descartes's treatment of sensory ideas is the alliance of a bold new theory of perception with what is for the most part a timidly conservative doctrine of causality. Curiously, it is this combination which generates Descartes's most radical expressions of innatism.

In his review of Descartes's main motives for reviving innate ideas, Louis Loeb largely ignores the role of this doctrine in Descartes's anti-scholastic theory of perception. This is a surprising omission. Innate ideas allow Descartes to propound a theory of perception which is consistent with his new mechanistic picture of the physical world, and the defence of this picture was surely at the very heart of Descartes's concerns. If innate ideas solved a problem which was otherwise intractable (at least without serious rethinking of causality), then this was a great merit of the doctrine.

Should we go further and claim that Descartes revives innate ideas primarily in order to explain perception, and that other uses of the doctrine are secondary? In some ways this is an attractive suggestion; it receives support from the fact that Descartes's other arguments for innate ideas are more familiar and traditional. It might be argued, then, that Descartes insists on the innateness of mathematical and metaphysical concepts largely for tactical reasons; his aim is to remind his readers of a familiar, modest version of innatism in order to prepare the way for the radical and unfamiliar thesis that even sensory ideas are innate. Such an interpretation has an interesting parallel in a recent account of the role of scepticism in Descartes's philosophy. It has been argued that it is a mistake to suppose that Descartes really takes the sceptical challenge seriously; rather, Descartes employs the sceptical arguments of the 'First Meditation' largely as a tactical device for introducing the new physics.[18] The idea is that scepticism about the senses is a valuable propaedeutic for a philosopher who wishes to persuade his readers that the physical world is radically unlike the manifest image. In the same way, it might be argued, Descartes draws on traditional arguments for innate ideas in the service of his new anti-scholastic theory of perception.

This is a tempting hypothesis, but it should, I think, be resisted. For one thing, it is plausible to suppose that, as a mathematician,

[18] M. D. Wilson, 'Skepticism without Indubitability', *Journal of Philosophy*, 81 (1984), 537–44.

Descartes was moved by the same sorts of considerations in the philosophy of mathematics which led Plato to argue for a theory of innate ideas. Further, as we shall see and as Loeb points out, a powerful case can be made for saying that Descartes needs innate ideas in connection with his strange doctrine of the creation of the eternal truths. So instead of supposing that there is one motive which is primary, it seems wiser to claim that a variety of heterogeneous considerations all converge on a doctrine of innate ideas. What is still unclear is whether it is one and the same conception of innateness which is involved throughout.

Innate Intellectual Ideas

Descartes's theory of perception may have played a major role in his revival of the doctrine of innate ideas; none the less, it remains true that when most people think of innate ideas in Descartes, they think not of sense-perception but of intellectual ideas, especially the ideas of mathematics and metaphysics. It has been said that such ideas are innate in a stronger sense than sensory ideas, and this claim seems correct.[19] We have seen that, according to Descartes's core theory, an innate idea is one which is proximately caused by a mental disposition; by contrast, adventitious ideas (if there are any) are proximately caused by external physical objects. Yet, for Descartes, intellectual ideas are innate in the stronger sense that they are neither abstracted from nor given in sense-experience. Now what is in question here is clearly mental content, so if we are to compare like with like, we should strictly say that intellectual ideas are innate in the sense that their content is neither abstracted from nor given in sense-experience. We can see that this is a stronger sense of innateness in the following way. According to the *Comments on a Certain Broadsheet*, sensory ideas are innate in the former sense but not in the latter, for they are straightforwardly given in sense-experience. By contrast, the innate ideas of mathematics and metaphysics are innate in both senses; they are neither abstracted from nor given in sense-experience, and they are proximately caused by a mental disposition—i.e. by the faculty of thinking.

The most prominent place where Descartes seems to invoke this stronger conception of innateness is in the 'Fifth Replies'. Here

[19] B. Williams, *Descartes: The Project of Pure Enquiry* (Hassocks, 1978), 133–4.

Descartes tries to persuade Gassendi that the idea of a triangle is not derived from the senses but is rather innate:

I do not, incidentally, concede that the ideas of these figures ever came into our mind via the senses, as everyone commonly believes. For although the world could undoubtedly contain figures such as those the geometers study, I nonetheless maintain that there are no such figures in our environment except perhaps ones so small that they cannot in any way impinge on our senses. Geometrical figures are composed for the most part of straight lines; yet no part of a line that was really straight could ever affect our senses, since when we examine through a magnifying glass those lines which appear most straight, we find they are quite irregular and always form wavy curves. Hence, when in our childhood we first happened to see a triangular figure drawn on paper, it cannot have been this figure that showed us how we should conceive of the true triangle studied by the geometers, since the true triangle is contained in the figure only in the way in which a statue of Mercury is contained in a rough block of wood. But since the idea of the true triangle was already in us, and could be conceived by our mind more easily than the more composite figure of the triangle drawn on paper, when we saw the composite figure we did not apprehend the figure we saw, but rather the true triangle . . . Thus we could not recognize the geometrical triangle from the diagram on the paper unless our mind already possessed the idea of it from some other source.[20]

At first sight it may seem that Descartes is guilty of a muddle here. It is perhaps a logical truth that we cannot recognize an *x* as an F unless we have the concept of F, and we might infer that Descartes conflates this with the non-logical truth that we cannot recognize an *x* as an F unless we already have the concept of F innately. But we can, I think, reconstruct the argument in such a way as to show that Descartes is not guilty of this conflation:

(1) We recognize the geometrical triangle from the diagram.

(2) If we recognize the geometrical triangle from the diagram, we have the idea of the triangle.

(3) If we have the idea of the triangle, either we have acquired it through the senses or it is innate.

(4) Therefore, either we have acquired the idea of the triangle through the senses or it is innate (from (1) to (3)).

(5) If we acquired it through the senses, then a triangle was presented to the senses.

(6) But no triangle was presented to the senses.

[20] 'Fifth Replies', AT vii. 381–2; CSM ii. 262.

(7) Therefore, the idea of the triangle was not acquired through the senses (from (5) and (6)).

(8) Therefore, the idea of the triangle is innate (from (4) and (7)).

This argument is not immune to criticism, but it is not obviously muddled.

Ideas of triangles are innate in a stronger sense than ideas of pain or colours. None the less, it may appear from Descartes's argument in reply to Gassendi that they have something important in common; in both cases there is a disposition which needs to be activated by a stimulus. For Descartes allows in his argument that his thought of a triangle was at least triggered off by seeing the diagram on the paper. Now in one way there is an important disanalogy between the two cases. With regard to sensory ideas, the stimulus is purely physical. With regard to the idea of a triangle, however, the immediate stimulus is mental; it is my experience of seeing the diagram on the paper which activates my disposition to think of the true triangle. Yet that sensory experience of seeing the diagram was in turn triggered off by a physical cause (unless at least the malicious demon was playing tricks). It thus appears that geometrical and sensory ideas are alike dependent on physical stimulation.

At first sight it seems easy to spell out a difference between the two kinds of case with regard to the physical stimulus. In the case of my idea of green, that which typically activates my disposition is a green object, such as grass. In the case of my idea of a triangle, that which activates my mental disposition is never itself triangular; the basic assumption of Descartes's argument in reply to Gassendi is that no triangular objects or figures ever stimulate the senses. Yet on reflection we can see that this contrast is misconceived. According to some interpretations Descartes denies that the grass is green at all. And even if we insist that, in Descartes's considered view, secondary qualities inhere in physical objects, they do so only as powers,[21] and it is still true to say that what activates the disposition is very unlike the content of my perception. In this respect the physical stimuli in the two cases are on a par.

Where the stimulus is concerned, perhaps the difference between the two classes of ideas comes down to this. Sensory ideas are

---

[21] For the view that secondary qualities are powers, see *Principles of Philosophy*, IV. 198 (AT ix/B. 322–3; CSM i. 285).

essentially dependent on physical stimulation, at least in the common order of nature; it may be logically possible for a malicious demon to cause me to see red, even if I had no body, but it is not causally possible in our world. Intellectual ideas can also be elicited by physical stimuli, and perhaps typically are; my thought of a triangle, for instance, may be triggered off by seeing a crudely drawn diagram on paper. But the existence of a physical stimulus is not a causally necessary condition for the occurrence of intellectual ideas. We do not have to invoke the malicious demon to explain this possibility. This is not necessarily to say that no stimulus is required to activate the disposition; it is only to say that the stimulus need not be physical.

Intellectual ideas may be innate, for Descartes, in an even stronger sense than any we have yet considered. So far we have assumed that Descartes's theory of innate ideas makes essential reference to dispositions, even if the ideas themselves are not identified with dispositions. But this assumption can be, and has been, challenged. It can hardly be denied that dispositions figure prominently in much of Descartes's writing about innate ideas, but there are occasions where Descartes seems to abandon the dispositional account altogether; he seems to suggest that innate ideas are present in the mind from birth as submerged, but occurrent, thoughts. After telling his correspondent, Hyperaspistes, that an infant's mind is mainly occupied in perceiving sensations, Descartes adds significantly:

Nonetheless, it has in itself the ideas of God, itself, and all such truths as are called self-evident, in the same way as adult humans have when they are not attending to them [*Nec minus tamen in se habet ideas Dei, sui et earum veritatum, quae per se notae esse dicuntur, quam easdem habent homines adulti, cum ad ipsas non attendunt*]; it does not acquire these ideas later on, as it grows older. I have no doubt that if it were taken out of the prison of the body it would find them within itself.[22]

This is obviously an important text, but it is not easy to interpret. As Kenny suggests, Descartes seems to advance a stronger claim than the position he develops in the *Comments on a Certain Broadsheet*;[23] what is not clear is just how strong a claim he is making in the letter to Hyperaspistes. Kenny himself deals with this issue in terms of the Aristotelian distinctions between mere

---

[22] Descartes to Hyperaspistes, Aug. 1641, AT iii. 424; K, p. 111.
[23] Kenny, *Descartes*, p. 102.

potentiality, first actuality, and second actuality. Kenny suggests that in the *Comments on a Certain Broadsheet* what is innate is a mere potentiality; it is the unrealized capacity to acquire knowledge. In the letter to Hyperaspistes, by contrast, it is more like Aristotle's 'first actuality'—in other words, the non-exercise of knowledge already acquired.[24] But Kenny may not have accurately located the contrast, for it is doubtful whether in the letter to Hyperaspistes Descartes is thinking in terms of the Aristotelian notion of first actuality. Descartes may intend a stronger claim than Kenny believes. Consider the implications of Descartes's comparison between innate ideas and ideas which adults have when they are not attending to them. It is not, I think, natural to interpret Descartes's talk of 'attention' here in terms of the activating of a disposition, even an acquired disposition such as my modest ability to speak French. When I start attending to my headache, I do not activate a disposition; rather, I start to notice a sensation which was present all the time in a straightforwardly non-dispositional form.

The difficulty of interpreting the letter to Hyperaspistes may be symptomatic of a deeper problem. Margaret Wilson has shown that there is an unclarity in Descartes's thinking in this area. Wilson observes that Descartes invokes the concept of attention to draw a distinction between explicit and implicit knowledge; both kinds of knowledge are actual, but implicit knowledge has the characteristic that it is not attended to.[25] Now at first sight this distinction appears to support our interpretation, for it seems that it is implicit knowledge that is in question in the letter to Hyperaspistes. But unfortunately, as Wilson shows, Descartes has difficulty holding on to this distinction; he tends to conflate it with the quite different distinction between actual and potential knowledge.[26] Thus it seems that Descartes was generally unclear about the difference between a thought which is occurrent but not attended to and a mere disposition to have such thoughts.

Perhaps the underlying difficulty for Descartes may be most vividly brought out in the following way. At a fundamental level Descartes is committed by his metaphysics to the thesis that the mind is essentially pure intellect. This thesis implies that if, counterfactually, the mind were taken out of the body, it would have purely intellectual, non-sensory properties. But it is perhaps

[24] Kenny, *Descartes*, p. 103.
[25] Wilson, *Descartes* (London, 1978), 158 ff.   [26] Ibid. 163.

not clear to Descartes exactly what this involves. In particular, he may be undecided on the issue whether in the counterfactual situation the mind would have merely a set of unactivated dispositions or whether it would have occurrent thoughts. Now Descartes is under strong philosophical pressure to embrace the latter horn of the dilemma; this seems to be entailed by his thesis that the mind always thinks (which surely holds for disembodied, as well as embodied, minds). But in that case Descartes is faced by the problem of explaining what would determine the mind to have occurrent thoughts with one content rather than another.

This problem is linked to a further hesitation in Descartes's thinking. Although they are not both fully spelt out, there are really two models of the role of the senses in relation to the intellect discernible in Descartes's writings. According to one account, the role of the senses is entirely negative; it consists in swamping, submerging, or—less metaphorically—distracting our attention away from our intellectual ideas. This view finds eloquent expression in Descartes's reply to Gassendi: 'The senses often impede the mind in its operations, and in no case do they help in the perception of ideas.'[27] Such a bleak view of the senses tends to suggest, though it does not quite entail, that it is essential to the intellect to have occurrent thoughts. But though this is perhaps Descartes's official and dominant view of the senses, there are surely at least suggestions of a more positive account; the senses play an important (indispensable?) role in activating the mind's dispositions so that it has occurrent intellectual ideas. Such a view would be consistent with supposing that the mind in itself has only dispositional properties. As we shall see, the claim that the mind could possess only dispositional properties is to be a major target of Malebranche's polemic.

Innate Ideas and the Creation of the Eternal Truths

In *From Descartes to Hume* Louis Loeb writes that 'apart from the special case of the idea of God, Descartes would have had no use for innate ideas were it not for his peculiar doctrine that the eternal truths are dependent upon God-willed essences'.[28] As we have seen, this is surely an overstatement. Descartes has other motives for

---

[27] 'Fifth Replies', AT vii. 375; CSM ii. 258.   [28] Loeb, p. 68.

advancing a doctrine of innate ideas such as his anti-scholastic theory of perception and his thesis that the mind is essentially pure intellect. But Loeb is right in what he asserts if not in what he denies; there is an important connection, for Descartes, between innate ideas and the creation of the eternal truths. We shall see that this dimension of Descartes's commitment to innate ideas is a major focus of Malebranche's polemic.

Loeb does not simply overstate his case; he sells it short in a curious way. Loeb draws on passages where Descartes says that our innate ideas represent true and immutable essences, but he is at pains to deny that Descartes advances a doctrine of innate propositional knowledge.[29] Loeb is not alone in denying this,[30] but it is none the less an odd position to take. In fact, on a number of occasions Descartes explicitly asserts that it is not only ideas but truths which are innate. As we have seen, Descartes tells Hyperaspistes that 'the mind has in itself the ideas of God, itself, and all such truths as are called self-evident'.[31] And in his letter to Voetius Descartes follows Plato in arguing for the innateness of geometrical truths, theorems as well as axioms:

It is to be noted that all those things of which the knowledge is said to be implanted in us by nature, are not thereby expressly known by us; but are only such that we can know them without any sense-experience through the powers of our own mind. All geometrical truths are of this sort, not only the very obvious ones but also the rest, however abstruse they may seem. And thus Socrates in Plato, by questioning a boy about the elements of geometry and by thus bringing it about that the boy drew out truths from his own mind, which he had not previously noticed to be in it, tried to prove his doctrine of reminiscence. And the knowledge of God is of this kind; and when you infer that there is no one who is speculatively an Atheist, you were not less silly [*ineptus*] than if from the fact that all Geometrical truths are in the same way innate in us, you had said that there is no one in the world who does not know Euclid's elements.[32]

Most surprisingly of all in view of his purposes, Loeb ignores Descartes's explicit assertions linking innate ideas with the creation

---

[29] 'While Descartes writes of innate ideas and innate faculties, he does not write explicitly of innate knowledge' (ibid. 67). Loeb's exegetical claim about Descartes is intended to cast doubt on the traditional view that Descartes is the target of Locke's polemic against innate knowledge.

[30] See e.g. W. Doney, 'Rationalism', G. H. Robinson (ed.), *The Rationalist Conception of Consciousness*, *Southern Journal of Philosophy*, 21 suppl. (1983), 7.

[31] Descartes to Hyperaspistes, Aug. 1641, AT iii. 424; K, p. 111.

[32] Letter to G. Voetius, viii/в. 166–7.

of the eternal truths. The famous letter where Descartes tells Mersenne that the eternal truths 'have been laid down by God' also contains his first known reference to innate ideas: 'They are all *inborn in our minds* [*mentibus nostris ingenitae*] just as a king would imprint his laws on the hearts of all his subjects if he had enough power to do so.'[33] There is thus direct textual evidence for the claim that Descartes saw a connection between innate ideas and the creation of the eternal truths. The connection does not need to be laboriously extrapolated from Descartes's remarks about true and immutable essences.

Descartes's doctrine of the creation of the eternal truths strikes many readers as bizarre, and its interpretation is of course controversial. One issue that has been debated is the implications of the doctrine for the Cartesian understanding of necessity. For some readers, Descartes's doctrine amounts to a denial that there are, strictly speaking, any necessary truths.[34] For others, Descartes's thesis is a weaker one; it should be taken merely as the denial that the necessity of necessary truths is itself necessary.[35] The second interpretation seems to be supported by a passage in a letter to Mesland:

And even if God has willed that some truths should be necessary, this does not mean that he willed them necessarily; for it is one thing to will that they be necessary, and quite another to will them necessarily, or to be necessitated to will them.[36]

But, in fact, Descartes stops significantly short here of committing himself outright to the necessity of the eternal truths. Descartes appears rather to be arguing concessively; even if it is granted that the eternal truths are necessary, it does not follow that they are necessarily necessary. But, in any case, the important point for our purposes is that the eternal truths could have been other than they are: for instance, God could have brought it about that two plus three equalled six. It is of course inconceivable to us that two plus

[33] Descartes to Mersenne, 15 Apr. 1630, AT i. 145; Kenny, p. 11.
[34] See e.g. H. Frankfurt, 'Descartes on the Creation of the Eternal Truths', *Philosophical Review*, 86 (1977), 36–57.
[35] E. Curley, 'Descartes on the Creation of the Eternal Truths', *Philosophical Review*, 93 (1984), 569–97. Cf. I. Hacking, 'Leibniz and Descartes: Proof and Eternal Truths', in A. Kenny (ed.), *Rationalism, Empiricism, and Idealism* (Oxford, 1986), 52–3.
[36] Descartes to Mesland, 2 May 1644, AT iv. 118–19; K, p. 151.

three should not equal five, but it is a mistake to infer from the fact that we cannot conceive it that it is impossible for God to bring it about.[37]

Some readers have felt that Descartes's doctrine of the eternal truths is connected in an interesting way with radical scepticism.[38] The nature of the connection is not easy to spell out. Clearly, the thesis that the eternal truths, such as 'Two plus three equal five', have been created by God does not of itself have sceptical implications. Consider, however, Descartes's claim cited at the end of the previous paragraph: from the fact that *p* is inconceivable to us it does not follow that God could not bring it about that *p*. In other words, the possibility of *p* is consistent with the inconceivability of *p*. Thus, our finite minds may not be reliable guides to the logical structure of reality.[39] It may be objected that there is a danger here of sliding from metaphysical to epistemic possibility.[40] In order to generate a sceptical position, it is the epistemic sense of 'possible' that is needed; however, when Descartes warns us not to suppose that it is impossible for God to bring about what is inconceivable to us, it is metaphysical possibility that is in question. It seems, however, that a sceptical problem can be generated in a way which does not involve any conflation. Recall the position of the enquirer in the 'First Meditation'. The enquirer may find it inconceivable that *p*—e.g. that two plus three are equal to six—but as yet he cannot be certain that there is not a deceiving god, or malicious demon, who has the power to make *p* true.[41] Indeed, the demon may actually have exercised such power. It is thus at this stage epistemically possible for him that *p*.

Descartes of course believes that he has the resources to defeat sceptical worries of this kind. Such scepticism is to be defeated by proving the existence of a benevolent, non-deceiving God. The goodness of God guarantees that what is psychologically necessary for us to believe coincides with what he has freely and contingently

---

[37] See Descartes to Arnauld, 29 July 1648, AT v. 223–4; K, pp. 236–7.

[38] For different views on the connection, see E. Bréhier, 'The Creation of the Eternal Truths in Descartes's System', in W. Doney (ed.), *Descartes: A Collection of Critical Essays* (London, 1967), 192–208, esp. pp. 200–1; M. Wilson, *Descartes* (London, 1978), 127–8.

[39] Cf. Frankfurt, p. 45.

[40] This objection is made by Wilson, *Descartes*, p. 128.

[41] See 'First Meditation', AT vii. 21; CSM ii. 14. Descartes does not introduce the 'malicious demon' until later in the meditation.

willed. Indeed, such necessities of thought have actually been implanted by God in our minds:

I have noticed certain laws which God has so established in nature, and of which he has implanted such notions in our minds, that after adequate reflection we cannot doubt that they are exactly observed in everything which exists or occurs in the world.[42]

In other words, the eternal truths are innate in us.

Descartes's theory of the eternal truths is thus psychologistic; necessary truths, if we continue to speak of necessity at all, are simply those which we are psychologically compelled to believe. But any account of this kind may seem obviously and fatally flawed. Surely, it may be objected, even the most elementary laws of logic are not psychologically necessary for us; most people's reasoning is fallacious much of the time. It may well be the case that Descartes's theory is ultimately unsatisfactory, but it is not without resources for dealing with objections of this sort. Descartes can reply by clarifying his concept of psychological necessity. The eternal truths are necessities of thought for us in the sense that we are compelled to assent to them if we are perceiving clearly and distinctly. Descartes can cheerfully concede that for much of the time people's thinking is not clear and distinct; on such occasions they can be mistaken about the content of the eternal truths. Thus Descartes would grant that there is a real sense in which we can be mistaken about what is conceivable and inconceivable for us. There is textual support of an indirect kind for such a suggestion. In the letter to Voetius and elsewhere Descartes claims that the fact that ideas and truths are innate in us does not imply that we cannot fail to discover them; indeed, Descartes remarks that someone may not notice their innate idea of God even after the thousandth reading of the *Meditations*.[43] Now the eternal truths are among the items that are innate in us. Thus, just as someone can fail to discover their innate idea of God, so too they can fail to discover the eternal truths which are innate in their minds. Part of what Descartes is saying is simply that people can be ignorant of eternal truths such as abstruse geometrical theorems. But for the purposes of defeating the objection he clearly needs a stronger claim: we can be in error even in regard to eternal truths of an elementary kind. In this sense we

---

[42] *Discourse on Method*, AT vi. 41; CSM i. 131.
[43] Descartes to Hyperaspistes, Aug. 1641, AT iii. 430; K, p. 117.

can be mistaken about what is psychologically necessary and impossible for us.

In this chapter we have seen that Descartes invokes innate ideas in response to a bewildering variety of philosophical issues, and we have resisted the temptation to impose a unity on his pronouncements which they do not seem to possess. To say this is not necessarily to accuse Descartes of a fundamental inconsistency; much of what he says can be defended by attributing to him a distinction—which he does not explicitly draw—between a strong and a weak sense of 'innateness'. But it is easy to see why philosophers in the Cartesian tradition should have been dissatisfied with Descartes's teaching concerning innate ideas. In the eyes of Malebranche, Descartes's teaching on this issue is flawed in a number of ways. For one thing, it relies heavily on an appeal to psychological dispositions, and, for Malebranche, the very notion of a dispositional property is suspect. But Malebranche's fundamental criticism cuts deeper. By attributing innateness to both concepts and sensations, Descartes has muddled things which should be kept quite separate; he has made the mistake of confusing logic and psychology. For Malebranche, the most serious weakness of Descartes's doctrine of innate ideas is one that it inherits from his doctrine of ideas in general.

4

Malebranche
The Theory of Ideas

MANY philosophers are aware that Malebranche held a distinctive theory of ideas, but the nature of the theory is not well understood. Malebranche's insistence on locating ideas in God is sometimes presented as gratuitous obscurantism or as a largely unmotivated, conservative reaction to the Cartesian revolution in philosophy. It is true that Malebranche's theory of ideas is an attempt to return to an older tradition in philosophy, but it is quite wrong to suppose that it is philosophically unmotivated. On the contrary, the theory is addressed to serious weaknesses in Descartes's philosophy. In the 'Tenth Elucidation' of *The Search after Truth* Malebranche deftly suggests that Descartes's theory of ideas is the source of three related problems:

> We can see clearly . . . that to maintain that ideas that are eternal, immutable, and common to all intelligences, are only perceptions or momentary particular modifications of the mind, is to establish Pyrrhonism and to make room for the belief that what is moral or immoral is not necessarily so, which is the most dangerous error of all.[1]

In other words, the Cartesian doctrine of ideas not merely conflates logic and psychology, but it thereby opens the door to scepticism and to a voluntarist theory of the eternal truths which Malebranche regards as both incoherent in itself and dangerous in ethics. We shall see, then, how Malebranche attempts to solve these problems by means of his theory of ideas; we shall also examine the difficulties raised by Malebranche's insistence on locating ideas in God.

Malebranche's theory of knowledge calls to mind not merely a distinctive theory of ideas, but the famous doctrine that we see all things in God. Since Malebranche locates all ideas in God, there is a sense in which all mental activity involving ideas might be described as 'vision in God'. But the term 'vision in God' may also be taken in

---

[1] 'Tenth Elucidation', *OCM* iii. 140; *SAT*, 620.

a narrower sense to denote Malebranche's theory of visual perception; thus, for Malebranche, it is in God that we perceive the primary quality features of physical objects such as tables and chairs. In the following chapter we shall examine Malebranche's doctrine of 'vision in God' in the narrower sense; in other words, we shall see how Malebranche applies his theory of ideas to the special case of sense-perception. But in the present chapter we shall be concerned with his theory of ideas in general.

Anti-Psychologism: Ideas and Perceptions

Perhaps the most basic feature of Malebranche's theory of ideas is its resolute anti-psychologism. Far more than any other seventeenth-century philosopher in the Cartesian tradition, Malebranche insists that logic and psychology must not be conflated. In particular, we need to distinguish carefully between the thought (i.e. thinking) of x and the concept or idea of x. The former is a particular mental event which occurs at a particular time; in Malebranche's terms, it is a modification or modality of the human mind. The latter, by contrast, is an abstract entity which exists over and above these modifications. It is true that Malebranche locates ideas, the abstract items, in God, and this may seem to qualify his anti-psychologism. But we shall see that Malebranche resists any attempt to reduce ideas or concepts to divine thinkings. Although it is obscure just how ideas are supposed to be in God, it is clear that they are not events in his mind; indeed, they do not seem to be mental contents at all.

Malebranche's theory of ideas naturally invites comparison with Descartes's. As we have seen in an earlier chapter, Descartes was aware of an ambiguity in his use of the term 'idea'; ideas, for Descartes, are sometimes mental events (ideas$_m$) and sometimes contents (ideas$_o$). It is tempting to say that Malebranche is simply resolving this ambiguity in favour of ideas$_o$, and it is certainly true that Malebranche's ideas are objects or contents of thought. But to leave the matter here is seriously misleading, for it fails to bring out the fundamental disagreement over ontology between Malebranche and Descartes. We can clarify the difference by considering how the two philosophers would analyse the case of someone thinking of a triangle in general. Descartes will say that there is one item here which has two irreducible aspects. On the one hand, there is its aspect as a particular thought or modification of the mind; on the other hand, there is its representational content, namely, the triangle in general.[2] Malebranche, by contrast, will claim that there is not one item here but two which need to be carefully distinguished; there is both thought or perception (the modification of the mind) and idea (the abstract entity). For Malebranche, when two people think of a triangle in general, they may be said to be thinking of the very same idea, although their thoughts (i.e. thinkings) are numerically distinct and peculiar to their minds.

Malebranche's theory of ideas was the subject of a famous attack from a Cartesian standpoint by Arnauld; Malebranche replied, and a controversy ensued which lasted many years. In his opening salvo, *On True and False Ideas*, Arnauld sharply criticized Malebranche's view of ideas as representative entities which are ontologically distinct from the mind's perceptions. Although the question is a controversial one, it does not seem that Arnauld is opposed to all representative entities. In the following passage Arnauld makes it clear that he is attacking only the thesis that ideas are entities over and above perceptions:

What I understand by representative beings, in so far as I attack them as superfluous entities, are only those which are supposed to be really distinct from ideas taken for perceptions. For I am not concerned to attack all sorts of representative beings or modalities; since I maintain that it is clear to whoever engages in reflection on what passes in his own mind, that all our perceptions are essentially representative modalities.[3]

Although Arnauld does not put it in these terms, we can say that what he opposes is the thesis that, in thinking, the mind is related to irreducibly abstract entities. Arnauld holds that we can explain the nature of thought without postulating the existence of any entities which are not psychological. For Arnauld, as for Descartes, to talk about the object or content of thought is simply to talk about an

---

[2] This is not to deny that Descartes may sometimes think of ideas$_0$ as abstract entities.

[3] A. Arnauld, *Des vraies et des fausses idées*, ch. iv, in *Œuvres de Messire Antoine Arnauld*, xxxviii (Paris, 1780; repr. Brussels, 1967), 199. On the question of Arnauld's own positive views, see A. O. Lovejoy, ' "Representative Ideas" in Malebranche and Arnauld', *Mind*, 32 (1923), 449–61; M. Cook, 'Arnauld's Alleged Representationalism', *Journal of the History of Philosophy*, 12 (1974), 53–62; D. Radner, 'Representationalism in Arnauld's Act Theory of Perception', *Journal of the History of Philosophy*, 14 (1976), 96–8; S. Nadler, *Arnauld and the Cartesian Philosophy of Ideas* (Princeton, 1989).

aspect of mental events. Indeed, for Arnauld as perhaps for
Descartes, it is essential to all perceptions to have representational
content. This does not of course mean that we can think only
of actually existing beings; it means that the psychological is
inherently intentional.

In order to bring out the importance of the Malebranche–Arnauld
controversy, it is helpful to stress two points. First, the issue
between Malebranche and Arnauld is not merely verbal; it does not
centre on the meaning of the term 'idea'. Although Malebranche
believes that his sense of 'idea' is the standard one, he is prepared to
allow Arnauld to define the term in whatever way he chooses:

If he claims only to define what he means by the terms, it is permitted to
him to name *idea* the modification or perception of the mind, for one can
say that nominal definitions are arbitrary. But in claiming to conclude from
that that the modifications of the mind are representative of objects, or that
the *idea*, the immediate object of the mind when it thinks for example of the
perfect square, is only the perception which it has of it, only its own
modification; it is clear that he abuses his nominal definition, that he
changes it into a real definition [*definition de chose*], and that he supposes
what he must prove.[4]

Thus, Arnauld may use the term 'idea' for perception if he wishes,
but there remains a substantive issue about the ontology of thought.
Secondly, and relatedly, Malebranche and Arnauld are not merely
debating the correct interpretation of Descartes. As a matter of fact
both philosophers spend much time trying to establish that their
own interpretation of Descartes is the correct one. But with
Malebranche, in particular, it is clear that the central issue is not
exegetical but philosophical.

For strategic reasons Malebranche tries hard to enlist Descartes
on his side. On a number of occasions Malebranche claims that he is
seeking to clarify Descartes's own theory of ideas. Malebranche
admits that Descartes's pronouncements on ideas are ambiguous,
but he denies that Descartes is committed to the theory which
Arnauld attributes to him.[5] On other occasions, Malebranche
concedes that he is making major revisions in Cartesian theory.
Descartes, he claims, did not get to the bottom of the nature of
ideas.[6] Malebranche brings out his difference from his predecessor
in terms of the terminology which Descartes himself employed:

[4] Lettre III, 19 Mar. 1699, *OCM* ix. 913.
[5] *Réponse au livre*, ch. XXIV (*OCM* vi. 172).
[6] *Trois Lettres*, I (*OCM* vi. 214).

Mr Descartes says that ideas are modalities of minds. That is true [i.e. that Descartes says this]; but it is because, unlike me, he does not take the word 'idea' to signify exclusively the 'representative reality', but for those sorts of thoughts by which one perceives a man, an angel, etc.[7]

Malebranche would like to be able to show that he is merely following Descartes, but fortunately he does not rest his case on the claim that his theory of ideas coincides with his predecessor's.

Malebranche is right to insist that the issue between him and Arnauld is neither merely verbal nor exegetical. However, a candid reader must admit that, even so, his presentation of his case against Arnauld is not entirely successful. There are points at which Malebranche can be suspected of misrepresenting Arnauld for polemical purposes. Thus on one occasion Malebranche seems to attribute to Arnauld the view that ideas, *qua* modifications of the mind, are essentially representative.[8] But Arnauld need not admit this. Arnauld's position is only that ideas essentially have two aspects, namely, both objective and formal reality; in other words, it is essential to ideas to have representational content, just as it is essential to ideas to be mental events or modifications. We can bring out the nature of Malebranche's mistake by means of an analogy with the more familiar case of Spinoza's metaphysics. It is as if someone were to saddle Spinoza with the claim that it is essential to substance, *qua* extended, to think. In fact, of course, Spinoza's thesis is only that it is essential to substance to think and to be extended.

Malebranche's defence of his position against Arnauld leaves something to be desired; none the less, he has powerful criticisms to make of the Cartesian doctrine of ideas. First of all, Malebranche is surely right that there is a fundamental unclarity in Descartes's position. In Descartes's writings, questions of the form 'How many ideas have I had during the last five minutes?' tend to be systematically ambiguous. Secondly, Malebranche would insist that, even when this muddle is straightened out, Descartes's theory cannot explain adequately how two people can be said to have the very same idea; for Descartes, this would seem to be a mere *façon de parler*. Nor can Descartes explain how ideas can pre-exist and post-exist particular acts of thinking. For the idea of a triangle did not

---

[7] Ibid. (*OCM* vi. 217).
[8] See ibid. (*OCM* vi. 216–17).

come into existence when someone first thought of a triangle, and it will not cease to exist when the last triangle-thinker has expired.

Finally, perhaps the most original of Malebranche's criticisms is implicit in his insistence that the mind's modifications are not essentially representative. We have seen that there is a tendency in Descartes's philosophy to ascribe intentionality to all mental phenomena. Malebranche, like Rorty, believes that this tendency is fundamentally mistaken. In the first place, Malebranche wishes to draw our attention to a class of mental phenomena which have no objects or content at all; these phenomena he calls *sentiments*. The paradigm of a *sentiment*, for Malebranche, is a pain sensation, for pains are perhaps the clearest case of mental events which do not represent, which are not about anything. But Malebranche thinks that lack of representational content is not limited to pains and other bodily sensations; it is characteristic of the whole class of secondary qualities. This is the serious philosophical point behind Malebranche's notorious remark that 'the soul actually becomes blue, red, or yellow, and . . . the soul is painted with the colours of the rainbow when looking at it.'[9] It is not surprising that on the strength of this remark Malebranche was ridiculed as a believer in the rainbow-coloured soul. Of course, Malebranche's remark *sounds* odd, because ordinary language embodies the pre-Cartesian assumption that secondary qualities are properties of bodies, not of minds. But in fact, however paradoxical it may sound, Malebranche's remark is intelligible and even defensible in the context of seventeenth-century philosophy; he can claim to be simply trading on and extending the widely recognized affinity between secondary qualities and bodily sensations.

Malebranche thus recognizes a class of mental modifications which have no content, and these modifications, *sentiments*, play a major role in all perceptual experience.[10] In candour, we must admit that Malebranche wishes to go further than this. He wants to argue, against Descartes, that no mental modifications—as such—are representational; on the contrary, they are representational only in so far as they are related to ideas. But even if we do not follow Malebranche as far as this, we can concede that he mounts a powerful critique of some of the most fundamental tendencies of Descartes's philosophy.

---

[9] 'Eleventh Elucidation', *OCM* iii. 166; *SAT* 634. Cf. McCracken, p. 60.
[10] See e.g. *Search after Truth*, III, 2. 6 (*OCM* i. 445; *SAT* 234).

Anti-Psychologism and Anti-Scepticism

For Malebranche, Descartes's psychologistic tendency to conflate ideas and perceptions is one of the roots of his inability to conquer scepticism. Malebranche claims that, by contrast, his own theory of ideas offers an antidote to scepticism (Pyrrhonism).[11] It is important to note that the scepticism in question here is not scepticism about the existence of the external world; for Malebranche holds that scepticism of this kind can be defeated, not by philosophical analysis, but only by an appeal to revelation. The sceptical problem which, for Malebranche, Descartes's psychologism renders him unable to solve is the problem of knowing that my clear and distinct ideas are true. In other words, how do I know that my clearest intellectual intuitions are a reliable guide to the structure of reality?

Consider, says Malebranche, the Cartesian rule that whatever I clearly and distinctly perceive is true, or, as Malebranche puts it, I can affirm of a thing whatever I clearly perceive to be contained in the idea of the thing. Such a rule can be interpreted in two ways, depending on whether the term 'idea' is taken in the logical or the psychological sense. If interpreted in the former way, then the rule is perfectly good; I can affirm of a thing whatever I clearly perceive to be contained in the concept or idea of a thing. For example, I can affirm of a Euclidean triangle that its internal angles must add up to one hundred and eighty degrees, for I can clearly perceive that this property is timelessly contained in the idea of a triangle. But if the rule is interpreted in the latter way, so that the term 'idea' is understood in a psychological sense, then the rule is useless. In the *Conversations chrétiennes* (*Christian Conversations*) Malebranche's spokesman even claims that it reduces to a tautology:

One can, you say, affirm of such a sphere whatever you clearly conceive to be contained in the idea; that is to say, still according to you, in the modality of your mind in so far as it is representative of a sphere. But this rigmarole, to which your opinion reduces, can mean only that you can affirm that you perceive what you perceive, and not that what you perceive is in itself such as you perceive it, since you say that your ideas are not distinguished from your perceptions.[12]

It is not clear why Malebranche thinks that on the psychologistic interpretation the rule must reduce to a tautology, but we can see at

---

[11] *Conversations chrétiennes*, III (*OCM* iv. 71).
[12] Ibid. (*OCM* iv. 71).

least why he thinks that it leads to scepticism. For on this interpretation the rule that whatever I clearly and distinctly perceive is true stands in need of justification; thus the Cartesian is driven to invoke God as the external guarantor of clear and distinct perceptions. But, notoriously, if we try to prove that God guarantees the truth of our clear and distinct perceptions, we fall into the trap of the Cartesian circle.

Malebranche seems right that if the Cartesian rule is to stand on its own, then it is the logical, not the psychological, sense of 'idea' that is needed. But though this is a necessary condition of defeating scepticism, it is not clear that it is sufficient; even when ideas are taken to be concepts, it is still surely possible to mount an effective case for scepticism about the structure of reality. It is true, of course, that ideas, in the logical sense of the term 'idea', have necessary consequences. Prima facie, then, it would seem to make no sense to worry whether triangular figures in the real world have the properties that are contained in *the* idea or concept of a Euclidean triangle. But the geometrical example is illuminating here, for in the light of subsequent developments in mathematics, we can see that some real sceptical questions remain in the field. We now know, for instance, that there are non-Euclidean geometries, and it is a serious question whether the space of the actual world is Euclidean in character. Of course, it is still true that the theorems of Euclidean geometry follow logically from the axioms and definitions, but it is an empirical question whether the axioms are true of the actual world. It may be objected that this criticism is a little unfair, for the existence of alternative geometries was unknown in the seventeenth century; Euclidean geometry was understood on all sides to constitute a system of necessary truths. But we need not run the risk of anachronism to see that Malebranche has not defeated scepticism about the structure of reality even on his own terms. Even if we waive the possibility of non-Euclidean geometries, it still has to be shown that the physical world possesses *only* geometrical properties. Perhaps I can clearly and distinctly perceive that the theorems of Euclidean geometry are true of the actual world, but what guarantee do I have that geometrical concepts are an adequate basis for physics?

To sceptical worries of this kind Malebranche's answer is clear. We can be sure that our ideas constitute an adequate conceptual framework for understanding the world because they are God's archetypes; they are, as it were, the blueprints which God either has followed, or would follow, in creating the physical world.[13] It is important to realize that Malebranche's reply is still addressed to scepticism concerning the structure of reality. For Malebranche, the fact that ideas, in the logical sense, are God's archetypes does not guarantee the existence of a physical world; for God may never have created such a world at all. But if physical objects do exist, then they must have the structural properties which can be deduced from the ideas to which our minds are related in thinking. Indeed, the status of ideas as God's archetypes is intended to establish a stronger claim; if physical objects exist at all, then the ideas to which we are related must constitute a wholly adequate framework for physics. The world has no general structural features which are not captured by these ideas.

Malebranche's appeal to the status of ideas as divine archetypes is ingenious, and has a long tradition behind it. But as a strategy for refuting scepticism, it is unsatisfactory. For it is clear that with his talk of archetypes Malebranche is simply smuggling in a new thesis about ideas. From the fact that ideas are logical, 'third realm' entities, it does not follow that they are divine archetypes in the required sense. It is true that since our ideas are eternal and immutable, a case can be made, as we shall see later, for saying that they are in God. Moreover, ideas might be said to be divine archetypes in the minimal sense that the structure of the world must conform to the laws of logic. But in order to defeat scepticism, Malebranche requires ideas to be archetypes in a stronger sense; he needs to show that significant structural features of the world can be discovered on the basis of ideas. To the sceptic who asks 'Is space Euclidean?', he needs to be able to show that the axioms of Euclidean geometry would be chosen by God for the creation of the world. Again, to the sceptic who asks whether geometry is an adequate basis for physics, he should be able to establish that God would employ only geometrical models in constructing the world. To satisfy such a sceptic it is not enough to say that the theorems of Euclidean geometry follow logically from the axioms and definitions. Yet it is not clear that Malebranche's theory of ideas offers reasons for going beyond this.

---

[13] *Conversations chrétiennes*, III (*OCM* iv. 72); *Dialogues on Metaphysics*, II (D, pp. 44–5). See D. Radner, *Malebranche* (Assen, 1978), p. 61.

In fact, by itself, Malebranche's anti-psychologism seems to provide little help with the conquest of scepticism. We can see this by taking note of a problem which also arises in Descartes's philosophy. For Malebranche, the paradigm ideas are geometrical concepts such as triangles and circles, but it is difficult to see how the privileged status of such concepts is justified by Malebranche's legitimate insistence on the distinction between psychology and logic. It is true, of course, that I can distinguish between my thought (i.e. thinking) of a triangle and the idea or concept of a triangle which is the timeless, abstract entity; but it would seem that I can similarly distinguish between the thought of a unicorn and the idea of a unicorn. It may be that, like Descartes, Malebranche would insist that the idea of a triangle, unlike the idea of a unicorn, is a true and immutable nature; but it is notoriously difficult to formulate a criterion which produces this desired result.[14] For the idea of a unicorn seems to have logical consequences just as surely as the idea of a triangle. It would seem, then, that Malebranche is under philosophical pressure to allow that there is an idea of a unicorn. Now we have seen that, even in the case of geometrical concepts, it does not follow that they are divine archetypes in a sense strong enough to defeat scepticism. And the point is even clearer in the present case. For if it is allowed that there is an idea of a unicorn, then obviously there are ideas which are not in any interesting sense archetypes for God's creation of the world. It is true of course that if God created a unicorn, then he would be obliged to create an animal that was one-horned; but Malebranche is after bigger quarry with his claim that ideas are archetypes.

Malebranche's attack on psychologism is important, but it does not seem to have the interesting anti-sceptical consequences that he ascribes to it. Malebranche tries to mask this uncomfortable fact by moving from logic to theology. Ideas are not merely logical entities; by virtue of their logical status, they also possess properties, such as being eternal and immutable, which make them divine. But even if we grant that they possess these properties, and are thus 'in God', it does not follow that they are divine archetypes for the creation of the world in a sense which is strong enough to defeat scepticism.

---

[14] On true and immutable natures, see 'Fifth Meditation', AT vii. 64–8; CSM ii. 44–7. On Descartes's difficulty in formulating a criterion for distinguishing true and immutable natures from fictitious ideas, see M. D. Wilson, *Descartes* (London, 1978), 168–76.

Anti-Psychologism and Anti-Voluntarism

Like Leibniz, Malebranche indignantly rejects Descartes's notorious doctrine of the creation of the eternal truths. Here, too, Malebranche's polemic against Descartes's psychologism is at work. Indeed, it is not too much to say that Malebranche's rejection of Cartesian voluntarism is really part of his overall attack on psychologism. In a letter to Regis, Malebranche argues with some irony that the Cartesian doctrine of the eternal truths is rooted in the conflation of logic and psychology:

> I cannot persuade myself that ideas depend on God as on their efficient cause. For being eternal, immutable, and necessary, they have no need of an efficient cause; although I admit that the perception I have of these ideas depends on God as its efficient cause. I am also in this error of believing that geometrical and numerical truths such as two times two are four are eternal, independent, and prior [*préalables*] to the free decrees of God.[15]

Thus, for Malebranche, once we distinguish logic from psychology, we will see that it makes no sense to look for the efficient cause of ideas. And similarly in the case of the eternal truths; once we make this distinction, we will see that it makes no sense to look for the efficient cause of the truths of logic and mathematics. Yet Descartes teaches that the eternal truths have been created by God; he is thus committed to the thesis that they have efficient causes, and it is this assumption that Malebranche traces to a general Cartesian tendency to conflate logic and psychology. It is not surprising that Malebranche should trace Descartes's voluntarism and his theory of ideas to a common source, for, according to Malebranche, there is a tight logical connection between ideas and necessary truths.[16]

Malebranche is not claiming that Descartes's teaching concerning the eternal truths is entailed simply by his psychologism. This of course would be a mistake. From the fact that ideas and truths have causes, it does not follow that they are created by God; consistently with psychologism, for instance, one might suppose that a complete causal explanation can be given in terms of the brute, contingent structure of the human mind. Malebranche's point is simply that if logic and psychology are conflated, then it becomes permissible to look for the efficient causes of the eternal truths. And once one allows that this enquiry is a proper one, it is natural to suppose that

---

[15] Réponse à Regis, *OCM* xvii/1. 308.
[16] See 'Tenth Elucidation', *OCM* iii. 136; *SAT* 617.

the efficient cause is to be found in the free will of an omnipotent God. Descartes's doctrine of the creation of the eternal truths gives a theistic twist to the claims of psychologism.

Malebranche's diagnosis of Cartesian voluntarism is highly suggestive, and throws new light on the vexed issue of Descartes's teaching concerning the eternal truths. Malebranche is surely right that Descartes's position on this issue is of a piece with his theory of ideas; indeed, the parallels between the two doctrines are quite striking. In the 'Third Meditation' Descartes denies that ideas are objects over and above mental events and states; to talk about the contents of thought is simply to talk about an aspect of our perceptions. And in his teaching concerning the eternal truths Descartes denies the existence of an irreducible realm of logical necessity; he dispenses with the notions of logical necessity and impossibility altogether, and proposes that instead we should talk simply in psychological terms. Thus to Arnauld he suggests that we should say merely that the falsity of certain propositions is inconceivable to us:

I do not think that we should ever say of anything that it cannot be brought about by God. For since everything involved in truth and goodness depends on His omnipotence, I would not dare to say that God cannot make a mountain without a valley, or that one and two should not be three. I merely say that He has given me such a mind that I cannot conceive a mountain without a valley, or an aggregate of one and two which is not three, and that such things involve a contradiction in my conception.[17]

The charge of conflating logic and psychology is not the only basis for Malebranche's case against Descartes's voluntarism. In the 'Tenth Elucidation' Malebranche in effect offers the following argument for the thesis that the eternal truths are independent of the will of God. We are certain, he claims, that 'Two plus two equal four' is true at all times and in all places. But we could not be certain of this unless it were the case that the eternal truths are independent of God's will. Therefore, the eternal truths are independent of God's will.[18]

The Cartesian will of course seek to block the argument by denying the second premiss; he will support this denial by appealing to divine immutability. The claim that the eternal truths have been created by God does not have the sceptical consequences Malebranche

[17] Descartes for Arnauld, 29 July 1648, AT v. 223–4; K, pp. 236–7.
[18] 'Tenth Elucidation', *OCM* i. 132; *SAT*, 615.

fears; we know that the eternal truths are unchanging because we know that the divine will is immutable.[19] For Descartes, to say that the divine will is immutable cannot mean that it is absolutely impossible for God to change his will; it must mean rather that a change of will would be inconsistent with divine benevolence. Even so, however, Descartes's reply would hardly satisfy Malebranche. For it is open to Malebranche to grant that God's will is immutable in this sense; in other words, the unchanging nature of the divine will is hypothetically necessary on the assumption of God's benevolence. But Malebranche can argue that a change in the laws of logic is consistent with the concept of divine immutability so construed. It is one thing to say that God's will is immutable; it is another thing to say that he wills an immutable set of laws. It may be part of God's eternal plan that different logics should prevail before and after t.[20] If Descartes then argues that this scenario is excluded by God's benevolence, Malebranche at least has a ready fall-back position; even Descartes admits that the purposes of God are inscrutable.

We can now see how the various strands in Malebranche's critique of Descartes's theory of ideas come together in the case of the eternal truths. Malebranche diagnoses the source of Descartes's voluntarism in a conflation of logic and psychology; only by making such a mistake could one come to believe that it even makes sense to look for the efficient causes of ideas and eternal truths. And once the efficient cause of the eternal truths is located in the divine will, no certainty about them is possible. Although Descartes does not admit it, his voluntarism, when thought through, entails a radical scepticism about logic and mathematics.

The Case against Innate Ideas

Malebranche is aware that Descartes is not without resources for replying to the charge that he cannot escape scepticism. As we have seen in the previous section, Descartes will rely on the benevolence of God established in the 'Third Meditation'. But divine benevolence is only part of the answer; the important point is

---

[19] See Descartes to Mersenne, 15 Apr. 1630, AT i. 145–6; K, pp. 11–12.
[20] See 'Tenth Elucidation', *OCM* iii. 132; *SAT* 615. Cf. M. Gueroult, *Malebranche*, i. (Paris, 1955–9), 114–15.

that God has manifested his benevolence by endowing our minds with a contingent structure so that no room for scepticism remains. Thus to the question 'How do I know that my geometrical ideas are adequate for physics?' Descartes can reply 'Because a benevolent God has implanted ideas in our minds which are designed to reflect the structure of physical reality'. And to the more radical sceptical question 'How do I know that what I take to be eternal truths of logic and mathematics really are so?' Descartes can reply 'Because a benevolent God has structured our minds in such a way that what is psychologically necessary for us to believe conforms to what he has freely and contingently, but immutably, ordained'.

As Malebranche sees it, Descartes's commitment to the thesis of contingent mental structure plays a major role in his philosophy; indeed, it serves to define one of the major issues between himself and his predecessor. It is not surprising, then, that Malebranche finds it necessary to attack Descartes's famous doctrine of innate ideas. Malebranche's attack is really two-pronged. For, first, Malebranche clearly holds that even if the doctrine of innate ideas were true, it could not play the role that Descartes assigns to it in his philosophy; in other words, even if Descartes could show that our minds possessed an innate structure, he is prevented by the problem of circularity from establishing that this structure is the result of a benevolent God. Thus Descartes is not in a good position to deploy the doctrine of innate ideas as a counter to scepticism. Secondly, Malebranche holds that the doctrine of innate ideas is in fact false, and it is this case which we must examine.

Although Malebranche has an effective case against innate ideas, it is not well presented in his most famous work, *La Recherche de la verité* (*The Search after Truth*). Arnauld complained with some justice that in the central epistemological section of this work, Malebranche seems to run together two questions; he does not clearly distinguish between the question of the origin of ideas and the question of their nature.[21] Malebranche confuses the reader by tackling the latter issue as if he shared basic Cartesian assumptions about the nature of ideas; the famous doctrine of vision in God is introduced as if it offered a superior account of idea-acquisition from within the Cartesian framework. In fact, as we have seen, Malebranche's epistemology is such that the whole question of the

[21] Arnauld, ch. XXVI, p. 340.

origin of ideas turns out to be misconceived. Relatedly, the objections to innate ideas which Malebranche does parade in this section are by no means his most powerful; they are almost in the nature of afterthoughts to his real case. Despite these failures of presentation, a major case against innate ideas can be derived from Malebranche's writings as a whole.

(1) Malebranche's most basic argument against innateness flows directly from his doctrine of the nature of ideas. In the simplicity of its structure it resembles his fundamental argument against Cartesian voluntarism. According to Malebranche, once we resist the temptation to conflate ideas and thoughts or perceptions, we must realize that the question of whether there are any innate ideas makes no sense. Indeed, the whole doctrine of innate ideas turns out to be based on a conflation of logic and psychology. If a person speaks of items as being in the mind—e.g. saying that they are there from birth—then he must be talking about modifications of the mind. But ideas are not modifications of the mind. Thus there are, and can be, no innate ideas.

As an initial response to this line of argument one might grant the distinction between ideas and thoughts, and then insist that what is at issue is whether there are any innate thoughts. Now, Malebranche sometimes seems to play down the need for thoughts or perceptions corresponding to our apprehension of ideas. But his considered view, I take it, is that when I think of a triangle, my mind is modified in a certain way, and this modification is what he calls a 'pure perception'.[22] Malebranche can reply to his opponent that he cannot be satisfied with innate perceptions. For it is surely an essential part of the doctrine of innate ideas that they persist through time; to have an innate idea is to be in a persistent mental *state*. Indeed, the defender of the doctrine will no doubt claim that the mind is in this state from birth and remains in it throughout its history. But perceptions are essentially transitory; in a favourite phrase of Malebranche's, they are *passagères*.[23] Thus the champion of innate ideas cannot rescue his thesis by simply replacing 'ideas' with 'perceptions'. Malebranche in fact can confront his opponent with a dilemma. The items that are supposed to be innate are either ideas or perceptions. If they are ideas, then the whole issue is misconceived; if they are perceptions, they cannot have the degree

[22] *Conversations chrétiennes*, III (*OCM* iv. 75). See Radner, p. 86.
[23] See e.g. *Conversations chrétiennes*, III (*OCM* iv. 74).

of permanence which they are required to have. Malebranche might perhaps reinforce the second horn of the dilemma in a Lockean way: he might argue that it is empirically false that there are innate perceptions of ideas such as triangles.

(2) Simply substituting talk of perceptions for talk of ideas is thus a mere provisional move which Malebranche can easily counter. But Descartes is likely to opt for a different strategy; he will reformulate his claim in a more basic way. Descartes might grant everything that Malebranche says so far, but he will insist that the mind has innate ideas in the sense that it has a faculty or disposition to form certain thoughts. Recall Descartes's defence of this position in the *Comments on a Certain Broadsheet*:

I have never written or taken the view that the mind requires innate ideas which are something distinct from its own faculty of thinking. I did, however, observe that there were certain thoughts within me which neither came to me from external objects nor were determined by my will, but which came solely from the power of thinking within me; so I applied the term 'innate' to the ideas or notions which are the forms of these thoughts in order to distinguish them from others, which I called 'adventitious' or 'made up'. This is the same sense as that in which we say that generosity is 'innate' in certain families, or that certain diseases such as gout or stones are innate in others: it is not so much that the babies of such families suffer from these diseases in their mother's womb, but simply that they are born with a certain 'faculty' or tendency to contract them.[24]

In this way Descartes can meet the objections which Malebranche has pressed so far. This version of the doctrine avoids the charge of at least crude psychologism, for it is clear that despite his terminology, Descartes is talking about a disposition to have certain mental events under certain conditions. And it also does justice to the claim that innate ideas persist through time, for what persists is not particular thoughts or perceptions, but rather the disposition to have those thoughts. The appeal to talk of faculties or dispositions also enables Descartes to meet the empirical worry that infants do not seem to engage in abstract thought of a mathematical or metaphysical variety.

The champion of innate ideas is almost forced to fall back on this second line of defence, but Malebranche is waiting for him. We now come to Malebranche's second major criticism of Descartes. In the 'Tenth Elucidation' of *The Search after Truth* Malebranche

---

[24] *Comments on a Certain Broadsheet*, AT viii/B. 357–8; CSM i. 303–4.

complains that there is a serious inconsistency in Descartes's meta-explanatory principles. In his physics, of course, Descartes insists that all appeal to faculties, natures, or occult qualities must be banished; in their place will be explanations which appeal solely to the actual, quantifiable properties of bodies. Yet when it comes to the mind, Descartes gets cold feet; he is indulgent towards the pseudo-explanatory talk of faculties, which he had rightly dismissed in the case of physical phenomena:

> I am amazed that the Cartesian gentlemen who so rightly reject the general terms *nature* and *faculty* should so willingly employ them on this occasion. They criticize those who say that fire burns by its *nature* or that it changes certain bodies into glass by a natural *faculty*, and yet some of them do not hesitate to say that the human mind produces in itself the ideas of all things by its *nature*, because it has the *faculty* of thinking. But, with all due respect, these terms are no more meaningful in their mouth than in the mouth of the Peripatetics.[25]

Malebranche's attack is perhaps too sweeping, but we can restate and develop his objection in the following way. The theory of innate ideas, if it is anything at all, is put forward as an explanatory hypothesis about idea-acquisition. Purged of objectionable psychologism, this means that it is an explanatory hypothesis about the occurrence of certain thoughts in human minds: for example, John's thought of a triangle at *t*. Malebranche may concede to his opponents that innate ideas are not intended to tell the whole causal story: some external stimulus will be additionally required. But he will still insist that the innatist hypothesis is intended to state at least a causally necessary condition for the existence of certain thoughts, and thus must have content. But when the defender of innate ideas resorts to talk of faculties, his claim must be empty unless such faculties can be grounded in non-dispositional properties of the mind. In the case of physical objects it is possible to see how such a grounding requirement for faculties or dispositions can be satisfied; the non-dispositional properties will typically be persistent structural modifications of the kind discovered by science. But no such solution seems readily available to the defender of innate ideas, for it is not clear how one can speak of persistent structural modifications in the case of immaterial minds. Thus the hypothesis of innate ideas is in danger of being explanatorily empty.

---

[25] 'Tenth Elucidation', *OCM* iii. 144; *SAT* 622.

Malebranche's anti-psychologism and his attack on faculty explanations are the core of his case against innate ideas; taken together, they form a powerful two-stage argument against the doctrine. However, in the section of *The Search after Truth* explicitly devoted to innate ideas, Malebranche argues in a more popular and superficial manner. He does not choose to submit the presuppositions of the doctrine to any searching scrutiny; indeed, given his strategy of presentation, he is not really in a good position to do so, for he has not yet fully explained his anti-Cartesian theory of ideas. Instead he argues largely on his opponents' own ground; he seems to accept that one can coherently conceive of a stock (*magasin*) of innate ideas. Malebranche in fact advances two arguments which he admits are less than conclusive. Since they are not central to his case, we can afford to deal with them quite briefly. As we shall see in a later chapter, however, each is fully countered by Leibniz, and this is perhaps their chief claim to importance.

(3) According to Malebranche, the doctrine of innate ideas is a clumsy hypothesis which is inconsistent with the simplicity of the divine ways. Malebranche invites us to consider the implications of the claim that *all* ideas are innate:

[The mind], then, has an infinite number of ideas—what am I saying?—it has as many infinite numbers of ideas as there are different figures; consequently, since there is an infinite number of different figures, the mind must have an infinity of infinite numbers of ideas just to know the figures.[26]

Malebranche's opponent is thus forced to postulate that the mind is created with an infinitely large stock of innate ideas. But since God always acts in the simplest ways, it is probable at least that he chose some other way of stocking the mind with its contents.

(4) Even if such a store is granted, Malebranche argues, his opponent cannot explain how the mind can select among its ideas. Suppose a person is perceiving the sun; a sensory idea, then, must be drawn out of the storehouse. If this selection is not to be arbitrary, the mind must follow a rule. What Malebranche seems to envisage is that the rule would specify the selection of the idea which maximally resembles some given pattern; consider, analogously, the role of samples in choosing a colour. But, according to Malebranche, it is difficult to see what such a pattern could be. It cannot be the retinal image, for there is no resemblance between

[26] *Search after Truth*, III. 2. 4. (*OCM* i. 430; *SAT* 227).

retinal images and ideas, and in any case, the mind does not perceive such images.[27] Nor will it help to suggest that the pattern in question could be an idea. For if all ideas have to be selected, and only ideas can guide the selection, then we are involved in an infinite regress.[28]

A difficulty with these arguments is to decide exactly what version of the doctrine is their target. Superficially, this should not be a problem. Malebranche is explicit that he is attacking a strong version of the doctrine which holds that '*all* ideas are innate or created with us'.[29] The second argument, in particular, seems to be directed against an opponent who holds that all our sensory ideas— i.e. sense-perceptions—are innate. Such a thesis may be espoused by a philosopher who, with Malebranche, denies that there is any causal interaction between mind and body. Descartes himself seems to flirt with such a thesis on occasion, and it is confidently embraced by Leibniz in his deep metaphysics (in contrast with more popular works such as the *New Essays*).

But it is not entirely clear that this is the right identification of Malebranche's target, and the problem of interpretation stems from his refusal, at this stage, to specify how far he is accommodating himself to the Cartesian theory of ideas. Recall that when Descartes seems to advance a strong version of innatism, he leaves no doubt about what is involved; he is explicit that colour perceptions and pain sensations are included:

the very ideas of the motions themselves and of the figures are innate in us. The ideas of pain, colours, sounds, and the like must be all the more innate if, on the occasion of certain corporeal motions, our mind is to be capable of representing them to itself, for there is no similarity between these ideas and the corporeal motions.[30]

For Malebranche, however, there are in strictness no *ideas* of pain or colour, but only sensations (*sentiments*) of them. For it is of the nature of ideas to represent truly the properties of objects, and Malebranche holds a strong version of the doctrine that physical objects have only primary qualities. We are now concerned with a different contrast between Descartes and Malebranche from the one

[27] Ibid. (*OCM* i. 431; *SAT* 227).
[28] Cf. W. Doney, 'Malebranche', in P. Edwards (ed.) *Encyclopedia of Philosophy*, v (New York, 1967), 142.
[29] *Search after Truth*, III. 2. 4 (*OCM* i. 429; *SAT* 226).
[30] *Comments on a Certain Broadsheet*, AT viii/B. 359; CSM i. 304.

we discussed earlier. The point here is not that, for Malebranche, ideas are abstract entities; it is that, being representative by their nature, they must correspond to properties which either actually are or could be instantiated by external, physical objects.

There is no doubt, then, that Malebranche is attacking a strong version of the innatist hypothesis. But unless he is adapting totally to the Cartesian terminology at this stage, it is not clear that the thesis he opposes allows room for innate ideas of pain and colour. To this extent the thesis in question is not as strong as that which Descartes sometimes entertains, and to which Leibniz is committed in his deep metaphysics. But it is clear that Malebranche is attacking a thesis which maintains that sense-perceptions of *primary* qualities are innate; for these figure explicitly in the discussion. To this extent Malebranche's target is importantly similar to Cartesian and Leibnizian versions of the thesis that all ideas are innate.

Ideas and God: Problems

It is not difficult in general terms to see why Malebranche locates ideas in God. Ideas, as abstract entities, possess certain properties which are traditionally ascribed to God, and to God alone; they are eternal, immutable, and necessary.[31] Perhaps the key claim here is that ideas are necessary, but, unfortunately, Malebranche does not seem to explain the precise sense in which he intends it. Historically, to say that God is the necessary being was to say that he could not come into existence or pass away; on this interpretation, necessity seems to be equivalent to eternity in the sense of 'sempiternity'. A good case can be made for saying that ideas are necessary in this sense; for, as we have seen, Malebranche thinks that it is absurd to suppose that the idea of a triangle could come into or go out of existence. But there is another sense in which, for Malebranche, ideas might be regarded as necessary. As Bennett has said, true propositions of the form: 'There is an F type essence' are absolutely necessary; in other words, truths about the consistency of concepts are necessary truths.[32] On this interpretation, necessity entails eternity (i.e. sempiternity), but is not entailed by it.

---

[31] 'La Raison qui nous éclaire par ses divines idées, par des idées immuables, nécessaires, éternelles' (*Dialogues on Metaphysics*, III (D, pp. 74–5)).

[32] J. Bennett, *A Study of Spinoza's* Ethics (Cambridge, 1984), 358.

Eternity, immutability, and necessity can be predicated of ideas by virtue of the fact that they are 'third realm' entities. But Malebranche also says things about ideas which are more puzzling. In addition to the properties we have mentioned, ideas possess another godlike property; they are said to be infinite.[33] Malebranche does not just mean by this that there is an infinite number of ideas—a claim which in any case he may have abandoned in his later philosophy; he means that each idea is in itself infinite. But in what sense are ideas supposed to be infinite, and why does Malebranche advance this claim? It has sometimes been suggested that Malebranche is committed to the principle that if the object is F, then the idea must also be F.[34] On this basis, then, it might be supposed that Malebranche inferred the infinity of the idea of extension from the infinity of extension itself. But it is difficult to believe that Malebranche is really committed to this principle, for it entails the unwelcome consequence that since space is extended, the idea of space must also be extended. In any case, there is clear evidence that Malebranche did not infer the infinity of the idea of extension from the infinity of extension; on a number of occasions, Malebranche asserts the infinity of the idea, but expresses doubts about the infinity of extension itself. Thus, in the course of making his familiar criticism of Spinoza that he confuses ideas and things, Malebranche tells his young correspondent, de Mairan: 'The idea of extension is infinite, but its *ideatum* [in the Spinozist sense] is perhaps not'.[35] Indeed, Malebranche further remarks that, contrary to Spinoza, this *ideatum* may not even exist. It is scarcely credible that a philosopher who could criticize Spinoza in these terms should seek to ground the infinity of the idea of extension in the infinity of extension itself. Even if Malebranche grants that the idea of extension is the idea of a substance which can be infinite, it still seems clear that he is not thinking along these lines.

A more promising approach to the problem has been proposed by Gueroult.[36] Gueroult seems to hold that the infinity of ideas should be explained in terms of the extension of concepts in possible worlds. For instance, the class of circles in the actual world may be

[33] *Dialogues on Metaphysics*, II (D, pp. 50–1); *Conversations chrétiennes*, III (*OCM* iv. 74).
[34] Radner, *Malebranche*, p. 110.
[35] Malebranche to de Mairan, 6 Sept. 1714, *OCM* xix. 910; cf. Réponse à Regis, *OCM* xvii/1. 286–7.
[36] Gueroult, p. 38.

finite or even empty, but the class of possible circles is infinitely large. There are occasions when Malebranche seems to have such a claim in mind,[37] but the bulk of the evidence seems to favour an intensional interpretation; ideas—geometrical concepts, for instance—are infinitely complex. Thus Malebranche writes of ideas being 'inexhaustible';[38] again, he remarks that one can 'ceaselessly' derive new truths from our ideas of geometrical figures.[39] It is a merit of the intensional interpretation that it explains, or helps to explain, why geometrical concepts are, for Malebranche, the paradigm ideas. For it is indeed plausible to say that geometrical concepts are infinite or inexhaustible in this sense. We expect that mathematicians will continue to discover all sorts of new properties of triangles, and we do not seriously suppose that this process will ever come to an end.[40]

Perhaps the most puzzling of Malebranche's claims about ideas is that they have causal properties; ideas have the power to cause perceptions in finite minds.[41] But if ideas are 'third realm' entities, it is hard to see how they can have causal properties of any sort. It is true that ideas are located in God, and God is traditionally thought of as causally active; but if God is causally active, it is surely not *qua* region of ideas. As Gueroult has shrewdly observed, Malebranche seems to be guilty here of equivocating on the term 'immaterial'.[42] Ideas are of course in one sense immaterial: they are immaterial in the straightforward sense of being non-physical; they are not at all like atoms, tables, or chairs. But the fact that they are non-material in this sense does not entail that they are immaterial in the sense of being mental or spiritual; yet this is the kind of immateriality which God is supposed to enjoy and which is relevant to his causal activity. If Malebranche thinks that this entailment holds, he seems to have fallen victim to the very mistake for which he castigates Descartes. Moreover, as Gueroult notes, if Malebranche holds that there must be a 'common measure' between cause and effect, this condition is not really satisfied by ideas.[43]

---

[37] See e.g. *Dialogues on Metaphysics*, II (D, pp. 50–1).
[38] Ibid. I (D, pp. 36–7).
[39] *Réponse au livre*, ch. XXII (*OCM* vi. 153, 159).
[40] Cf. I. Hacking, *Why Does Language Matter to Philosophy?* (Cambridge, 1975), 63.
[41] *Conversations chrétiennes*, III (*OCM* iv. 75–6).
[42] Gueroult, p. 171.
[43] Ibid.

It is, I believe, futile to attempt a real defence of Malebranche's claim that ideas have causal properties. None the less, it is possible to reconstruct a line of reasoning by which Malebranche might have been led to this conclusion. A clue is provided by Malebranche's frequent claim that ideas are prior (*préalables*) to perceptions.[44] Suppose that this means that ideas are logically prior to perceptions; the existence of a perception is logically dependent on the existence of an idea. In other words, a perception is always a perception of some object (= idea); as Malebranche puts it, 'to see nothing is not to see'.[45] Now, despite his original and highly fertile views on causality, Malebranche is still, at least formally, a causal rationalist in Bennett's terminology; Malebranche resembles Spinoza and perhaps Leibniz in assimilating causal relations to logical relations.[46] Thus, given Malebranche's causal rationalism, the thesis that perceptions are logically dependent on ideas becomes the thesis that perceptions are causally dependent on ideas. It is true that this result may be not as strong as the thesis Malebranche intends to assert; for our argument establishes only that ideas are causally necessary conditions of perceptions; it does not establish that they are causally sufficient. None the less, this line of reasoning does establish a causal connection of some kind between ideas and perceptions.

A possible objection to this reconstruction is that it renders Malebranche needlessly incoherent. For if one thing emerges clearly from the controversy with Arnauld, it is that perceptions and ideas, for Malebranche, are ontologically distinct; Malebranche does not challenge Arnauld's claim that his 'representative entities' exist over and above mental events. But if ideas and perceptions are ontologically distinct, it may then be wondered how Malebranche can also consistently claim that ideas are logically prior to perceptions, and thus that perceptions are logically dependent on ideas. The perception/idea relation cannot be like the property/substance relation as it is traditionally conceived; properties are supposed to depend logically on substance, but they are not ontologically distinct from the substance in which they inhere.

This objection is a natural one, but it is none the less misguided; it mistakenly conflates logical and ontological dependence. The truth

---

[44] See e.g. *Conversations chrétiennes*, III (*OCM* iv. 71).
[45] *Trois Lettres*, I (*OCM* vi. 202). Malebranche, however, denies that in the case of *sentiments* there must be some correlative object.
[46] Bennett, p. 30.

is that logical dependence is a function of the way things or events are described, and has no implications for the question of whether they are ontologically distinct. Davidson and Anscombe have both made this point in connection with causal relations.[47] Suppose that the lighting of a match causes an explosion. Then the lighting of the match is the cause of the explosion. Thus the cause of the explosion caused the explosion. But this is a logical truth, and we can truly say that the cause of the explosion is logically dependent on the explosion. But this has no tendency to show that Hume was wrong in thinking that cause and effect are ontologically distinct events.

Ideas: The Problem of Ontology

In order to show that they are in God, Malebranche attributes properties to ideas which it is not clear that they can possess. But Malebranche's doctrine of ideas raises a more fundamental problem of ontology. Nominally, at least, Malebranche accepts the framework of Cartesian metaphysics: everything is either a substance or a mode, and there are just two kinds of substances, minds, and bodies. But unlike Descartes, Malebranche cannot really accommodate ideas within such a framework; for unlike the Descartes of the 'Third Meditation', Malebranche cannot say that ideas are modes of finite, human minds. Foucher put his finger on the problem when he asked Malebranche why God was a more satisfactory location for ideas than the human mind.[48] As Radner writes, 'if it is inconceivable that the human mind, a simple and immaterial being, can have in itself ideas representative of material objects, surely it is no more conceivable that God, who is, after all, a being even more simple and immaterial, should have such ideas in himself'.[49] As Foucher sees, Malebranche is faced with an unappealing range of choices. Malebranche clearly denies that ideas are modes of God, for as he insists in the 'Tenth Elucidation', Infinite Being is incapable of modifications.[50] Equally clearly,

---

[47] D. Davidson, 'Actions, Reasons, and Causes', in *Essays on Actions and Events* (Oxford, 1980), 14; G. E. M. Anscombe, 'Times, Beginnings, and Causes', in A. Kenny (ed.), Rationalism, *Empiricism, and Idealism* (Oxford, 1986), p. 87.

[48] Foucher, *Critique de* La recherche de la vérité (Paris, 1675), 117–18. See Radner, *Malebranche*, p. 114.

[49] Radner, *Malebranche*, p. 114.

[50] 'Tenth Elucidation', *OCM*, iii. 149; *SAT* 625.

Malebranche must deny that ideas are themselves substances in God, for such a claim would be inconsistent with the simplicity of the divine nature. The only remaining alternative is that ideas are the substance of God himself, and this is the solution that Malebranche seems to have embraced. In the 'Tenth Elucidation' and elsewhere Malebranche says that ideas are God's essence in so far as it is participable by creatures.[51]

Malebranche may appear to have solved the problem of the status of ideas within the Cartesian framework, but the appearance is deceptive. The most that Malebranche has really achieved is to satisfy one requirement of Cartesian ontology, while falling foul of another. For if ideas are identified with the substance of God, then the infinite, uncreated *res cogitans* of Descartes's metaphysics is converted into an abstract entity or perhaps the realm of abstract entities. Such a position is really inconsistent with the framework of Cartesian dualism. And apart from the problem of philosophical consistency, it also generates theological difficulties; it is fundamentally at odds with the orthodox Christian conception of God as a personal being who watches over us and cares for us.

In retrospect it is tempting to say that Malebranche could have made his philosophy more consistent by breaking openly with the framework of Cartesian ontology. In the first place, Malebranche could have given up the pretence that his philosophy is dualistic; he could have admitted that his philosophy is really a version of trialism: in addition to minds and bodies, there is a third realm of abstract, logical entities. Secondly, Malebranche could have given up the Cartesian assumption that everything there is, is either a substance or a mode. To questioning like Foucher's, Malebranche could simply have declined to play the game of classifying ideas as either substances or modes; like Locke, he could have been sceptical of the value of such metaphysical categories.[52] None the less, it would still have been possible for him to insist that the realm of ideas is not reducible to either the mental or the physical.

Malebranche of course never made an open break with the fundamental tenets of Cartesian ontology; at least nominally, he remained committed to substantial dualism and to the framework of substance and mode. It is worth asking why Malebranche remained

---

[51] Ibid. Cf. *Dialogues on Metaphysics*, II (D, pp. 44–5).
[52] See e.g. Locke's discussion of the question whether space is a substance: *Essay*, II. xiii. 18.

loyal to his predecessor in these respects. It may seem that
Malebranche could have embraced a form of trialism without
theological embarrassment, and even indeed with some theological
gain; one can obviously admit the existence of an irreducible third
realm without identifying this realm with God. So Malebranche
could have located ideas outside God while agreeing with Descartes
that He is a thinking substance. Perhaps part of the reason why
Malebranche did not take this step is to be found in his concern with
scepticism: Malebranche believed that by locating ideas in God, he
had found the solution to the sceptical challenge which had eluded
Descartes. But once this strategic decision had been taken,
there were insuperable philosophical and theological objections to
identifying the divine locus of ideas with the realm of abstract
objects.

An unkind judgement on Malebranche's theory of ideas would be
that it replaces one muddle with another. For the Cartesian
conflation of logic and psychology, Malebranche substitutes the
conflation of logic and theology. It is not surprising that theology
leads Malebranche in directions we may regret, for theological
considerations were surely a major motive behind his critique of
Descartes's theory of ideas. For Malebranche, the Cartesian mind is
altogether too godlike; in spite of Descartes's assurances that all
knowledge depends on God, the Cartesian mind is really 'a light
to itself'.[53] Gueroult even suggests that, for Malebranche, the
Cartesian mind usurps the divine prerogative of creation.[54] Perhaps
Gueroult overplays his hand here. It is true that Descartes endows
the mind with a power of thinking, and that for Malebranche, this
claim is philosophically objectionable; but it is no less true that, for
Descartes, innate ideas are implanted by God, and that this
Cartesian conception of a divinely ordered, contingent mental
structure is one of the main targets of Malebranche's critique. But in
his general claim Gueroult is surely right: there is a theological
dimension to Malebranche's theory of ideas which we ignore only
at the price of serious distortion.

---

[53] *Dialogues on Metaphysics*, III (D, pp. 56–7).
[54] Gueroult, pp. 136–7.

5

Malebranche
Vision in God

'IT is an opinion that spreads not and is like to die of itself, or at least do no great harm.'[1] In these words, written just three days before his death, Locke accurately predicted the long-term fate of Malebranche's doctrine of vision in God, at least in the English-speaking world. Although it was influential early in the eighteenth century, since that time the doctrine has fallen into almost total neglect. Philosophers who have studied the theory are aware that it attempts to marry the views of Descartes and Augustine, but few have committed themselves on the question whether the marriage is a success or a disaster. Within the wider philosophical community, the doctrine that we see all things in God is no doubt regarded as a paradigm of obscurity and mysticism in philosophy. As Locke's friend Molyneux commented, 'as there are Enthusiasmes in Divinity, so there are in Philosophy'.[2]

Such a verdict on the central doctrine in Malebranche's epistemology is grossly unfair; neither the charge of mysticism nor that of obscurity is warranted. To call a doctrine mystical suggests that, as a whole or in large part, it is unsupported by philosophical arguments; in this respect Malebranche is no more mystical than Spinoza or Plato. Nor is the doctrine particularly obscure. On the contrary, it offers a theory of perception which can be understood as a logical result of introducing certain changes into Descartes's teaching. In the first part of this chapter I shall argue that Malebranche takes over three central doctrines from Descartes, and transforms at least two of them; when they are combined, the result is vision in God. In the second half of the chapter, I shall show how Malebranche uses Cartesian innovations to extend Augustine's theory of divine illumination. With the help of Descartes's teaching,

---

[1] Quoted in M. Cranston, *John Locke: A Biography* (London, 1957), p. 478.
[2] Molyneux to Locke, 18 Apr. 1693, *Correspondence of John Locke*, ed. E. S. de Beer, iv (Oxford, 1979), 668.

Malebranche is able to argue that we can see bodies—changing and corruptible things—in God, without falling foul of divine immutability. In this way he can overcome Augustine's scruples about the theological dangers of seeking to extend his theory of divine illumination.

Let us now unveil the three Cartesian doctrines which Malebranche needs in order to develop his theory of vision in God. They are: the distinction between primary and secondary qualities; the representative theory of perception; and the conclusion of the wax meditation—the thesis that bodies are perceived through the intellect, not the senses. We shall examine in turn the use that Malebranche makes of each of them.

The Distinction between Primary and Secondary Qualities

The first thing to note about Malebranche's use of Cartesian teachings is that it enables him to limit the scope of his thesis. When Malebranche claims that we see all things in God, he means that we see bodies in God, but his claim is more restricted than one might suppose. According to Malebranche, it is only the primary qualities that we see in God, for these are the only properties that bodies possess. Secondary qualities are not properties of bodies at all; they are merely sensations in the human mind.[3] Thus colours, tastes, smells, etc. do not fall within the scope of the thesis that we see all things in God.

In distinguishing between primary and secondary qualities, Malebranche sees himself of course as in the Cartesian tradition. For Malebranche, Descartes (and others) had made a major philosophical discovery; even his hero Augustine had been unable to escape the prejudice that colours, for instance, are genuine properties of bodies. Indeed, Malebranche may have thought that he was simply following Descartes's own teaching here. But in fact, Malebranche's position on the status of secondary qualities is more radical than Descartes's own. For Descartes's considered view seems to be that secondary qualities are in bodies as dispositional and relational qualities:

In view of all this we have every reason to conclude that the properties in external objects to which we apply the terms light, colour, smell, taste,

---

[3] 'Eleventh Elucidation', *OCM* iii. 165; *SAT* 634.

sound, heat and cold—as well as the other tactile qualities and even what are called 'substantial forms'—are, so far as we can see, simply various dispositions in those objects which make them able to set up various kinds of motions in our nerves which are required to produce all the various sensations in our souls.[4]

Descartes thus anticipates the more famous account of secondary qualities which Locke was to give in the *Essay concerning Human Understanding*: secondary qualities are powers in bodies to produce ideas (i.e. sensations) in the human mind.[5] It is true that, for Descartes, it is possible to give a complete description of the physical world which mentions only primary qualities, but it does not follow from this that secondary qualities are not genuine physical properties. Malebranche, by contrast, foreshadows Berkeley in regarding secondary qualities as purely mind-dependent.

Malebranche departs from Descartes's actual teaching on the status of secondary qualities in the interest of a purer Cartesianism. In his view, what we may call Descartes's Lockean view of secondary qualities is inconsistent with a strict interpretation of Cartesian ontology. There are two reasons, in particular, why Malebranche finds it objectionable. In the first place, Descartes's Lockean thesis implies that secondary qualities are relational; they involve a hypothetical relation to the human mind. For Malebranche, there is no place for such properties in the Cartesian metaphysic; on the contrary, as he understands Descartes's teaching, the only properties which extended substances can have are various figures and motions.[6] Such a claim might suggest that Malebranche would exclude all relational properties of bodies from the Cartesian ontology, but in fact this does not seem to be his considered position. The thesis he wishes to defend is that every property of bodies either is, or is at least reducible to, a non-relational property which involves only figure and motion. But even this weaker thesis is sufficient to exclude secondary qualities, on the Lockean view, from a strict Cartesian ontology. For if the analysis of a proposition of the form 'The grass is green' essentially involves a reference to the human mind, then it cannot be derived from other propositions about bodies which specify only monadic, primary-quality predicates; it would thus fail Malebranche's test for

---

[4] *Principles of Philosophy*, IV. 198 (AT viii/A. 322–3; CSM i. 285).
[5] Locke, *Essay*, II. viii. 10.
[6] 'Eleventh Elucidation', OCM iii. 165; SAT 634.

reducibility. By contrast, a proposition such as 'Smith is taller than Jones' would pass the test, for it can be derived from other non-relational propositions such as 'Smith is six foot' and 'Jones is five foot ten'. Thus Malebranche does not object to secondary qualities on the ground that they are relational; rather, he objects to them because they involve a special kind of relation, namely, a relation to the human mind. For this reason they fail to satisfy the fundamental principle of Cartesian ontology that properties split cleanly into two exclusive groups, the mental and the physical. As Malebranche sees them, secondary qualities, as understood by Locke and the historical Descartes, are monstrous hybrids.

Malebranche's second reason for rejecting Descartes's Lockean view of secondary qualities is that it makes them into dispositional properties. Here, too, Malebranche sees himself as the defender of a purer Cartesianism. Malebranche shares the Cartesian contempt for the circular, faculty explanations of the scholastics; like so many seventeenth-century philosophers, he ridicules his predecessors for solemnly informing us that clocks tell the time by virtue of a horodeictic power or faculty. Unlike some of his contemporaries, however, Malebranche has a radical hostility to dispositions; he seems to regard them as pseudo-properties which have no place in ontology. At times he even says that talk of dispositions is strictly meaningless:

when we say that bodies tend toward their center, that they fall by their gravity, that they rise by their levity, that they move by their nature, that they are hard or fluid by themselves, that they successively change their forms, that they act by their virtues, qualities, faculties, and so on, we use terms signifying nothing, and all these propositions are absolutely false in the sense philosophers give them.[7]

It is natural to suppose that Malebranche is unwilling to regard a physical property as genuine if it can play no role in a causal explanation, and that, as Malebranche sees it, dispositions fail this test. It may be objected, however, that this is not a position which Malebranche can consistently hold, for in his metaphysics not even non-dispositional properties meet the standard. For, according to the teaching of occasionalism, no physical object, indeed no creature, is a genuine cause. Thus in this respect dispositional properties are no worse off than non-dispositional properties. But

---

[7] 'Twelfth Elucidation', *OCM* iii. 179; *SAT* 642–3.

this objection is misguided. It is true that the crystalline structure of the sugar is not a genuine cause of the sugar's dissolving in the hot liquid, for there is no necessary connection between the possession of this property and the event to be explained. But as we shall see in the next chapter, for Malebranche, the crystalline structure has a non-trivial role to play in explaining why the sugar dissolves; it may not be a genuine cause, but unlike the solubility, it is at least an occasional cause. Thus Malebranche can legitimately claim that there is an important distinction between dispositional and non-dispositional properties. There is, then, no inconsistency between his rejection of the former and his occasionalist metaphysics.

By concluding that secondary qualities are not properties of bodies, Malebranche has not only made a significant change in Descartes's teaching; he has also laid an important, if negative, foundation for his doctrine of vision in God. For if secondary qualities are not properties of bodies, then they do not fall within the scope of the doctrine. Thus, for the purposes of understanding vision in God, we can now afford to put such qualities on one side.

The Representative Theory of Perception

It is well known that Malebranche subscribes to a version of the representative theory of perception. In other words, like Descartes, at least as he is traditionally understood, he holds that our perception of physical objects needs to be mediated; directly we perceive ideas, and indirectly we perceive the physical world. In *The Search after Truth* Malebranche provides one of the famous formulations of the doctrine:

I think everyone agrees that we do not perceive objects external to us by themselves. We see the sun, the stars, and an infinity of objects external to us; and it is not likely that the soul should leave the body to stroll about the heavens, as it were, in order to behold all these objects. Thus, it does not see them by themselves, and our mind's immediate object when it sees the sun, for example, is not the sun, but something that is intimately joined to our soul and this is what I call an idea. Thus by the word 'idea', I mean here nothing other than the immediate object, or the object closest to the mind, when it perceives something, i.e. that which affects and modifies the mind with the perception it has of an object.[8]

It is difficult to know whether Malebranche seriously intends to offer an argument here for the representative theory of

---

[8] *Search after Truth*, III. 2. 1 (*OCM* iii. 413–14; *SAT* 217).

perception; in response to Arnauld's criticism Malebranche tended to emphasize the element of raillery in the passage.[9] But taken at face value, the passage seems to offer the following argument:

(1) Whatever we directly perceive must be present to the mind.

(2) Bodies are not present to the mind.

(3) Therefore, we do not directly perceive bodies.

If this is the argument Malebranche intends, then, as Arnauld observed, it appears to commit a fallacy of equivocation; the equivocation is between 'locally present' and 'objectively present'.[10] The first premiss seems to rely on the notion of objective presence; whatever we perceive must be in our minds. The second premiss, however, seems to rely on the notion of physical presence; my mind does not take a stroll in the heavens or, in other words, it is not physically present in the heavens:

(1) Whatever we directly perceive must be (objectively) present to the mind.

(2) Bodies are not (locally) present to the mind.

(3) Therefore, we do not directly perceive bodies.

Thus Malebranche may fare no better than other seventeenth-century philosophers in advancing direct arguments for the representative theory of perception, but as we shall see, in fact he can afford to dispense with this argument.

For our present purposes, the most important feature of Malebranche's representationalism is his account of the direct objects of perception. For Malebranche, these objects are of course ideas, and Malebranche defines the term 'idea' in a way that is reminiscent of Locke. Thus, the unwary reader might suppose that, for Malebranche, the immediate objects of perception are mental items which form a screen or veil between us and physical objects; such a supposition was indeed made by the unfortunate Foucher.[11] But, as we have seen in the previous chapter, this supposition is mistaken. Ideas, for Malebranche, are not mental entities of any

---

[9] *Réponse au livre*, ch. IX (*OCM* vi. 95).

[10] A. Arnauld, *Des vraies et des fausses idées*, ch. VIII, in *Œuvres de Messire Antoine Arnauld*, xxxviii (Paris, 1780; rep. Brussels, 1967), 216. See D. Radner, *Malebranche* (Assen, 1978), 96–101. I am grateful to Godfrey Vesey for help with this issue.

[11] See Radner, *Malebranche* p. 102.

kind; they are concepts—abstract, logical items to which the mind is related in thinking.

We can now see that Malebranche gives a new twist to the representative theory of perception; indeed, his uncompromising insistence that ideas are not psychological entities transforms the theory almost beyond recognition. Like Locke or Descartes, Malebranche can still make the familiar contrast between the direct and indirect objects of perception, and of course (leaving occasionalism on one side), the objects that are indirectly perceived are unaffected. But we can see the extent of the change if we employ the metaphor of the veil of perception. The objects on the far side of the veil may be unaffected, but the nature of the veil has become unfamiliar; it is constituted not by mental objects or events, but by concepts in God; characteristically, they are geometrical concepts such as squares and triangles. It is worth insisting on the point that Malebranche's theological language should be given an austere interpretation. To say that we directly perceive ideas in God is to say that we directly perceive items in logical space.

Malebranche's logicist version of the representative theory of perception has certain advantages which were to be perceived by Reid;[12] it enables him to avoid some of the difficulties which beset Descartes and Locke and even idealist critics of the representative theory such as Berkeley. For Locke and Descartes, as they are traditionally understood, the immediate objects of perception are mental items which are private to the perceiver; thus they must admit that, strictly speaking, no two people ever directly perceive the same object. Malebranche's theory of ideas does not commit him to this counter-intuitive position, for Malebranche's ideas are not private, mental items at all; they are objects to which all minds can be related. Thus Malebranche can agree with common sense in holding that when you and I perceive a table, we directly perceive numerically the same object.

We can see, then, that once again Malebranche has appropriated one of Descartes's doctrines, and transformed it in a remarkable way; he has made it peculiarly his own. By logicizing ideas, Malebranche has given new content to the representative theory of perception. Of course the nature and extent of Malebranche's departure from the Cartesian teaching is controversial. I have

[12] See ch. 11 below.

assumed that (1) Descartes subscribes to a representative theory of perception, and that (2) for Descartes the immediate objects of perception are psychological or mental items. However, both these assumptions might be, and indeed have been, challenged. Not all scholars are convinced today that Descartes was a representationalist;[13] moreover, there are places where Descartes seems to understand ideas, in an almost Malebranchean way, as abstract objects. But in spite of the problems in interpreting Descartes, two things are not in doubt; Malebranche's version of the representative theory of perception owes something to Descartes, and yet corresponds to nothing which Descartes himself ever held.

The Intellectual Perception of Bodies

For anyone brought up in the Lockean tradition, the present interpretation should raise an obvious question. For Malebranche, the immediate objects of perception are ideas, and ideas are abstract objects; they are universals, of which the paradigm examples are geometrical concepts such as triangles and circles. But in that case, Malebranche's ideas must be objects of purely intellectual awareness, for universals can be thought about, but *qua* universals, cannot be sensed; in this respect they resemble what Bennett calls 'logical concepts'.[14] But if Malebranche's ideas are objects of the intellect, then one may wonder how they can play their required role in the representative theory of perception. A representative theory of perception, is, after all, a theory of *perception*; yet it seems as if on Malebranche's version it is more like a theory of abstract thought. We may wonder, then, whether vision in God is merely vision in some strange Pickwickian sense. Or to put the point another way: what have abstract objects got to do with a theory of sense-perception?

The answer to the last question is of course: everything, or almost everything. It is perfectly correct that Malebranche's ideas are abstract entities, and as such, must be objects of the intellect; it is also true that Malebranche's doctrine of vision in God is a theory of sense-perception. The solution to the problem of reconciling these

---

[13] The traditional reading is called into question by J. W. Yolton, *Perceptual Acquaintance from Descartes to Reid* (Minneapolis, 1984).

[14] RB (1982), introd., p. xxi.

two claims is again to be found in Malebranche's Cartesian inheritance; Malebranche agrees with Descartes that, in some sense, 'even bodies are not strictly perceived by the senses or the faculty of imagination, but by the intellect alone'.[15] As Lennon has written, '[Malebranche's] view of Ideas offers a consistent and plausible reading of, for instance, the difficult example of the piece of wax from *Meditations* II'.[16]

The thesis of the wax meditation is thus the third doctrine which Malebranche takes over from Descartes, and presses into service of vision in God. But in some ways this doctrine is the odd man out; for in this case Malebranche's relationship to his predecessor is more problematic than in the other two examples. With regard to the status of secondary qualities and the representative theory of perception, it is reasonably clear that Malebranche makes Cartesian teaching his own by introducing significant changes; it is less clear, however, that this is true in the case of the wax meditation. And this is because, despite its fame and prominence, the wax meditation is one of the most controversial and puzzling issues in Descartes scholarship.

Recent literature on Descartes's wax meditation has shown some tendency to move towards a consensus. Most scholars now agree that Descartes's main intention in the wax meditation is not metaphysical but epistemological; in other words, Descartes is not here concerned to establish the thesis that the essence of matter is extension; rather, he seeks to establish a thesis about how the wax is known.[17] Yet even this degree of consensus still leaves us with a major problem of interpretation on our hands; Descartes insists that 'the nature of this piece of wax is in no way revealed by my imagination, but is perceived by my mind alone',[18] and again, 'even bodies are not strictly perceived by the senses or the faculty of imagination but by the intellect alone';[19] but we may wonder what precisely this thesis amounts to. In particular, it is not clear just how strong a thesis Descartes seeks to establish.

One commentator who has grappled with this problem is Bernard Williams. Williams mounts his interpretation by focusing

---

[15] 'Second Meditation', AT vii. 34; CSM ii. 22.
[16] *Philosophical Commentary*, SAT 787.
[17] See B. Williams, *Descartes: The Project of Pure Enquiry* (Hassocks, 1978), 222; M. D. Wilson, *Descartes* (London, 1978), 77.
[18] 'Second Meditation', AT vii. 31; CSM ii. 21.
[19] Ibid., AT vii. 34; CSM ii. 22.

on the most obvious feature of the wax meditation, namely, Descartes's preoccupation with the understanding of change. As Williams emphasizes, Descartes sees that the wax can remain the same through an infinite number of changes, and that this is a piece of intellectual awareness; it cannot be grasped by the imagination. On this basis Williams argues that the thesis which Descartes seeks to establish is a relatively weak one:

Thus my conception of the wax is an intellectual conception, a conception of the understanding; this is what Descartes means when he says 'I perceive it with my understanding.' 'Perception' here means the comprehension of a thing's nature, one's mental conception of the thing and of what it is. So when Descartes says that 'perception of the wax is not sight, nor touch, nor imagination, and it never was . . . but an inspection of the mind alone, which can be either imperfect or confused, as it was at first, or clear and distinct, as it is now', he does not mean (as he might easily be taken to mean) that there is *no such thing* as perception, in the ordinary sense, of the wax by sight or touch, but only confused perception by the intellect.[20]

On Williams's interpretation, Descartes's thesis that bodies are perceived through the intellect alone is not nearly as strong as it might look; to put the point bluntly, Descartes does not really mean what he says. If Descartes's main point is that it is through the intellect that we grasp the wax's capacity to remain the same through an infinity of changes, then the thesis is true but relatively uncontroversial; and its connection with perception—in the ordinary sense—is somewhat tangential, for we can form such a conception when we are not—in the ordinary sense—perceiving at all.

There is reason to believe, however, that Williams does not do justice to Descartes's position. The trouble with Williams's reading is that it ignores the wider, scientific context of the wax meditation; it ignores Descartes's preoccupation with the psychology of perception. Hatfield and Epstein have shown how in the *Optics* and elsewhere Descartes seeks to develop a theory of perception which is consistent with his austere, radically anti-scholastic ontology; in other words, he argues for a theory which distinguishes sharply between mechanically conceived physiological processes and mental activity, and has no room for the transmission of sensible forms from bodies into the soul.[21] In spite of its radical ontological

[20] Williams, pp. 223–4.
[21] G. Hatfield and W. Epstein, 'The Sensory Core and the Medieval Foundations of Early Modern Perceptual Theory', *Isis*, 70 (1979), 374–9.

setting, Descartes's theory none the less accommodates some traditional claims about perception. In the 'Sixth Replies' Descartes gives a concise and illuminating account of his position. Here he distinguishes three grades of sensory response: (1) 'the immediate stimulation of the bodily organs by external objects'; (2) 'all the immediate effects produced in the mind as a result of its being united with a bodily organ which is affected in this way'; (3) 'all the judgements about things outside us which we have been accustomed to make from our earliest years'.[22] Descartes then illustrates his position with the example of seeing a stick:

For example, when I see a stick, it should not be supposed that certain 'intentional forms' fly off the stick towards the eye, but simply that rays of light are reflected off the stick and set up certain movements in the optic nerve and, via the optic nerve, in the brain, as I have explained at some length in the *Optics*. The movement in the brain, which is common to us and brutes, is the first grade of sensory response. This leads to the second grade, which extends to the mere perception of colour and light reflected from the stick; it arises from the fact that the mind is so intimately conjoined with the body that it is affected by the movements which occur in it. Nothing more than this should be referred to the sensory faculty, if we wish to distinguish it carefully from the intellect. But suppose that, as a result of being affected by this sensation of colour, I judge that a stick, located outside me, is coloured; and suppose that on the basis of the extension of the colour and its boundaries together with its position in relation to the parts of the brain, I make a rational calculation about the size, shape and distance of the stick: although such reasoning is commonly assigned to the senses (which is why I have here referred it to the third grade of sensory response), it is clear that it depends solely on the intellect.[23]

Descartes follows tradition here in holding that, strictly speaking, we sense only colour and light; on the basis of these sensations we reason to the size, shape, and distance of the physical object. As Hatfield and Epstein note, Descartes's distinction between the second and third grades of sensory response corresponds to the well-established distinction in psychology between the sensory core and the visual world.[24]

There is thus a real sense in which Descartes holds that our perception of bodies is intellectual; we construct our visual world of three-dimensional objects in space by reasoning from the sensory core. We know that Malebranche was a keen student of Descartes's

---

[22] 'Sixth Replies', AT vii. 436–7; CSM ii. 294–5.
[23] Ibid., AT vii. 437–8; CSM ii. 295.   [24] Hatfield and Epstein, p. 377.

scientific writings, and there can be little doubt that he takes over these elements of Cartesian theory into his own doctrine of vision in God.[25] Like Descartes, Malebranche holds that whereas our perception of secondary qualities is sensory, our perception of primary qualities is, strictly speaking, intellectual in the sense that it involves judgement and inference. We may wonder, however, whether Descartes's position is quite strong enough for Malebranche's purposes. For although Descartes follows tradition in holding that only light and colour are really sensed, it becomes clear that primary qualities must also be involved in the sensory core; for according to Descartes, we calculate the size, shape, and distance of the stick on the basis of 'the *extension* of the colour and its boundaries together with its position in relation to the parts of the brain'. Thus, it seems that, for Descartes, we do, after all, sense primary qualities; for example, I judge or see that the coin is circular on the basis of a sensation which represents it as elliptical. Malebranche, by contrast, seems to hold that only secondary qualities can be sensed, for primary qualities are perceived only through ideas, and ideas are objects of intellectual awareness. It would thus be wrong to claim that on this issue there is an exact fit between Descartes's and Malebranche's teachings, or that no puzzles of interpretation remain unsolved. But we have now reached a position where we can summarize the broad outlines of Malebranche's case for vision in God. For Malebranche, visual perception involves an intellectual, interpretative element; it involves judging, for instance, that the coin is circular. Judgements of this kind involve the mind's relation to concepts. Concepts are not mental but abstract, logical items. The realm of abstract objects is God. It follows, then, that we perceive bodies in God.

The Augustinian Challenge: The Problem of Change

Vision in God is a theory of perception which is rooted firmly in Cartesian teaching. But of course Malebranche is no mere disciple of Descartes; on the contrary, he is engaged in a creative synthesis of Cartesian and Augustinian teaching. As Daisie Radner writes, 'Malebranche sees himself as using the philosophical innovations of Descartes to improve on the teaching of Augustine'.[26] In particular,

---

[25] See C. J. McCracken, *Malebranche and British Philosophy* (Oxford, 1983), 54.
[26] Radner, *Malebranche*, p. 84.

he seeks to improve on and extend Augustine's theory of divine illumination. Malebranche himself seems well aware of the nature of the change he is proposing to make. Whereas Augustine believes only that we see eternal truths in God, Malebranche seeks to go further:

> We further believe that changeable and corruptible things are known in God, though Saint Augustine speaks only of immutable and incorruptible things, because for this to be so, no imperfection need be placed in God, since, as we have already said, it is enough that God should reveal to us what in Him is related to these things.[27]

As Malebranche sees it, for Augustine divine illumination can be no more than an account of our knowledge of necessary truths. The Cartesian revolution in philosophy provides an opportunity to transform the theory of divine illumination into something more radical; with the aid of Descartes's discoveries, it can be incorporated in a general theory of perception

Malebranche is well aware of the scruples which Augustine felt about seeking to extend his doctrine of divine illumination. Augustine was restrained by theological considerations. Whatever is in God must be unchanging and incorruptible. But if we say that we see bodies in God, we risk making God subject to change and corruption. Thus, as Malebranche sees it, Augustine has issued a challenge which must be met: vision in God poses a threat to the immutability of the divine nature. We shall see how Malebranche seeks to meet this challenge with the aid of weapons derived from Descartes.

In controversy with Arnauld, Malebranche spells out the nature of his strategy:

> I conclude at the same time that if Augustine had not been in this common prejudice, from which one is now delivered, that colours belong to bodies, and in this other prejudice that we see bodies in themselves, or by the species which come from them or are received from them; I conclude, I say, that his principles, which he has certainly well proved, would have obliged him to recognize that one sees in God created bodies as well as their uncreated ideas; that one sees them, I say, as far as one can see them.[28]

In other words, Malebranche adopts a double-barrelled strategy for replying to the Augustinian challenge, and each barrel is in origin

---

[27] *Search after Truth*, III. 2. 6 (*OCM* i. 444–5; *SAT* 234).
[28] *Contre la prévention*, OCM ix. 1066–7. Cf. Lettre III, 19 Mar. 1699, *OCM* ix. 951.

Cartesian. In the first place, Malebranche will appeal to the subjectivity of secondary qualities; in the second place, he will appeal to the representative theory of perception.

We have seen that Malebranche credited Descartes and other moderns with a major discovery concerning the status of secondary qualities; Descartes had liberated philosophers from the prejudice that colours, and secondary qualities in general, are in bodies. As we have also seen, Malebranche may have misrepresented Descartes's views, but he is right at least that Descartes had broken with tradition; colours are not properties of bodies in a straightforward, non-dispositional way. As Malebranche sees it, on this issue Augustine was in the grip of pre-Cartesian prejudice:

What prevented this holy doctor from speaking as I have done [i.e. from saying that we see all things in God] is that being in the prejudice that colours are in objects . . . as one sees objects only by colours, he believed that it was the object itself that one saw. He could not then say that one saw in God these colours which are not immutable, intelligible natures common to all minds, but sensible and particular modifications of the soul, and according to St Augustine, a quality which is spread on the surface of objects.[29]

Thus, according to Malebranche, because of his pre-Cartesian prejudice, Augustine had reasoned as follows. Colours and other secondary qualities are genuine properties of bodies. But the colours of bodies change. So if we see colours in God, then it seems that there is something in God which is subject to change. And this runs foul of the immutability of the divine nature.

Malebranche meets this objection in the following way. He admits, of course, that colours and secondary qualities in general are subject to change. But, according to Malebranche, secondary qualities are not properties of bodies; they are merely sensations in human minds. So to talk about the changing colour of the grass is simply to talk about a sequence of sensations in the minds of human observers. Thus the mutability of secondary qualities has no tendency to rub off on the divine nature; it therefore poses no threat to the thesis that we see all things in God.

The appeal to the mind-dependency of secondary qualities is only a stopgap, however; it cannot provide a complete reply to Augustine's scruples. For a defender of Augustine can simply make the familiar point that primary qualities are also affected by change;

[29] *Réponse au livre*, ch. VII (*OCM* vi. 68).

as even Descartes noted, the piece of wax expands and changes shape when it is brought near the fire. Thus, even if we grant Malebranche his account of secondary qualities, we have not yet disposed of Augustine's theological scruples; the doctrine of seeing all things in God still threatens the immutability of the divine nature.

At this point Malebranche must fall back on his second line of defence; he must invoke the representative theory of perception. Despite the eccentric features of Malebranche's version of the theory, he can still distinguish between the direct and indirect objects of perception, and this distinction is crucial for meeting the Augustinian challenge. Consider this clearly Augustinian argument:

(1) Whatever we see in God is immutable.

(2) But bodies are not immutable.

(3) Therefore, we do not see bodies in God.

Malebranche of course can have no quarrel with (2); and at first sight it may seem that theological orthodoxy would compel him to accept (1). But in fact, armed with Cartesian weapons, Malebranche can detect an ambiguity in (1) of which Augustine was unaware. The first premiss is capable of two interpretations:

(1*a*) Whatever we see directly in God is immutable.

(1*b*) Whatever we see indirectly in God is immutable.

Malebranche can accept (1) when it is construed in the sense of (1*a*): what we perceive directly in God is ideas, and ideas are eternal and immutable. So from this premiss in conjunction with (2), we can validly conclude that we do not directly see bodies in God. But this conclusion need not worry Malebranche, for it leaves his own doctrine quite untouched. If, however, the first premiss is construed in the sense of (1*b*), then Malebranche can claim that it expresses a false proposition. To say that we indirectly see bodies in God is to say that we see them by means of representative ideas. But bodies themselves are not in God, and of course they are not immutable. The Augustinian argument appears to refute Malebranche's doctrine only if we commit the following fallacy of equivocation:

(1) Whatever we see (directly) in God is immutable.

(2) But bodies are not immutable.

(3) Therefore, we do not (indirectly) see bodies in God.

When this equivocation is detected, the Augustinian challenge can be met.

By appealing to the representative theory of perception, Malebranche can explain how changes in the physical world do not, as it were, rub off on God. But it may seem that Malebranche has paid an extremely high price for this result. Recall that in response to the Augustinian argument, Malebranche concedes that whatever we perceive directly in God is immutable; in other words, the ideas which represent the physical world to us are eternal, unchanging abstract objects in God. But in that case it may seem difficult to see how Malebranche's 'ideas' can fulfil their representative function; it is hard to see how they can reflect changes in primary qualities. The peculiar status of ideas in Malebranche's philosophy appears to place him at a disadvantage as compared with other seventeenth-century philosophers. More conventional advocates of the representative theory can allow that the content of our ideas changes in a way that reflects events in the physical world. But it is not open to Malebranche to say this, for his ideas are not mental items at all; they are unchanging abstract objects. Thus, where primary qualities are concerned, Malebranche may seem to condemn us to contemplating immutable archetypes in God, while the flux of the physical world passes us by unnoticed.

In fact, however, the problem is not as difficult as it seems; it can be solved by making a straightforward distinction. The geometrical concepts or ideas in God are, of course, eternal and immutable; in this sense the objects of our perception are unchanging. But in another sense the objects of our perception may be said to change. Although a circle is an eternal idea in God, it does not follow that God always displays this idea to me, or that he displays it in the same way. Thus, when I perceive a change of shape in the wax, God simply displays to me the appropriate ideas in the appropriate order; for example, I have intellectual perceptions of a circle at t and of a square at t_1. But this difference in the content of my perceptions has no tendency to imply that there is any corresponding change in God. It is not the ideas themselves that change, but my perceptual relationship to them.

There is no doubt that Malebranche ingeniously deploys Cartesian resources in order to fight off the Augustinian challenge. Indeed, vision in God as a whole is one of the most brilliant works of synthesis in the history of philosophy. Yet, as Gueroult has noted, there is a certain tension between the two sides of Malebranche's inheritance; indeed, to some extent they are associated with competing models of mind. As Gueroult writes:

The mind, on the one hand, must be conceived as a created substance deprived of all light of its own, as a pure affectivity which receives from God its light and its objects of knowledge; on the other hand, it must be conceived as a faculty of knowing, as endowed with an intellect, a pure understanding which indeed belongs to it and which obeys its will.[30]

To appreciate the force of this charge, let us recall the status of ideas in Malebranche's philosophy. We have seen that, for Malebranche, ideas are abstract items; they correspond to what Bennett calls 'logical concepts'. But in that case they must be objects of intellectual awareness; they can be thought about, but they cannot be sensed. It thus becomes natural to suppose that Malebranche must have a doctrine of pure intellect, that he must regard intellectual activity as one of the mind's main functions. Yet, curiously enough, Malebranche has rather little to say explicitly about intellectual activity. When Malebranche wishes to distinguish between the two sides of our epistemic condition, the poles of the opposition are ideas and sensations. One might infer that Malebranche is hereby drawing a contrast between the intellectual and the sensory, but in fact this is only indirectly the case; what is explicitly contrasted is abstract—i.e. non-psychological—entities with a certain kind of psychological activity. We may read into this a contrast between the intellectual and the sensory aspects of the human condition, but we do so only by making an inference which Malebranche himself is strangely reluctant to draw: ideas, being abstract objects, require intellectual acts (thinkings) by which they may be apprehended.

Confronted with Malebranche's contrast between ideas and sensations, an unsympathetic reader might conclude that he is guilty of muddle after all: he has conflated the distinction between the logical and the psychological with the quite different distinction between the sensory and the intellectual. But that, I think, is not the root of the problem; it is rather, as Gueroult notes, that

---

[30] M. Gueroult, *Malebranche*, i. (Paris, 1955–9), 197.

Malebranche is working with two models of mind which are in tension. On the one hand, like Descartes, Malebranche requires a doctrine of pure intellect; on the other hand, under the influence of Augustine, he is drawn to a model of the mind which seems to have no room for it. On the second, 'Augustinian' model, the mind has no natural capacity for knowledge;[31] on the contrary, its essence consists in having sensations which are devoid of representational content. It is true that, on this model, the mind can achieve knowledge by being illuminated by an external source, namely, by the light of God's ideas, but Malebranche does not really provide us with a way of unpacking this metaphor. At least, if the nature of the mind consists in having sensations, it is not clear how the illumination metaphor is to be unpacked in such a way that Malebranche can consistently admit that the mind is also capable of intellectual activity.

Ultimately, then, Malebranche may not have succeeded in reconciling the two sides of his thought; the pulls of Descartes and Augustine generate a certain tension in his model of mind. But it would be wrong to end this chapter on a negative note. At the minimum estimate, the doctrine of vision in God constitutes an ingenious application of Malebranche's theory of ideas to the problem of visual perception. Once we appreciate Malebranche's basic concept of 'idea', the most serious problems of interpretation can be solved with the help of Cartesian resources. To Locke and his disciples, the doctrine of vision in God may have appeared mystical and unintelligible, and in a later chapter we shall examine the reasons for their incomprehension. But we should not lose sight of the fact that Malebranche's theory of ideas is in many ways more coherent and consistent than Locke's.

---

[31] I do not mean to imply that Malebranche's theory of mind is in fact faithful to that of the historical Augustine. As Gueroult points out (p. 137), Malebranche attributes a degree of passivity to the mind which Augustine, no less than Descartes, would deny.

6

Malebranche
Vision in God and Occasionalism

MALEBRANCHE'S name is widely associated with two famous doctrines, occasionalism and vision in God, but the relationship between them is not well understood. It is true that there are obvious and superficial parallels which can be drawn. Both doctrines concern the union of the mind with something other than itself. Vision in God is of course a thesis about the mind's union with God; occasionalism, at least in its specific form, is a thesis about the mind's relationship with its body. More strikingly perhaps, it is characteristic of both doctrines that they place man in a condition of extreme dependence on God; indeed, they might be seen as respectively ontological and epistemological versions of this theme. According to occasionalism, God alone is a true cause; thus, man by himself is causally impotent. According to vision in God, God alone has ideas; thus, the human mind by itself is, as it were, cognitively impotent. Further, both doctrines can be seen as pushing Cartesian themes to extreme lengths. Occasionalism is a radical version of the continuous creation doctrine of the 'Third Meditation';[1] vision in God is a radical version of Descartes's thesis in the 'Fifth Meditation' that all knowledge depends on the prior knowledge of God.[2]

The comparison with Descartes, however, is in one important respect misleading. For underlying the doctrines of vision in God and occasionalism is also a profoundly anti-Cartesian intuition. We have seen that Descartes brings such seemingly disparate items as concepts, sense-perceptions, and sensations under the heading 'idea', and he thereby signals his determination to regard them all as psychological entities for which it is appropriate to seek a causal explanation. The doctrine of innateness is one such answer to the causal question; Descartes arguably compounds his problems by

[1] 'Third Meditation', AT vii. 48–9; CSM ii. 33.
[2] 'Fifth Meditation', AT vii. 69–71; CSM ii. 48–9.

failing to distinguish between different senses of the term 'innate'. Malebranche, by contrast, is much more sensitive to the distinction between logical and psychological issues, and for this reason he refuses to regard concepts as psychological items which we may come to possess. The doctrines of vision in God and occasionalism express Malebranche's insistence on staking out boundaries in a way that Descartes did not. Yet if Malebranche is clear about the difference between logic and psychology, he is not so clear about the relations between different kinds of mental events, and this unclarity is reflected in a puzzle about the relationship between the two famous doctrines.

Occasionalism in General

Occasionalism is a doctrine which has been widely misunderstood ever since it was grossly caricatured by Leibniz. Contrary to popular textbook accounts, occasionalism is not simply an *ad hoc* solution to the mind-body problem bequeathed by Descartes; it is a general theory of causality which, none the less, has a specific application to the mind–body problem. As some English-speaking scholars are beginning to realize, occasionalism is in fact a brilliant theory which is at least half-way to Hume.[3]

For an understanding of occasionalism, it is best to begin with something familiar. Like so many of his contemporaries Malebranche rejects the faculty explanations of the scholastics in favour of the mechanical explanations of Descartes and others. On several occasions Malebranche uses the following example to bring out his partisanship for the new explanatory model:

If one asks me, for example, how it comes about that a piece of linen dries when one exposes it to the fire: I should not be a philosopher [i.e. a natural philosopher] if I reply that God wills it; for one knows well enough that everything which happens, happens because God wills it. One is not asking for the general cause, but the particular cause of a particular effect. I must then say that the small parts of the fire or of the wood that is set in motion, coming into contact with the linen, communicate their movement to the parts of the water that are in it, and detach them from the linen; and then I shall have given the particular cause of a particular effect.[4]

    [3] See e.g. C. J. McCracken, *Malebranche and British Philosophy* (Oxford, 1983), ch. 3; L. E. Loeb, *From Descartes to Hume: Continental Metaphysics and the Development of Modern Philosophy* (Ithaca and London, 1981), ch. 5.
    [4] *Conversations chrétiennes*, III (*OCM* iv. 77).

Although he does not put it in these terms, it seems fair to say that Malebranche's overall concept of explanation is deductive-nomological; particular effects, such as the drying of the linen, are explained by deriving them from covering laws in conjunction with particular statements of fact. Where the physical world is concerned, the covering law will be mechanistic; it will be one of what Malebranche calls the laws of the communication of movements.

Malebranche is as committed as any of his contemporaries to mechanistic explanations, but he sees that they are in a way problematic. Like Hume, Malebranche is aware that the laws of nature which are cited in the explanations to which he is committed are not absolutely necessary; it is logically possible, for instance, that the particles of water should not be detached from the linen when it comes into contact with the small parts of the burning wood. Yet Malebranche is wedded to the traditional view that genuine causality involves necessary connections; as he puts it in *The Search after Truth*, 'a true cause as I understand it is one such that the mind perceives a necessary connection between it and its effect'.[5] Hume, of course, confronted the problem of necessary connection by distinguishing sharply between causal and logical relations; he then preserved the traditional view of causality by simply locating the necessity in a subjective disposition of the mind.[6] Malebranche, by contrast, refuses to take this step, and to this extent he can be correctly described as a rationalist and a pre-Humean. Malebranche responds to the problem which his assumptions create for him in an entirely natural way; he draws the conclusion that the laws of nature cannot be genuinely causal.

For reasons which anticipate Hume, then, Malebranche holds that no physical processes can be truly causal. But of course Malebranche does not wish to hold that the concept of genuine causality is nowhere instantiated; he thinks that there is one case where the conditions of genuine causality are satisfied. Consider again the case of the linen. As we have seen, the particular effect is explained by deductive subsumption under a covering law, and the covering law in question will be a law of the communication of movements. But, for Malebranche, such an explanation does not exhaust all that can be said about the case; it is legitimate to seek an

---

[5] *Search after Truth*, VI. 2. 3 (*OCM* ii. 316; *SAT* 450).
[6] Hume, *Treatise of Human Nature*, I. III. xiv.

explanation of the law of nature itself. Thus Malebranche, like Leibniz and Spinoza, holds that there are no brute facts:

> But if one asked me how it comes about that the parts of the wood set in motion those of the water, or generally that the bodies communicate their movement to those which they encounter: I should not be a philosopher if I sought some particular cause of this general effect. I must have recourse to the general cause which is the will of God, and not to particular *faculties* or *qualities*.[7]

In some ways Malebranche's position is remarkably close to Leibniz's. Laws of nature are not simply brute facts; they can be explained by appealing to the will of God. The will of God is not arbitrary, however; it is guided by considerations of reason and order.[8] But in one crucial respect Malebranche differs from Leibniz. For Malebranche stresses that in explaining general laws by reference to the will of God, we finally arrive at a true cause. For God is omnipotent, and it is only in the case of an omnipotent being that we find the necessary connection we are looking for. In other words, it is a contradiction to suppose that something should be willed by God and not take place. Thus Malebranche subscribes to the following principle:

$$N(p) \text{ (If God wills that } p, p)$$

Although God must will some particular events, the values of p that Malebranche characteristically stresses are laws of nature; they comprise not only the laws of physics, but also, as we shall see, the psycho-physical laws which govern the relations of mind and body. Although they appear as the consequents of absolutely necessary propositions, the laws themselves are only hypothetically necessary; they are necessary on the assumption that God wills them. On Malebranche's understanding of causality, this implies that they are not genuinely causal; in his terms they describe the workings of merely occasional causality.

Malebranche's doctrine of causality is original and coherent, but we can see in retrospect that it involves a certain tension. On the one hand, Malebranche agrees with his contemporaries that mechanical explanations are genuinely explanatory; indeed, he regards them as paradigm explanations to be contrasted unfavourably with the circular, faculty explanations of the scholastics. On the other hand,

---

[7] *Conversations chrétiennes*, III (*OCM* iv. 77).
[8] Cf. Leibniz, *Discourse on Metaphysics*, 6 (G iv. 431–2; L, p. 306).

Malebranche subscribes to the traditional thesis that causal relations are necessary; thus, as we have seen, Malebranche is led to the conclusion that the new mechanical explanations are not genuinely causal. Yet, ironically, the faculty explanations of the scholastics did involve necessary connections, and to that extent they satisfied the conditions of genuine causality better than the mechanical explanations which superseded them. We can see this by means of a stock example. Suppose, in scholastic style, we seek to answer the question 'Why did the glass break when dropped?' by citing the fact of its fragility. Now it is plausible to suppose that to say the glass is fragile is merely to say that there is a law of nature to the effect that whenever the glass is dropped, it breaks.[9] So when we analyse the concept of fragility in this way, we see that our explanation is really circular, and hence, we are inclined to say, unsatisfactory. But precisely because it is circular, it involves a necessary connection, and as we have seen, for Malebranche, necessary connection is an essential component of genuine causality. Thus Malebranche is in the curious position of deriding the faculty explanations of the scholastics, even though, in one way at least, they are more nearly causal than the mechanical explanations with which he wishes to replace them.

Malebranche's position is not formally inconsistent. It is open to Malebranche to reply that although genuine causal explanations invoke necessary connections, they are also non-circular, and it is their failure to satisfy this requirement that vitiates the explanations of the scholastics. Malebranche is, of course, right to think that there can be necessary connections without circularity; he would point to the example of geometry which he would regard as a science of necessary truths. For Malebranche, not merely do the theorems follow logically from the axioms and definitions, but the axioms are themselves necessary. What Malebranche sees is that the mechanical explanations to which he is committed do not conform to the model of geometry, for the covering laws which figure as premises in such explanations are not necessary but contingent. None the less, Malebranche retained a concept of causality which the new science could not possibly satisfy. Perhaps this is merely another way of saying that occasionalism is a half-way house on the road to Hume.

[9] For a valuable discussion of dispositional properties, see D. H. Mellor, 'In Defense of Dispositions', *Philosophical Review*, 81 (1974), 157–81.

Occasionalism and the Mind–Body Problem

Occasionalism is a general thesis about causality, but of course it has a specific application to the mind–body problem; to this extent at least the received picture is correct. Just as there are laws of the communication of movements, so there are laws of the union of mind and body. As we might say, there are not only laws of physics; there are also psycho-physical laws. As we shall see later, the interpretation of these psycho-physical laws presents problems, but for the moment we can be content with an approximation. The laws of the union of mind and body run, as we would expect, in two directions: brain states are the occasional causes of sensations, and volitions are the occasional causes of voluntary physical movements.

Scholars who are aware that occasionalism is not simply an *ad hoc* solution to the mind–body problem have faced the problem of deciding on the exact nature of the relationship between the general and the specific forms of the doctrine. An influential answer to this question has been proposed by Louis Loeb. According to Loeb, the mind–body problem which Descartes bequeathed to his successors has a mainly strategic importance for Malebranche. Malebranche's chief interest is in advancing a general thesis about causality, but he exploits the widely felt difficulty of mind–body interaction as a way of preparing his readers for acceptance of the more general thesis:

> The thesis that mind and body do not or cannot interact did not require much argument. Malebranche could rely upon the reader to agree with, or at least be sympathetic to, or at the very least understand the grounds for, the denial of mind–body interaction. This provides a wedge. At section 11 [of *Dialogues on Metaphysics*, IV] Malebranche is saying: 'The denial of interaction between mind and body is familiar enough; I go even further and deny interaction between any two created entities, between two minds, or two bodies. I realize this may sound extravagant. But you agree that there can be persuasive grounds for denying interaction between certain entities, minds and bodies. Read on, and I will show you that there are persuasive grounds for denying other interactions as well.'[10]

Loeb may be right about the strategy which Malebranche adopts in the *Dialogues on Metaphysics*, but he is wrong if he wishes to imply that Malebranche always argues in this way. The *Meditations chrétiennes* (*Christian Meditations*) provides a striking counter-

---

[10] Loeb, p. 227.

example; in this work Malebranche adopts almost the opposite tack. Here the Word begins by proving to the meditator that matter in general is powerless, and then proceeds to argue that created minds are also causally impotent. In other words, Malebranche introduces the mind–body problem only after presenting a general thesis about matter:

You are sufficiently persuaded that matter is a powerless nature which acts only by the efficacy of the movement which I impress upon it. But I clearly see that you are not sufficiently persuaded that minds [*esprits*] have no power over bodies, or over inferior spirits. You are still inclined to believe that your soul animates your body in this sense, that it is from it that it receives all the movements which are produced in it, or at least those which one calls voluntary, and which depend effectively on your volitions. Give up your prejudices, my son, and never judge with regard to natural effects that one thing is the effect of another because experience teaches one that it never fails to follow it.[11]

Of course, if body is completely powerless, then the causal action of body on mind must be just as obviously impossible as the causal action of body on body; to this extent mind–body interaction is as problematic as interaction in the physical world. But as this passage reminds us, there are aspects of Malebranche's philosophy which tend to drive a wedge between the two sides of the mind–body problem. For one thing, as we have seen, Malebranche stresses, as Berkeley was later to do for rather different purposes, that on the new physics matter is completely passive;[12] by contrast, there is nothing in the new science which implies that the same is true of minds. Secondly, Malebranche subscribes to the Augustinian principle that the lower substance (matter) cannot act causally on the higher substance (mind);[13] there is, however, nothing in Malebranche's Augustinian inheritance which implies that the converse is also true. Thus, for both these reasons, the action of mind on body is less obviously problematic than the action of body on body or of body on mind.

Loeb, then, is wrong to suggest that Malebranche has a single strategy of argument for unqualified occasionalism; on the contrary, the truth seems to be that Malebranche adopts different

---

[11] *Meditations chrétiennes*, VI (*OCM* x. 58–9).

[12] G. Berkeley, *Three Dialogues Between Hylas and Philonous*, 2, in Berkeley, *Philosophical Works*, ed. M. R. Ayers (London, 1975).

[13] See e.g. *Conversations chrétiennes*, I (*OCM* iv. 20). See D. Radner, *Malebranche* (Assen, 1978), 19.

strategies on different occasions. It is not difficult to think of an historical explanation for this variation; the answer may be that Malebranche suits his method of argument to the assumptions of particular audiences. When, as in the *Dialogues on Metaphysics*, Malebranche is addressing a mainly Cartesian and secular audience, he adopts the strategy described by Loeb; he exploits the widely felt difficulty of the mind–body problem as a way of preparing his readers for unqualified occasionalism. But when, as in the *Christian Meditations*, Malebranche is addressing a mainly Augustinian and religious audience, he adopts the opposite strategy; he exploits the generally accepted belief in the causal impotence of matter as a way of preparing his readers for the causal impotence of created minds.

Occasionalism is not the only general thesis about causality which has a specific application to the mind–body problem: Leibniz's doctrine of pre-established harmony is another prominent example in the period. This fact is perhaps one of the main reasons why, from the very first, readers have seen close parallels between the two doctrines; in particular, they have wondered whether there is any real difference between occasionalism and the pre-established harmony in their specific forms as solutions to the mind–body problem. As Woolhouse shrewdly observes, there is one answer to this question which will not do: it is Foucher's suggestion that the pre-established harmony is simply occasionalism with all the adjustments made at once;[14] in other words, the pre-established harmony improves on occasionalism by substituting God's programming of mind and body for the series of discrete acts of divine intervention that Malebranche supposedly envisages. This answer is wrong because it rests on a gross misrepresentation of Malebranche which even Leibniz encouraged. With his characteristic refusal to be bullied, Arnauld tried to make this clear to Leibniz. Confronted with Leibniz's own account of voluntary movement, Arnauld remarks:

It seems to me that it is saying the same thing in other terms as those who claim that my will is the occasional cause of the movement of my arm, and that God is the real cause of it. For they do not claim that God does that in time by a new act of will, which he has each time I will to raise my arm; but that he does it by this single act of the eternal will by which he has willed to

---

[14] R. S. Woolhouse, 'Leibniz's Reaction to Cartesian Interactionism', *Proceedings of the Aristotelian Society*, 86 (1985–6), 69–70.

do everything which he has foreseen that it would be necessary that he did in order that the universe be such as he judged that it had to be.[15]

In other words, for Malebranche just as much as for Leibniz, God acts through general laws, not through a series of particular volitions. On this issue Malebranche could hardly be more explicit; indeed, Malebranche was accused (for example, by Arnauld himself) of going so far in this direction that he left no room for the suspension of natural laws in the case of miracles.[16] Thus there is no basis whatever for the suggestion that Malebranche's occasionalism appeals to God simply as a *Deus ex machina*.[17] When Leibniz encourages this view, he is probably indulging in polemical exaggeration; if he really thought this was an issue between him and Malebranche, then he had a very poor understanding of occasionalism.

We should not, however, conclude with Arnauld that there is no real difference between occasionalism and the pre-established harmony. On this issue the correct answer seems to have been provided by Roger Woolhouse.[18] The real difference between the two doctrines turns on the question of psycho-physical laws, or what Malebranche calls the laws of the union of mind and body. In other words, for Malebranche, where mind and body are concerned, there are strictly nomological propositions of two distinct kinds; propositions which refer to physical events in the antecedent and mental events in the consequent, and propositions which refer to mental events in the antecedent and physical events in the consequent. For Leibniz, by contrast, the admission of such hybrid nomological propositions leads to conceptual incoherence; it leads to what he calls a 'derangement' of the laws of physics.[19] To this extent Leibniz seeks to do justice to the common intuition that every physical event has a physical cause. As Woolhouse remarks, Leibniz is closer here to Spinoza than he is to Malebranche, inasmuch as he regards the physical and the mental as closed systems with their own sacrosanct laws.[20] It may be a slight

---

[15] Arnauld to Leibniz, 4 Mar. 1687, G ii. 84.

[16] On this issue see H. Gouhier, *La Philosophie de Malebranche et son expérience religieuse* (Paris, 1948), 56.

[17] This suggestion is frequently made by Leibniz. See e.g. *New System*, G iv. 483; L, p. 457; and 'A Specimen of Discoveries', G vii. 313; P, pp. 80–1.

[18] Woolhouse, pp. 77–82.

[19] *Theodicy*, 61 (G vi. 136). See Woolhouse, p. 76.

[20] Woolhouse, pp. 77–8, 82.

exaggeration to claim, as Woolhouse does, that Leibniz is as clear on this point as Spinoza, for the status of bodies is at times problematic in Leibniz, especially perhaps in his later philosophy. But there is little doubt that, unlike Malebranche, Leibniz has serious reservations about the whole notion of psycho-physical laws.

Vision in God and Mind–Body Occasionalism

We are now in a position to go back to our starting-point, and consider the relationship between Malebranche's two most famous doctrines. In its application to the mind–body problem, occasionalism holds that there are non-causal psycho-physical laws; not to beg any questions at this stage, let us say, then, that at least some mental phenomena can be explained in terms of the conjunction of these laws and antecedent physical states. Malebranche is further committed to the thesis that the mind is united, not just to its body, but also to God; and it is by virtue of this latter union that we perceive ideas. Thus both the doctrines of occasionalism and vision in God bear on mental phenomena, and we need to know how the field is divided between them. Let us begin by considering two kinds of mental event which involve only one of the two doctrines.

Suppose that I am engaged in proving theorems of Euclidean geometry. Malebranche will analyse such a case by saying that I am engaged in perceiving ideas, and that these ideas are displayed to me by God. Such perception is obviously not visual perception, and is thus not vision in God in the narrow sense we distinguished in Chapter 4. But it is none the less a clear case of vision in God, inasmuch as God is the locus of the ideas to which my mind is related. Of course, concurrently with my intellectual activity, I may have certain sensations; I may be aware of a tickle in my leg, or I may make use of visual diagrams to assist me in my proofs. But abstract thought, *qua* abstract thought, is not governed by the laws of the union of mind and body, or as we might say, by psycho-physical laws.

Suppose, on the other hand, that I am experiencing a violent toothache. In such a case, as Loeb notes with regard to a similar example, there is no vision in God, for there is no idea;[21] unlike

---

[21] Loeb, p. 225.

Descartes, Malebranche feels no temptation to say that a pain is a confused idea because it is a confused representation of damage to a part of my body. We have seen that my pain, for Malebranche, has no representational content at all; it is simply a sensation (i.e. sensing), and is thus governed by psycho-physical laws. Again, concurrently with my pain experience, I may do some thinking; for instance, I may calculate the cost of a visit to my dentist. But this intellectual activity of course is not an essential feature of the pain experience. Thus sensations, *qua* sensations, do not involve vision in God; they are governed exclusively by the laws of the union of mind and body.

It is possible, then, to isolate two kinds of mental event, each of which involves only one of Malebranche's two most famous doctrines. Indeed, it is even possible to conceive of two kinds of mind, each of which enjoys only one kind of union. If a mind is disembodied and united only with God, then its mental life would be restricted to purely intellectual activity; if, on the other hand, a mind is united only with its body by means of psycho-physical laws, then its experience would be restricted to sensations and secondary-quality perceptions. In some respects these two kinds of union would parallel the poles of the Spinozistic life, freedom and bondage. But between abstract thought and pure sensation there is another kind of mental activity which human minds enjoy by virtue of being united both to God and to their bodies; in other words, it involves both vision in God and the psycho-physical laws. This of course is sense-perception.

Malebranche seems very clear that sense-perception is a combination of heterogeneous elements. In *The Search after Truth* he offers a concise account of his position:

When we perceive something sensible, two things are found in our perception: *sensation* and pure *idea*. The sensation is a modification of our soul, and it is God who causes it in us. He can cause this modification even though He does not have it Himself, because He sees in the idea He has of our soul that it is capable of it. As for the idea found in conjunction with the sensation, it is in God, and we see it because it pleases God to reveal it to us. God joins the sensation to the idea when objects are present so that we may believe them to be present and that we may have all the feelings and passions that we should have in relation to them.[22]

---

[22] *Search after Truth*, III. 2. 6 (*OCM* i. 445; *SAT*, 234).

We can once again flesh out Malebranche's analysis by means of an example. Supposing that I am perceiving the top of my desk. An essential ingredient of my experience is the perception of primary qualities; Malebranche would analyse this perception in terms of seeing that—of seeing that, for example, the top of my desk is rectangular. To this extent I am engaged in contemplating ideas in God. But a further, no less essential, feature of the total situation is the perception of secondary qualities; Malebranche would analyse this perception by saying that I have a sensation or *sentiment* of brown, for example. Such secondary-quality perceptions, like pains and tickles, have no representational content; they are simply sensations which are caused by God in accordance with the laws of the union of mind and body. Thus Malebranche's two most famous doctrines are both involved in the analysis of sense-perception.

Conceiving and Perceiving: Two Different Accounts

In *The Search after Truth*, then, Malebranche offers the following picture of sense-perception: when I am seeing the top of my desk, God displays to me the idea of a rectangle at the same time that my mind is modified by the appropriate sensations in accordance with the laws of the union of mind and body. There is thus, as it were, a pre-established harmony between vision in God and the psycho-physical laws, or specifically, between the intellectual and the sensory elements in sense-perception. Yet on occasions Malebranche tells a different story which seems inconsistent with the above account. In the *Christian Conversations*, for instance, Malebranche addresses the issue of the difference between conceiving and perceiving extension. In other words, he seeks to give a philosophical account of the difference between, for example, merely thinking of a rectangle and actually seeing a rectangular object such as my desk-top. The position that Malebranche defends in *The Search after Truth* would seem to furnish him with a ready way of explaining the difference. Malebranche could say that when I merely think of a rectangle, I see an idea in God; but when I see a rectangular object, such as the desk-top, my vision of the idea in God is additionally correlated with secondary-quality sensations in accordance with the laws of the union of mind and body. Malebranche of course need not deny that in the former case I must be having some sensations; the psycho-physical laws are never silent. All he needs to deny is that these sensations are correlated with my vision of the idea in God in the way that is characteristic of sense-perception. But in the *Christian Conversations* Malebranche seems to take a quite different tack:

> When the idea of extension affects or modifies the mind with a pure perception, then the mind simply conceives this extension. But when the idea of extension touches the mind in a livelier fashion, and affects it with a sensible perception, then the mind sees or senses extension. The mind sees it [i.e. extension] when this perception is a sensation of colour; and it senses or perceives it in a still more lively fashion when the perception with which intelligible extension modifies it is a pain. For colour, pain, and all the other sensations are only sensible perceptions produced in intelligences by intelligible ideas.[23]

In this passage Malebranche does not appeal to the relationship between vision in God and psycho-physical laws in order to explain the difference between conceiving and perceiving; rather, he seeks to explain the difference exclusively in terms of intelligible ideas and their relations to the mind. We are said to think or sense according to the different ways in which our minds are 'touched' by ideas. Malebranche's position in *The Search after Truth* might be called 'dualistic': vision in God and the laws of mind–body union are distinct, but they are capable of being correlated, as they are in sense-perception. By contrast, the position of the *Christian Conversations* is 'monistic': the doctrine of psycho-physical laws is simply collapsed into the doctrine of vision in God.

Malebranche's monistic position in the *Christian Conversations* seems fraught with difficulties. For one thing, it involves the attribution of causal properties to ideas—'third realm' items, and as we have seen, this seems a dubious notion; there are, of course, precedents in Plato, but the notion remains dubious. Moreover, it is difficult to see how the idea of extension can be invoked to explain sensations such as colour and pain. But although this doctrine is obscure, it is possible to do something to make it more intelligible, for the context of the discussion in the *Christian Conversations* indicates the direction in which Malebranche's mind was moving. We can see at least that there were reasons why Malebranche might have been dissatisfied with the dualistic position of *The Search after Truth*.

---

[23] *Conversations chrétiennes*, iii (*OCM* iv. 75–6).

Let us go back to the implications of Malebranche's doctrine of vision in God. The items that I see in God are ideas, and ideas, as we have seen, are not psychological but logical; as Malebranche insists again and again, they are not modifications or modalities of minds. None the less, if these ideas are to be anything to us, they require corresponding mental modifications; in other words, as Malebranche emphasizes in the *Christian Conversations*, we must have perceptions of the ideas in God's mind to which we are related.[24] Now such perceptions are in one way quite unlike pains or colour sensations, for they are intellectual, not sensory. But of course my thought of a rectangle is just as much a psychological item as a pain or a sensation of red; we must beware of conflating the distinction between the intellectual and the sensory with the quite different distinction between the logical and the psychological. Now it is just this recognition of the psychological nature of thinkings and conceivings which creates problems for Malebranche. For it is intrinsically plausible to suppose that all mental events, intellectual as well as sensory, are law-governed, and there is reason to believe that Malebranche shared this intuition.[25] But it is not clear that the dualistic model can accommodate it; sensations of course occur in accordance with the laws of the union of mind and body, but in *The Search after Truth* Malebranche does nothing to indicate that intellectual perceptions are comparably law-governed. Instead, we are told that God simply displays or reveals his ideas to us.

Malebranche could, of course, protest that he should not be read too literally. Talk of God's displaying or revealing ideas is metaphorical, and the metaphor can be unpacked in strictly nomological terms.[26] But if this is so, then Malebranche provides us with two parallel sets of laws; there is one set of laws for our intellectual perceptions, and another set of laws for sensations, namely, the laws of the union of mind and body. And Malebranche may well have supposed that this was simply uneconomical; why not instead postulate a single set of laws for all mental events, intellectual as well as sensory? Thus, by thinking through the problem of intellectual perceptions, Malebranche may have been led to the monistic position of the *Christian Conversations*. It cannot be

---

[24] *Conversations chrétiennes*, III (*OCM* iv. 74).
[25] See *Dialogues on Metaphysics*, XIII (D, pp. 320–1).
[26] Ibid.

claimed that all mysteries are hereby dispelled. For instance, if the dualistic position is to be abandoned, it might seem more natural to collapse vision in God into the laws of the union of mind and body, but instead, Malebranche goes the other way; he seems to bring the psycho-physical laws under the wing of vision in God. But at least we can see why Malebranche might have been dissatisfied with the position of *The Search after Truth*.

Malebranche, then, does not achieve a fully satisfactory account of the relations between his two most famous doctrines. Here, as elsewhere, it is the status of intellectual perceptions which is the source of his problems. Malebranche sometimes has difficulty acknowledging that the realm of the psychological is not simply coextensive with the sensory; when he does try to accommodate this insight, the result is that he sets up tensions with his most basic commitments. Even so, Malebranche's position is in many ways an imaginative and sensitive response to the problems that Descartes bequeathed his successors. Unlike Descartes, Malebranche is never tempted to treat concepts as straightforwardly psychological items on a par with sensations; nor does he find himself in Descartes's position of being forced to juggle with two incompatible doctrines of innateness. The doctrines of vision in God and occasionalism may be flawed, but they are free from the arguably more serious conflations and inconsistencies which bedevil Descartes's treatment of the same issues.

7
Malebranche
Ideas and Self-Knowledge

MALEBRANCHE is sometimes classified as a Cartesian, but on the issue of self-knowledge he departs radically from Descartes; Malebranche completely rejects the thesis that the mind is better known than body. Indeed, Malebranche stands Descartes's thesis on its head; he holds that in a certain sense body is better known than mind. Strictly speaking, Malebranche argues that mind and body are known in two different ways; bodies are known through ideas, but the mind is known only through consciousness or internal sensation. In this way Malebranche imposes an important restriction on his doctrine of vision in God; for if we do not know our mind through ideas, then we do not see it in God. Malebranche's account of self-knowledge thus occupies a central place in his philosophy; indeed, it constitutes one of the major, if negative, applications of his whole theory of ideas.

In his treatment of self-knowledge Malebranche is thus something of a radical. On this issue at least, he belongs, not with Descartes or the other 'rationalists', but with the 'empiricists' Gassendi, Locke, and perhaps even Hume.[1] Not surprisingly, Malebranche's position on self-knowledge was subjected to vehement criticism from a Cartesian standpoint; in *On True and False Ideas*, Arnauld singled out Malebranche's denial that we have an idea of our mind as one of the main targets of his polemic.[2] Among other criticisms Arnauld argued cogently that, on Malebranche's view, it is difficult to see how we can have knowledge of such vital truths about the mind as its freedom and immortality. But to a large extent the substance of Malebranche's views emerges unscathed from Arnauld's attack, for

[1] See C. J. McCracken, *Malebranche and British Philosophy* (Oxford, 1983), 80 1. Cf. R. W. Church, *A Study in the Philosophy of Malebranche* (London, 1931), 55. Unlike Church, however, McCracken warns against reducing Malebranche's view to Hume's.

[2] A. Arnauld, *Des vraies et des fausses idées*, chs. XXII–XXIV, in *Œuvres de Messire Antoine Arnauld*, xxxviii (Paris, 1780; repr. Brussels, 1967).

Arnauld failed to come to grips with his central claims. Arguably, Malebranche had more insight than any other seventeenth-century philosopher into the weaknesses of Descartes's philosophy of mind. For this reason alone Malebranche's discussion of self-knowledge is an important contribution to the subject.

Descartes

In the full title of the 'Second Meditation' Descartes promises to show that the mind is better known than body; he seeks to honour the promise at the very end of the meditation. In fact, Descartes is making not one promise but two; he undertakes to show, first, that the existence of the mind is better known than the existence of body, and secondly, that the nature of the mind is better known than the nature of body. Many readers, including Malebranche, have no difficulty accepting that Descartes has made good on his first promise; Descartes can argue convincingly that any judgement I make about the existence of a body—the piece of wax, for instance—implies a greater certainty about the existence of my mind. But Descartes's second claim has proved much more troublesome. Malebranche, like other contemporary critics, argued that Descartes had not succeeded in establishing this second thesis; indeed, according to Malebranche, this second thesis is actually false.[3]

How does Descartes in fact seek to establish his claim about the nature of the mind? In the 'Second Meditation' Descartes offers the following argument:

I now know that even bodies are not strictly perceived by the senses or the faculty of imagination but by the intellect alone, and that this perception derives not from their being touched or seen but from their being understood; and in view of this I know plainly that nothing can be more easily or evidently perceived by me than my mind [*aperte cognosco nihil facilius aut evidentius mea mente posse a me percipi*].[4]

As Margaret Wilson has argued, Descartes seems to be guilty of a 'thumping' *non sequitur* here.[5] We might try to come to Descartes's aid by supposing that he is relying tacitly on a premiss to the effect

---

[3] *Résponse au livre*, ch. xxiii (*OCM* vi. 161).
[4] 'Second Meditation', AT vii. 34; CSM ii. 22–3. I have somewhat altered Cottingham's translation.
[5] M. D. Wilson, *Descartes* (London, 1978), 94–5.

that if I use x as an instrument for knowing y, then the nature of x is as well known to me as the nature of y. Unfortunately, however, this general principle does not seem to be true; as far as the user is concerned, the instrument may be simply a black box. An entomologist may use microscopes for the study of insects, but this does not mean that he knows much about optics.

Descartes, then, seems to offer an invalid argument for the conclusion that nothing is better known than the nature of the mind. Yet in fact Descartes seeks to establish an even stronger thesis; he wants to argue that the nature of the mind is *better* known than the nature of anything else, including body. Descartes was pressed on this issue by Gassendi, who charged that Descartes had not succeeded in establishing this. 'Your intention was surely to establish that [the mind's] nature is better known than the nature of the body, and this you have not managed to do.'[6] Descartes's reply is puzzling:

As for me, I have never thought that anything more is required to reveal a substance than its various attributes; thus the more attributes of a given substance we know, the more perfectly we understand its nature. Now we can distinguish many different attributes in the wax: one, that it is white; two, that it is hard; three, that it can be melted; and so on. And there are correspondingly many attributes in the mind; one, that it has the power of knowing the whiteness of the wax; two, that it has the power of knowing its hardness; three, that it has the power of knowing that it can lose its hardness (i.e. melt), and so on . . . The clear inference from this is that we know more attributes in the case of our mind than we do in the case of anything else. For no matter how many attributes we recognize in any given thing, we can always list a corresponding number of attributes in the mind which it has in virtue of knowing the attributes of the thing; and hence that the nature of the mind is the one we know best of all.[7]

Thus Descartes gives an argument for the stronger thesis which relies on two main claims. First, he appeals to a general thesis about knowledge; secondly, he holds that for any property I know in a body, there is a corresponding property that I discover in my own mind. The converse, by contrast, does not hold; it is not the case that any knowledge I have of my own mind entails a corresponding piece of knowledge about body.

Critics of Descartes have not been satisfied by his answer to Gassendi. Margaret Wilson, for instance, observes that the general

---

[6] 'Fifth Objections', AT vii. 275; CSM ii. 192.
[7] 'Fifth Replies', AT vii. 360; CSM ii. 249.

principle to which Descartes appeals seems curiously simplistic; it equates the extension of knowledge with a mere lengthening of properties in a way that seems most un-Cartesian.[8] From Malebranche's standpoint, Descartes's reply has a further, related defect. When Descartes specifies the properties of the mind that are known in knowing the wax, the examples he cites are all powers— e.g. the power of knowing the whiteness of the wax. Barring difficulties we shall examine later, it is unlikely that Malebranche would agree with Descartes that he has thereby succeeded in adding to his knowledge of his mind. No genuine properties of bodies are identified when we speak of physical powers (such as dormitive powers), and in Malebranche's view, things are no different in the case of mental powers. Malebranche complains that Descartes and other Cartesians were guilty of a double standard here:

I am amazed that the Cartesian gentlemen who so rightly reject the general terms *nature* and *faculty* should so willingly employ them on this occasion. They criticise those who say that fire burns by its *nature* or that it changes certain bodies into glass by a natural *faculty*, and yet some of them do not hesitate to say that the human mind produces in itself the ideas of all things by its *nature*, because it has the faculty of thinking. But, with all due respect, these terms are no more meaningful in their mouth than in the mouth of the Peripatetics.[9]

It is true that Malebranche's primary reason for objecting to talk of powers is that it is explanatorily empty; mental powers can no more explain mental events than physical powers can explain physical events. Descartes might object that in the 'Fifth Replies' he is not seeking to explain anything in terms of his power to know the wax; none the less, the power in question is a genuine property of his mind. But in fact Malebranche would not accept this answer, for he seems to have held a quite radical view on the subject of dispositions; he regards all talk of powers, natures, and faculties as wholly empty. Thus, in Malebranche's eyes, Descartes has acquired no genuine self-knowledge when he claims to discover, for instance, a power in his mind of knowing the whiteness of the wax. Malebranche would agree with Gassendi that Descartes has done nothing to establish his thesis that the nature of mind is known better than the nature of body.

---

[8] Wilson, *Descartes*, pp. 96–7.
[9] 'Tenth Elucidation', *OCM* iii. 144; *SAT* 622.

Malebranche: Knowledge through Ideas and Knowledge through Consciousness

For Malebranche, the Cartesian claims for the superiority of self-knowledge rest on a fundamental mistake; they confuse two radically different kinds of knowledge. According to Malebranche, we know the nature of bodies through ideas, but we know the mind only through consciousness or what he also calls internal sensation. Commenting on Descartes's reply to Gassendi, Malebranche protests: 'Who does not see that there is quite a difference between knowing through a clear idea and knowing through consciousness?'[10] It is tempting to suppose that Malebranche is here anticipating Russell's distinction between knowledge by acquaintance and knowledge by description. On the whole, the temptation should be resisted, for as we shall see, Malebranche's concept of knowledge through idea does not correspond to Russell's knowledge by description. But the Russellian concept of knowledge by acquaintance does throw light on Malebranche's claims about self-knowledge. Malebranche does not deny that we have a peculiarly intimate and indeed incorrigible knowledge of our mental states; 'our consciousness of [our soul] does not involve us in error'.[11] But such consciousness is knowledge by acquaintaince only; the mistake of the Cartesians is to suppose that it has anything to do with their own conception of knowledge by means of clear and distinct ideas.

Malebranche formulates his negative thesis about self-knowledge in rather different ways on different occasions. In *The Search after Truth* he remarks that we do not know the mind through its idea—we do not see it in God.[12] In the 'Eleventh Elucidation', he writes that 'we have no clear idea of our soul's nature or of its modifications'.[13] At first sight the difference between the two formulations may appear trivial, but in fact it is important, for it bears on the wider issue of the whole nature of ideas. The second formulation is couched in the psychologistic mode; it suggests that ideas are mental entities, properties which can belong to the mind. By contrast, in *The Search after Truth* itself, Malebranche states his

---

[10] 'Eleventh Elucidation', *OCM* iii. 167; *SAT* 635.
[11] *Search after Truth*, iii. 2. 7 (*OCM* i. 453; *SAT* 239).
[12] Ibid. (*OCM* i. 451; *SAT* 237).
[13] 'Eleventh Elucidation', *OCM* iii. 163; *SAT* 633.

thesis about self-knowledge in terms of the theory of ideas towards which he was still struggling: ideas are not psychological, but abstract, logical, entities in God. In what follows I shall treat the logicist formulation as basic, and the psychologistic one as an aberration, or at least as a concession to the Cartesian framework. We shall see that Arnauld was to exploit Malebranche's occasional lapses into psychologism during the course of his polemic.

According to Malebranche, then, there is a radical asymmetry between our knowledge of mind and body. In the case of body we have cognitive access to ideas in God; in the case of the mind we do not. Malebranche is not saying that there is no idea of the mind in God; on the contrary, he is saying that there is such an idea, but we do not have access to it. Indeed, Malebranche is under considerable pressure from other parts of his system to postulate the existence of an idea of the human mind in God, for ideas, for Malebranche, are not just objects to which we can be related in thinking; they are also archetypes for God's creation of the world. With the example of Leibniz in mind, we might suppose that such archetypal ideas are like Leibnizian complete concepts of individuals. We might suppose, then, that when Malebranche says we do not know our soul through idea, he is thinking of an individual essence rather than a specific essence. This, however, is probably a mistake. Malebranche no doubt should have been more sensitive to the distinction between individual and specific essences, but it seems that when he says we have no idea of our mind, he is talking about the human mind in general. God's archetypal idea of the mind would thus be a blueprint for the creation of every human mind.[14]

The idea of the mind is thus a universal, but we still need to know what knowledge through such an idea would be like; in other words, what exactly are we deprived of by having no access to this idea in God? McCracken is surely right that what we lack, according to Malebranche, is a priori knowledge of the nature of the mind; as we might say, we lack an a priori science of psychology.[15] It is tempting to say that for Malebranche there can be no a priori science of psychology; there is no body of axioms and definitions from which substantive psychological theorems about the human

---

[14] It should be noted that Malebranche's thought developed in the direction of placing greater emphasis on the generality of ideas. On this issue, see D. Radner, *Malebranche* (Assen, 1978), ch. v.

[15] McCracken, p. 77.

mind could in principle be deduced. But here we must be careful, for it is not clear that Malebranche really allows us to say this. For Malebranche, as we have seen, does not deny that there is an idea of the soul; he denies that we have any kind of epistemic access to it. And this seems to suggest that there is an a priori science of human psychology for God; it seems as if God can know substantive truths about the human mind by deriving them from the idea to which he alone has access. As in the case of extension, when Malebranche talks about ideas, he seems to envisage a package of axioms and definitions which would serve as a basis for deriving a body of theorems.

Here there is an interesting comparison to be made with Leibniz's account of complete concepts. Despite the differences we have noted, Leibniz's complete concepts of individuals resemble Malebranche's idea of the mind in that God alone has epistemic access to them. Thus Leibniz holds that God is in a position to have a priori knowledge of truths about individuals simply by inspecting their complete concepts. We, by contrast, can only discover the truth of the proposition 'Julius Caesar crossed the Rubicon' a posteriori, i.e. by experience; we discover it through observation or through the reports of historians. To say that God knows such truths a priori, however, is not to say that in his eyes they are necessary truths. On the contrary, the distinction between necessary and contingent truths is absolute; it is not merely relative to human minds. Thus 'Julius Caesar crossed the Rubicon' is knowable a priori by God, but it is a contingent truth, even for him.[16]

Leibniz's insistence on the absolute nature of the distinction between necessary and contingent truths is one of the strengths of his system; it puts him in a position to explain why we cannot know factual truths about individuals a priori. For Leibniz, it is a mark of contingent truths that they involve an infinite analysis; in contrast to necessary truths, the inclusion of the predicate concept in the subject concept cannot be discovered by a finite analysis.[17] Leibniz can use this fact to explain why it is that, unlike God, we can have no a priori knowledge of complete concepts. Malebranche, by contrast, has no real explanation of why our minds are related to God's idea of body, but not to his idea of the mind. When

[16] See *On Freedom*, L, p. 266.
[17] Ibid. (L, p. 265).

Malebranche does venture an explanation, all he can offer is a few lame remarks which show him at his worst; he says that God has withheld this idea from us because it would prove too intellectually seductive; we should be tempted to spend all our time contemplating it to the neglect of our duties.[18] But Malebranche has no philosophical account of our ignorance of the idea of the soul. It seems that for God there must be an a priori science of psychology, but why it is not also a science for us is simply a mystery. Unlike Leibniz, Malebranche is not in a position to suggest that there is something about the logical structure of this science which puts it beyond our cognitive grasp. In this respect the idea of the soul is more like Spinoza's unknown attributes than Leibniz's complete concepts.

There is no evidence, then, that God's knowledge of the soul through ideas has any special logical peculiarities. To understand what an a priori psychology would be like there is no reason why we should not turn to the knowledge through idea which we do possess. Here, there seem to be significantly different candidates. Consider how McCracken explains Malebranche's negative thesis about self-knowledge:

In saying we have no *idea* of the soul, Malebranche did not mean we have no knowledge of it; he meant tht we have no a priori knowledge of it. The geometer, he supposed, begins with a clear a priori concept of extension from which he can deduce truths about the figures of two- and three-dimensional objects, and the physicist, recognizing that extended things are movable, can discover a priori the general laws governing motion and its communication. Euclid showed the properties of figures, in his *Elements*; Descartes, the laws of motion, in his *Principles*. But there will never be a Euclid or Descartes in psychology, for we lack an a priori idea of the mind from which to deduce its properties.[19]

To clarify Malebranche's negative thesis, McCracken here appeals to two examples of knowledge by idea, geometry and physics. It seems, however, that we get a rather different picture of what an a priori psychology would be like, depending on which of these two sciences we take as our paradigm. If we focus on the case of geometry, then we get a claim of the following type: if, and only if, we had access to the idea of the mind, we could derive its essential properties in the way that we can derive the essential properties of

---

[18] See e.g. *Meditations chrétiennes*, IX (*OCM* x. 104).
[19] McCracken, pp. 77–8.

geometrical figures from Euclidean axioms and definitions. I can know a priori that the Pythagorean theorem is true of any right-angled triangle, but since I do not know its idea, I cannot know a priori that the mind is capable of pain and pleasure; I find this out only by experience. If, however, we focus on the case of physics, then we get some such claim as the following: if, and only if, we had access to the idea of the mind, we could have a priori knowledge of laws of psychology which would enable us to make detailed predictions about particular mental states. The physicist has a priori knowledge of the laws of motion, and on this basis he can predict the positions of the planets, for instance, but nothing like this is possible for us in psychology. That I shall feel a twinge of toothache at 2.00 p.m. tomorrow is something I can only discover empirically. The difference between the two paradigms is of course clear; the second model represents an a priori psychology as a much more ambitious enterprise than does the first.

Interpreting Malebranche's negative thesis about self-knowledge thus seems to depend on the choice of paradigm; if McCracken is right, then an a priori psychology might be a predictive science like physics. The problem of interpretation is complicated by the question of Malebranche's view of the status of physics and its relation to geometry; in this respect Malebranche presents the same kind of difficulty as the other rationalists. It is clear, as McCracken suggests, that knowledge through idea is a priori knowledge, and that geometry, for Malebranche, is a paradigm case of an a priori science. But it is less clear than McCracken suggests that for Malebranche physics is also wholly an a priori discipline. Indeed, Malebranche's occasionalism seems to be prima-facie evidence against this interpretation. We saw in the previous chapter that, contrary to the textbook picture, occasionalism is not merely an *ad hoc* solution to the mind-body problem; it is a general thesis about created substances, and one of its main tenets is that the laws of nature are not logically necessary. But if physics is not a science of necessary truths, then there is an obvious problem as to how it can be known a priori.

In fact, there is no clear evidence that Malebranche was thinking in terms of the paradigm of physics. When Malebranche seeks to clarify his negative thesis about self-knowledge, he stops short of saying that an a priori psychology would be a predictive science:

Surely we have no idea of our mind which is such that, by consulting it, we can discover the modifications of which the mind is capable. If we had never felt pleasure or pain we could not know whether or not the soul could feel them. If a man had never eaten a melon, or seen red or blue, he would consult this alleged idea of his soul in vain and would never discover distinctly whether or not it was capable of these sensations or modifications.[20]

There is one way in which one might take Malebranche to be saying that a knowledge of the idea of the soul would yield predictions. In this passage Malebranche suggests that if we knew the idea of the soul, we would be able to derive its powers—the modifications of which the mind is capable. If we take Malebranche to be talking about fully-fledged dispositions, then such dispositions would provide a basis for predictions about mental states. Consider the case of physical dispositions. To say that a glass is fragile is to say that there is a law of nature roughly of the form: whenever the glass is dropped, it breaks. And this obviously provides a basis for making predictions about the behaviour of the glass. But there is no necessity to suppose that Malebranche is talking about fully-fledged dispositions. What he actually says is that we have no idea of the mind such that, by consulting it, we can discover the modifications of which it is capable. Consider again the case of physical dispositions. A physical object may be capable of the modification of breakage (in Malebranche's language) without thereby being fragile. In other words, unless a genuine disposition is in question, to say that a physical object can break is not to cite any law of nature. Similarly, Malebranche's suggestion that by knowing the idea of the soul, we could derive its capacities need not be taken to imply that we could thereby derive laws of psychology analogous to physical laws of nature.

Malebranche's negative account of self-knowledge also seems to raise a problem of consistency. We saw earlier that Malebranche has a radical hostility to dispositions; he regards them as pseudo-properties, and he criticizes the Cartesians for tolerating them in the mental sphere while correctly banishing them from physics. Yet in the present discussion Malebranche suggests that the idea of the mind would extend our knowledge by enabling us to derive the modifications of which it is capable. Now the powers in question may be less than fully-fledged dispositions, but this fact of course

---

[20] 'Eleventh Elucidation', *OCM* iii. 164; *SAT* 634.

would not help Malebranche; for if fully-fledged dispositions are not real properties, then *a fortiori* any powers or capacities which are less than fully-fledged dispositions are not real properties either. Thus it is not clear how Malebranche can consistently suppose that discovering the capacities of the mind would amount to a genuine extension of our knowledge. It may be that Malebranche was muddled on this issue. As we have seen, his primary objection to dispositional properties is that they have no explanatory power; and Malebranche could point to the fact (as Descartes also could) that he does not claim we would be in a position to explain anything by knowing the capacities of the mind. Yet Malebranche's attack on dispositions seems to be more than the familiar seventeenth-century complaint that they provide only circular pseudo-explanations. Did Malebranche confuse the common currency of his contemporaries with a more radical thesis?

Perhaps we could mount a partial defence of Malebranche in the following way. Suppose, for the sake of argument, that the capacities of which Malebranche speaks are fully-fledged dispositions. Then by knowing a priori that the mind has a certain disposition, we would thereby come to know that it is subject to a psychological law of nature. To that extent we would have made an undoubted addition to our knowledge of the nature of the mind. But this need not commit us to the view that the disposition in question is a genuine property; for it is possible to hold, as Ryle does, that dispositions merely license certain inferences.[21] In this way Malebranche could consistently hold that dispositions extend our knowledge without being genuine properties. Such a line of defence may not be adequate for all Malebranche's purposes, but it is probably the best that can be done.

Arnauld's Critique

Malebranche's radically anti-Cartesian account of self-knowledge was one of the chief targets of Arnauld's attack in *On True and False Ideas*. Arnauld's critique is important mainly because it is written from a Cartesian standpoint; Arnauld thus acts as a valuable surrogate for Descartes himself. Arnauld, of course, could not fail

---

[21] G. Ryle, *The Concept of Mind* (London, 1949), ch. 5.

to make some trenchant criticisms, and there is little doubt that he detects a number of bad arguments. But it is fair to say that, on the whole, Malebranche emerges from the assault without serious damage. Unfortunately, Arnauld never really succeeds in coming to grips with Malebranche's central thesis about self-knowledge.

Arnauld attacks Malebranche's thesis that while we have a clear idea of body, we have no clear idea of the mind. With the first part of the thesis Arnauld of course has no quarrel; what he wishes to defend is the Cartesian position that our idea of the mind is at least as clear as our idea of body. Now we have seen that, strictly speaking, Malebranche's thesis should be formulated in the logicist mode: we do not know the nature of the mind through its idea in God. And to say that we do not know the nature of x through its idea is to say that we cannot discover its essential properties a priori. When the real content of Malebranche's thesis is borne in mind, most of Arnauld's objections are seen to be beside the point.

Arnauld's criticisms are sometimes of a bluff, homespun character reminiscent of Locke. Surely, says Arnauld, a philosopher has a better knowledge of his mind than a peasant has of the sun:

> It must necessarily be the case either that material things can be known by peasants other than in God and by their idea, or that there is no proof that our soul is not known in God and by its idea from the fact that it is known imperfectly. For one cannot doubt that the knowledge which a peasant or a child has of the sun is incomparably more imperfect than that which a philosopher has of the soul.[22]

The peasant, of course, may indeed not know much geometry, but this is really irrelevant to Malebranche's thesis, for the peasant's ignorance has no tendency to impugn the fact that the properties of geometrical figures are derivable from the axioms and definitions of Euclidean geometry. By contrast, we have no comparable science of psychology. Of course Malebranche can bolster his thesis with an *ad hominem* argument; even the Cartesians (such as Arnauld) must admit that there is a sense in which the peasant does know geometry, for they postulate a dispositional knowledge of such truths in order to defend the doctrine of innate ideas. There is, in fact, a hint of such an argument in Malebranche's reply to Arnauld, but Malebranche has no real need to fall back on this line of defence.[23]

---

[22] Arnauld, ch. XXII, p. 302.
[23] See *Réponse au livre*, ch. XXII (*OCM* vi. 159).

Arnauld has a better point when he charges that Malebranche operates with a double standard.[24] When Malebranche wishes to argue that we have no clear idea of the soul, he makes the criterion for a clear idea extremely strong; having a clear idea is equated with 'simple vision' (*simple vue*). In other words, to have a clear idea of *x* is to have something like an intuitive knowledge of the essential properties of *x*. But when Malebranche seeks to argue that, by contrast, we do have a clear idea of body, he surreptitiously lowers the standard considerably, so that even pre-Pythagoreans could be said to have a clear idea of a right-angled triangle despite their ignorance of the famous theorem. Arnauld's charge has some substance; there are occasions (in the 'Eleventh Elucidation', for instance) where Malebranche seems to cheat in just this way.[25] But again Arnauld's criticism does not affect the core of Malebranche's thesis, for, as we have seen, he has a criterion of clear ideas which gives just the desired results.

Arnauld's strategy is well illustrated by his criticism of Malebranche for claiming that there is any opposition between clear ideas and internal sensations.[26] Here Arnauld reveals the extent of his commitment to the whole Cartesian framework. In characteristic fashion, Arnauld concentrates on Malebranche's psychologistic formulation of his thesis in the *Elucidations*; in other words, he prefers to attack Malebranche's claim that we have no clear idea of the mind. Arnauld then interprets the notion of a clear idea in the Cartesian manner so that any lively perception, such as a pain sensation, counts as a clear idea.[27] Thus Arnauld is in a position to say that Malebranche is wrong to oppose clear ideas and internal sensations. Arnauld seems to be smudging the line not just between psychology and logic but also between the sensory and the intellectual aspects of the human condition. At any rate, Arnauld's criticism again misfires, for Malebranche has a quite different understanding of the notion of clear ideas. For Malebranche, the notions of clear ideas and internal sensations are indeed opposed.

Perhaps Arnauld's most scathing criticism is reserved for an *ad hominem* argument that Malebranche deploys against the Cartesians. Malebranche argues that even the Cartesians are forced

---

[24] Arnauld, ch. XXIII, pp. 321–2.
[25] 'Eleventh Elucidation', *OCM* iii. 166; *SAT* 635.
[26] Arnauld, ch. XXIII, p. 317.
[27] See Descartes, *Principles of Philosophy*, I. 46 (AT viii (a). 22; CSM i. 208).

to recognize that they have no criterion of the mental which is not simply parasitic on the physical:

> In order to determine whether sensible qualities are modes of the mind, we do not consult the alleged idea of the soul—the Cartesians themselves consult, rather, the idea of extension, and they reason as follows. Heat, pain, and colour cannot be modifications of extension, for extension can have only various figures and motion. Now there are only two kinds of being, minds and bodies. Therefore pain, heat, color, and all other sensible qualities belong to the mind.[28]

Arnauld has nothing but contempt for this argument; he ridicules it as a travesty of the Cartesian position. Having quoted a passage from Descartes's *Principles*, he then comments:

> One sees, then, through what everyone can recognize in himself, as Descartes did, that no one has ever needed to consult the idea of extension in order to discover that sensations of colour and pain are modifications of our soul, for no one can ever have doubted it, since they are things of which everyone is internally convinced by his own experience.[29]

In other words, the status of pain and colour sensations as mental has never been in doubt; the issue between the Cartesians and the scholastics is whether there are any non-dispositional properties of bodies which resemble our pain and colour sensations, and it is to settle this issue that the Cartesians appeal to the idea of extension. Thus Arnauld charges Malebranche with a gross *ignoratio elenchi*.

Yet in fact it is not so clear that it is Malebranche who is guilty of *ignoratio elenchi*. The issue is complicated by the fact that Arnauld significantly misrepresents Malebranche's claim. Malebranche does not say that we can discover that *sensations* are mental only by consulting the idea of extension; he says that we can discover that *sensible qualities* are mental only by consulting the idea of extension, and then determining that colour, for example, cannot be a non-dispositional, physical property. Malebranche is, of course, right that the status of sensible qualities is at issue between the Cartesians and the scholastics; he is also correct in claiming that it is by consulting the idea of the extension that the Cartesians arrive at the conclusion that they are not properties of bodies, at least in a straightforwardly non-dispositional way. In fact Malebranche and Arnauld are really in agreement on this issue.

---

[28] 'Eleventh Elucidation', *OCM* iii. 165; *SAT* 634.
[29] Arnauld, ch. xxiii, pp. 310–11.

In spite of his unfairness to Malebranche, however, Arnauld has a point. It is enough for Arnauld's purpose of defeating the argument if the mental status of *sensations* can be established without reference to the physical, and if this can be done even on Cartesian principles. And Arnauld is surely right that it can. Indeed, the Cartesians do possess a criterion of the mental which is not parasitic on the physical; the criterion is incorrigibility. Thus Malebranche's *ad hominem* argument against the Cartesians is a failure.

Suppose, however, that we grant Arnauld that Malebranche's *ad hominem* argument fails. The consequences of this failure are less devastating than one might imagine. From the fact that we have a criterion of the mental such as incorrigibility, it does not follow that we have a clear idea of the soul in Malebranche's sense. Granted, if I am in possession of such a criterion, then with respect to any item that turns up (e.g. a pain sensation), I can decide whether it should be classified as mental without consulting the idea of extension. But this has no tendency to show that I can know a priori the properties of which the mind is capable; classification takes place after the event, as it were. The possession of a non-parasitic criterion of the mental may be a necessary condition of having a clear idea of the mind, but it is not a sufficient condition. The most that Arnauld has done is to knock away one of Malebranche's argumentative props for his central negative thesis about self-knowledge.

Freedom and Immortality

Perhaps the most serious of Arnauld's charges centred on the wider metaphysical and even theological implications of Malebranche's position. Arnauld observed that if we have no idea of the soul, then we surely cannot demonstrate its freedom and immortality; it is a contradiction, he claimed, to assert that we can demonstrate anything of what is known only obscurely and confusedly.[30] Malebranche could of course have admitted that, strictly speaking, we can have no a priori knowledge in this area; he could then have argued that our assurance of the mind's freedom and immortality depends on faith alone. Hobbes and Locke both adopted such a

---

[30] Arnauld, ch. xxiii, p. 326.

strategy with regard to the issue of personal immortality, but unlike them, Malebranche was not content with a fideistic solution.[31]

We can develop Arnauld's line of criticism by remarking that there seems to be something seriously misleading in Malebranche's claims about self-knowledge. In *The Search After Truth* Malebranche claims that 'although our knowledge of our soul is not complete, what we do know of it through consciousness or inner sensation is enough to demonstrate its immortality, spirituality, freedom, and several other attributes we need to know'.[32] A little earlier Malebranche similarly remarks that 'our knowledge [of the soul] is imperfect . . . [it] is limited to what we sense taking place in us'.[33] Here it may look as if Malebranche is guilty of equivocation. To say that our knowledge of the soul is incomplete may suggest that it differs only in degree from our knowledge of body, but of course, as we have seen, this is not Malebranche's position; his actual view is that the difference between the two cases is not a difference of degree only, but a difference of kind; we know the body through idea, but the soul only through consciousness or internal sensation. If we did have an incomplete knowledge of the soul through idea, then Malebranche would be in a good position to reply to Arnauld; he could have defended the consistency of his position by means of a geometrical analogy. A schoolboy geometer might have an incomplete and imperfect knowledge of right-angled triangles in the sense that he cannot demonstrate really complex and difficult theorems; but he might know just enough Euclidean geometry to be able to demonstrate the Pythagorean theorem. Similarly, Malebranche might argue, we know just enough of the idea of the soul to be able to demonstrate its immortality and freedom. But Malebranche, of course, cannot make use of this analogy; for his position is that we have no knowledge of the idea of the soul. Yet Malebranche may seem to fudge the issue by referring to our self-knowledge as imperfect and incomplete.

In reply to Arnauld, however, Malebranche does not simply take refuge in equivocation; he confronts the challenge head-on. He seeks to show how, consistently with his general thesis about self-

---

[31] See T. Hobbes, *Leviathan*, ed. C. B. MacPherson (Harmondsworth, 1968), pt. I, ch. 15, p. 206; J. Locke, *The Reasonableness of Christianity*, in *The Works of John Locke*, vii (London, 1823), 122.

[32] *Search after Truth*, III. 2. 7 (*OCM* i. 453; *SAT* 239).

[33] Ibid. (*OCM* i. 451; *SAT* 237).

knowledge, we can none the less demonstrate our freedom and immortality; in other words, he denies himself any recourse to the idea of the soul.[34] Malebranche adopts quite different strategies for the two cases. In the case of immortality, he bases his proof on the idea of extension, in conjunction with general considerations concerning the indestructibility of substances.[35] In the case of freedom, he does not give an a priori proof at all; he follows Descartes in seeking to ground our knowledge of free will in our own self-consciousness.[36] It is not really necessary to consider the merits of these 'proofs'; as McCracken remarks, Malebranche's treatment of these issues is perfunctory and derivative.[37] The important point is that Malebranche has a strategy which is at least consistent with his central thesis that we have no idea of the mind.

Arnauld is surely right that freedom and immortality pose problems for Malebranche. In his concern for such wider metaphysical and theological implications, Arnauld resembles the Leibniz of the *New Essays*; Leibniz was similarly worried that Locke's philosophy threatened traditional claims concerning the soul's immateriality and natural immortality.[38] Of course we might well feel tempted to say that even philosophers who take a more optimistic view of self-knowledge have not done very well in giving a priori proofs of immortality and freedom. But through the radicalism of his position, Malebranche effectively deprives himself of the resources that he needs.

Yet these are rather external criticisms; unlike Arnauld, we shall not worry much if Malebranche's teaching poses a threat to our knowledge of immortality. In spite of all Arnauld's objections, Malebranche's treatment of self-knowledge remains important and suggestive, for Malebranche has a clear diagnosis of the weaknesses of Descartes's philosophy of mind. Like other seventeenth-century philosophers, Malebranche sees that the thesis of the 'Second Meditation' is not well supported; Descartes gives us no real reason to believe that the nature of the mind is better known than the nature of body. But Malebranche also sees something which escaped most of his contemporaries, including Arnauld; he sees

---

[34] *Réponse au livre*, ch. XXIII (*OCM* vi. 162–4).
[35] Ibid. (*OCM* vi. 163).
[36] Ibid. (*OCM* vi. 163–4).   [37] McCracken, p. 80.
[38] See N. Jolley, *Leibniz and Locke: A Study of the* New Essays *on Human Understanding* (Oxford, 1984).

that, on the Cartesian conception, the mind is really a rag-bag which collects everything which remains once the physical world has been defined in terms of geometrical properties. Of course there are ways in which Descartes seeks to disguise this aspect of his philosophy; for instance, he seeks to impose some kind of spurious order on the mental by means of the incorrigibility criterion. None the less, the Cartesian mind remains a thoroughly heterogeneous collection of items. Malebranche is not satisfied with this situation; he seeks to do some tidying up. He makes a notable start on this task by insisting that not everything non-physical is mental; there is also the logical, the 'third realm'. Malebranche may get into difficulties of his own, but arguably he saw more clearly into the weaknesses of Descartes's conception of mind than any philosopher before Kant.

8
Leibniz
Ideas and Illumination

LEIBNIZ'S defence of innate ideas in the *New Essays* has been widely studied, but his views on the nature of ideas in general have received relatively little attention. This is unfortunate, for we cannot really understand his polemic against Locke unless we grasp Leibniz's concept of 'idea'. Moreover, the exclusive focus on the *New Essays* is historically misleading; it tends to obscure the fact that much of Leibniz's discussion of ideas is a response to issues raised by Malebranche and Arnauld. We shall see that Leibniz's discussion of ideas has wider philosophical significance, for his views are shaped by his nominalism; unlike Malebranche, Leibniz cannot tolerate irreducibly abstract entities.

Leibniz's nominalism has important implications for his treatment of the theological dimensions of the debate over ideas. Like Malebranche, Leibniz attempts to do justice to the Augustinian doctrine of divine illumination, but in adapting the doctrine to his own philosophical commitments, he tends to change its content; in fact, Leibniz deprives the doctrine of much of its real point. But it would be quite wrong to suppose that Leibniz's theory of mind has no significant theological dimensions. As we shall see, Leibniz's distinctive philosophical claims put him in a strong position to defend the Christian doctrine that the human mind is made in the image of God. Indeed, perhaps no other philosopher has ever made such a strenuous attempt as Leibniz to provide a philosophical gloss on this doctrine.

Ideas As Dispositions

As one would expect, Leibniz was well aware of seventeenth-century debates over the nature of ideas; his writings on the topic show that he has a firm grasp of the main lines of division. About the time of his first careful study of Malebranche's *The Search after*

Truth, Leibniz distinguishes between two main senses of the term 'idea' and warns against the dangers of equivocation:

'Idea' can be taken in two senses; namely, for the quality or form of thought, as velocity and direction are the quality and form of movement, or for the immediate or nearest object of perception. Thus the idea would not be a mode of being of our soul. This seems to be the opinion of Plato and the author of the *Recherche*. For when the soul thinks of being, identity, thought, or duration, it has a certain immediate object or nearest cause of its perception. In this sense it is possible that we see all things in God and that the ideas or immediate objects are the attributes of God himself. These formulas or modes of speaking contain some truth, but to speak correctly it is necessary to give constant meanings to the terms.[1]

In the *Discourse on Metaphysics*, written ten years later, Leibniz again distinguishes between two views of ideas, and repeats his warning against equivocation:

In order properly to conceive correctly what an idea is, we must forestall an ambiguity, for several thinkers take the idea for the form or differential of our thoughts, and thus we have an idea in our mind only in so far as we are thinking of it, and every time we think of it anew, we have another idea of the same thing, though it is similar to the preceding ones. But others, it seems, take the idea to be an immediate object of thought or for some permanent form which remains even when we no longer contemplate it.[2]

By the time of writing the *Discourse on Metaphysics* Leibniz had had the benefit of studying the controversy between Malebranche and Arnauld, and that controversy leaves its mark on the work. Although they are somewhat underdescribed, the two views which Leibniz sketches correspond at least roughly to the positions of the two antagonists; the first view of ideas is that of Arnauld, and the second is that of Malebranche.

Leibniz's own theory of ideas raises a problem of interpretation which can be expressed by the following question: does Leibniz agree with Arnauld or with Malebranche or with neither? At first sight it might seem that Leibniz must side with Malebranche, for like Malebranche, Leibniz is prepared to endorse the Platonic thesis that 'there is an intelligible world in the divine mind, which I also usually call the region of ideas'.[3] In passages like this it seems as if ideas, for Leibniz, must be irreducibly abstract, logical entities.

[1] R, p. 73; L, p. 155.
[2] *Discourse on Metaphysics*, 26 (G iv. 451; L, p. 320).
[3] Leibniz to Hansch, 25 June 1707, Dutens ii. 222; L, p. 592.

Moreover, in the *New Essays* Leibniz clearly expresses a preference for regarding ideas as objects of thought:

If the idea were the *form* of the thought, it would come into and go out of existence with the actual thoughts which correspond to it, but since it is the *object* of thought, it can exist before and after the thoughts.[4]

For Leibniz, as for Malebranche, there can be no straightforward identification of ideas with particular thoughts, for thoughts have properties which are not possessed by ideas. We can say of thoughts that they are transitory and that they occur at particular times, but we cannot say this of ideas.

There seems, then, to be an important measure of agreement between Leibniz and Malebranche; Leibniz seems to hold with Malebranche that ideas are objects to which the mind is related in thinking. Curiously, however, there are occasions when Leibniz takes Arnauld's side in the controversy. Before he had properly studied the debate, Leibniz announced that he was predisposed in Arnauld's favour: 'as far as I can judge by their other works', he wrote, 'Father Malebranche has much intelligence [*esprit*], but M. Arnauld writes with more judgement'.[5] Towards the end of his life Leibniz went much further; he explicitly endorsed Arnauld's claim, against Malebranche, that ideas are modifications of the mind:

There is more plausibility in attacking P. Malebranche's opinion about ideas. For there is no necessity (it seems) to take them for something which is outside us. It is sufficient to consider ideas as Notions, that is to say, as modifications of our mind [*des modifications de notre ame*]. This is how the Schools, M. Descartes, and M. Arnaud take them.[6]

Thus Leibniz seems to be simultaneously pulled in opposite directions by the views of Malebranche and Arnauld; it is no wonder, then, that Bennett writes of an unresolved tension in Leibniz's thought about ideas.[7] On the one hand, Leibniz agrees with Malebranche that ideas are objects, and that they cannot be identified with particular thoughts; on the other hand, he claims, with Arnauld, that they are modifications of the mind. The tension seems particularly marked in the paper entitled *Meditations on*

---

[4] *NE* II. i (A VI. vi; RB, p. 109).
[5] Leibniz to Tschirnhaus(?), 1685, R, p. 150.
[6] Leibniz to Remond, 4 Nov. 1715, G iii. 659.
[7] RB (1982), introd., p. xxiii.

Knowledge, Truth and Ideas; for here he remarks that even if we saw all things in God, we would still need our own ideas as affections or modifications of our mind.[8] And we may also note that in the *New Essays* Leibniz qualifies his claim that ideas are objects by adding that they are immediate internal objects; God, by contrast, is the immediate external object of our mind.[9] By insisting that ideas are 'internal', Leibniz seems to be taking at least one step away from Malebranche; he seems to be claiming that ideas are psychological items, not abstract or logical entities as they are for Malebranche.

It is, however, a mistake to suppose that there is a muddle in Leibniz's thought about ideas; indeed, it is even unfair to speak, as Bennett does, of an unresolved tension in his views. Leibniz in fact has a coherent position on the nature of ideas which is to be distinguished from that of both Malebranche and Arnauld. It is true that Leibniz takes something from both philosophers. From Malebranche he takes the claim that ideas are not particular mental events; from Arnauld he takes the claim that ideas are not abstract but psychological entities. But Leibniz's position is not so much a muddle as a genuine synthesis.

We have seen that, like Malebranche and Plato before him, Leibniz is prepared to say that there is an intelligible world in the mind of God; or, as Leibniz prefers to express it, God is the region of ideas. At first sight it may seem that Leibniz can have no objection to the existence of irreducibly abstract entities and, in particular, to regarding ideas as abstract objects. Indeed, Leibniz's metaphysics seems to proliferate with abstract entities. When Leibniz says that God is the region of ideas, he seems to be advancing a strong thesis: God is the region of infinitely many possible worlds, where possible worlds are constituted by complete concepts or ideas.[10] But in fact, despite his 'Platonic' language, it is a mistake to see Leibniz as a Platonist in this respect. As Mates observes, for all his fondness for talk of ideas, essences, and possible worlds, Leibniz is a nominalist who cannot countenance abstract entities as basic items of ontology.[11] In other words, Leibniz holds

---

[8] *Meditations*, G iv. 426; L, p. 294.   [9] *NE* ii. i (A vi. vi; RB, p. 109).

[10] There is some controversy as to whether in Leibniz's philosophy only individuals in the actual world have complete concepts. On this issue, see B. Mates, *The Philosophy of Leibniz: Metaphysics and Language* (Oxford, 1986), 66–7.

[11] Mates, esp. p. 246.

that there are no entities named by abstract nouns such as 'heat' and 'justice'. Thus, statements which appear to be about such entities should be rephrased as statements in which the abstract nouns are replaced by concrete nouns and adjectives. In a passage in which Leibniz explains his views, he is prepared to describe himself, at least tentatively, as a nominalist:

> Up to now I see no other way of avoiding these difficulties than by considering abstracta not as real things [*res*] but as abbreviated ways of talking [*compendia loquendi*]—so that when I use the name *heat* it is not required that I should be making mention of some vague subject but rather that I should be saying that something is hot—and to that extent I am a nominalist, at least provisionally.[12]

Leibniz may allow us to talk of ideas, essences, and possible worlds, but he holds that when we do so, we are using expressions which are mere *compendia loquendi*; they are convenient, abbreviated ways of speaking which do not accurately describe reality. In metaphysical rigour there are no abstract entities; there are only individual substances (including God) and their affections.

Leibniz's agreement with Malebranche is thus much less thorough-going than some of his statements might suggest. Ideas, for Leibniz, are not some 'third realm' existing over and above particular acts of thinking. Although he resists any straightforward identification of ideas with thoughts, Leibniz does believe that talk about ideas can be reduced to talk about the mental. Leibniz brings off the reduction by explaining that ideas are dispositions to think in certain ways. In the early paper entitled 'What is an Idea?', Leibniz expresses his core theory of ideas with admirable clarity:

> There are many things in our mind, however, which we know are not ideas, though they could not occur without ideas—for example, thoughts, perceptions, and affections. In my opinion, *an idea consists not in some act, but in the faculty of thinking*, and we are said to have an idea of a thing even if we do not think of it, if only, on a given occasion, we can think of it.[13]

Leibniz qualifies this definition of 'idea' by saying that the disposition must not merely lead to the thought of the object; it must also express the object. In the *Discourse on Metaphysics* Leibniz seems to state the same requirement:

---

[12] Gr ii. 547. Quoted in Mates, p. 171.
[13] 'What is an Idea?', G vii. 263; L, p. 207. This paper may have been prompted by Leibniz's reading of both Spinoza and Malebranche.

I believe that this disposition [*qualité*] of our soul in so far as it expresses some nature, form, or essence, is properly the idea of the thing, which is in us, and which is always in us, whether we think of it or not.[14]

Leibniz's concept of expression is a technical one, and thus requires some explanation. In 'What is an Idea?', Leibniz explains that 'what is common to [the various forms of] expression is that we can pass from a consideration of the properties [*habitudo*] of the expressing thing to a knowledge of the corresponding properties of the thing expressed'.[15] Thus Leibniz seems to be saying that if I have the idea of a triangle, I have a disposition to think of a triangle, and there is something about my disposition which would allow a supermind to read off the properties contained in the essence of a triangle. But if this is Leibniz's meaning, then it poses an obvious difficulty for his account of ideas. We have supposed that Leibniz is engaged in the project of trying to show how talk of seemingly abstract entities can be reduced to talk about the mental. But it now looks as if the project is threatened with circularity; the analysis makes reference to natures, forms, and essences, and these seem to be just the sort of abstract entities which Leibniz wants to analyse away.

The objection, however, is not as crippling as it appears. Suppose we ask 'What is it for a mental item to express a nature, form, or essence?' In one passage where Leibniz tries to find common ground with Malebranche, he hints at an answer:

Our perceptions have for *immediate external formal object* the ideas which are in [God], although there are also in us modifications which involve a relation to these ideas, and these relations would be what could be called ideas in us, and which are our *internal formal object*.[16]

At first sight, this passage may seem to offer no help, and even to be an embarrassment for the present interpretation; for it appears to offer a rival theory of ideas as relations of a certain sort. But in reality, I think, Leibniz is not so much offering a new theory of ideas, as clarifying his old one; he fills out that theory by showing that the natures, forms, or essences which are expressed by our

---

[14] *Discourse on Metaphysics*, G iv. 451; L, p. 320. Leibniz also states that an idea is a proximate, not a remote, faculty. See ch. 9 below.

[15] 'What is an Idea?', G vii. 263–4; L, p. 207. Cf. Leibniz to Arnauld, 9 Oct. 1687: 'Une chose *exprime* une autre (dans mon langage) lorsqu'il y a un rapport constant et reglé entre ce qui se peut dire de l'une et de l'autre' (G ii. 112; L, p. 339). On Leibniz's theory of expression, see M. Kulstad, 'Leibniz's Conception of Expression', *Studia Leibnitiana*, 9 (1977), 55–76.

[16] Draft of a letter to Remond (?), 1715, R, p. 490. Cf. R, p. 196.

mental dispositions are ideas in the mind of God. My idea of a triangle is a disposition to think of a triangle which is such that a supermind could read off the idea which God has of a triangle. Now Leibniz might be more reluctant than Mates concedes to allow that divine ideas are dispositions, for this may be difficult to reconcile with the traditional view that God is pure act.[17] Moreover, God's ideas, unlike human ideas, cannot be temporally extended, for God is not a sempiternal being. But Leibniz would surely hold that he can acknowledge both these differences without compromising the status of God's ideas as mental states of some kind which are expressed by ideas in human minds. Using a modern analogy, Leibniz could say that human ideas express God's ideas rather in the way that the playing of a gramophone record expresses the information that is timelessly encoded in the disc.[18] On this reconstruction, Leibniz's analysis of ideas may not be impeccable, but it should be clear that the reductive project is not threatened with any serious circularity.

We can now see how Leibniz would respond to Malebranche's claims about ideas. Malebranche argues that ideas are not in the mind because they are abstract objects. Leibniz can reply that Malebranche is setting up a false dichotomy between mental items (thoughts) and non-mental ones (ideas). Ideas are mental because they are dispositions to form certain thoughts under certain conditions, and these dispositions are predicated of individual minds. The very first point that Leibniz makes in the paper, 'What is an Idea?', is that an idea 'is something which is in the mind',[19] and he never retreats from this position.

Yet if Leibniz does not agree with Malebranche, he does not fully agree with Arnauld either. Since ideas, for Leibniz, are dispositions, they are persistent properties of the mind; thus they cannot be identified with transitory mental events. We may wonder, then, how Leibniz can feel entitled to tell Remond that he agrees with Arnauld in regarding ideas as modifications of the mind; for the term 'modification' tends to suggest something which comes into being and passes away. The answer seems to be that in writing to Remond Leibniz is guilty of a pardonable exaggeration; he has his eye on the point that ideas are psychological, not abstract or logical,

---

[17] See Mates, p. 246.
[18] I am grateful to George MacDonald Ross for this example.
[19] 'What is an Idea?', G vii. 263; L, p. 207.

items, and in making this point he fails to note that, in his view, ideas are psychological properties which persist through time. It is perhaps significant that in the *Meditations on Knowledge, Truth and Ideas* Leibniz speaks of ideas as 'affections or modifications of our mind [*affectiones sive modificationes mentis nostrae*]'.[20] *Affectio* here is a word which better captures his real position on ideas, for it is a more general term which has no tendency to suggest something fleeting or transitory. Alternatively, one might defend Leibniz by invoking his doctrine that dispositional properties need to be grounded in non-dispositional ones. As we shall see in the next chapter, Leibniz holds that this applies even to ideas, and that in this case the ground of the disposition is the mind's unconscious perceptions. We might, then, suppose that Leibniz is applying the term 'idea' to the ground of the disposition rather than the disposition itself; for unconscious perceptions, being fleeting, are indeed appropriately described as 'modifications of the mind'.

Ideas and Representation

Leibniz denies that the contents of thought are abstract entities over and above the mental states of God and finite minds; there is no irreducible 'third realm'. Ideas are simply dispositions to have certain thoughts under certain conditions. But Leibniz does not appear to envisage that the content of thought itself might be susceptible to reductionist treatment. On the contrary, as Adams has argued, Leibniz seems to regard the objective reality or representational content of thoughts as primitive features of those thoughts.[21] Indeed, for Leibniz, the property of being representational is not confined to ideas and occurrent thoughts; it appears to be of the very essence of the mental.

Here, then, as in his theory of ideas, Leibniz parts company from Malebranche on a fundamental issue, but it is not entirely clear how far he was aware of the fact. On this matter the evidence appears to point in different directions. Commenting on the Malebranche–Arnauld controversy, Leibniz insists, against Malebranche, that it is

---

[20] *Meditations*, G iv. 426; L, p. 294.
[21] R. M. Adams, 'Phenomenalism and Corporeal Substance in Leibniz', in P. A. French, T. E. Uehling, and H. K. Wettstein (eds.), *Contemporary Perspectives on the History of Philosophy* (*Midwest Studies in Philosophy*, 8; 1983), 221.

essential to our thoughts to be representative;[22] he thus seems to recognize that, for Malebranche, intentionality is not a mark of the mental. On the other hand, he does not appear to grasp what is involved in Malebranche's distinction between ideas and *sentiments*. In his critique of Locke's own *Examination of Malebranche*, Leibniz seems to regard the distinction as simply equivalent to the familiar Cartesian distinction between ideas and images, which he takes over in his own philosophy: 'I believe that the Father [Malebranche] understands by sentiment a perception of the imagination whereas one can have ideas of things which are not sensible or imaginable.'[23] Leibniz is right that Malebranche's idea/ *sentiment* distinction involves, or is related to, the Cartesian distinction between the intellectual and the sensory. But Leibniz does nothing to indicate that anything more than this is involved; he shows no awareness that Malebranche's *sentiments* are different from what he would call 'images'. For Leibniz's images or 'perceptions of the imagination' are clearly representative or about things in a way that Malebranche's sensations are not.

Perhaps the best way of approaching Leibniz's position is by way of Spinoza; this comparison will help us to define the nature and extent of Leibniz's disagreement with Malebranche. In Spinoza's philosophy it is useful to draw a distinction between the direct and indirect objects of ideas. Consider how Spinoza would analyse the case of someone perceiving the sun. By virtue of his mind–body parallelism, Spinoza is committed to saying that the mental state here is uniquely correlated with a state of the person's body under the attribute of extension; from this Spinoza infers that the mental state (idea) is a true representation of the physical state.[24] At the very least this implies that the mental state can be mapped on to the physical state. Following Bennett, let us say that this physical state is the direct object of the idea.[25] But Spinoza also tries to do justice to the common-sense intuition that the mental state represents or is about the sun. Let us say that the sun is the indirect object of the idea. Spinoza will further claim that while all ideas are true of their direct objects, not all ideas are true of their indirect objects; typically, indeed, ideas represent their indirect objects only

[22] R, p. 207.   [23] *Examination of Malebranche*, G vi. 577. Cf. R, p. 155.
[24] *Ethics*, part II, prop. 32.
[25] J. Bennett, *A Study of Spinoza's Ethics* (Cambridge, 1984), 155. Cf. D. Radner, 'Spinoza's Theory of Ideas', *Philosophical Review*, 80 (1971), 338–59.

confusedly. As Spinoza puts it, 'the ideas which we have of external bodies indicate the condition of our own body more than the nature of external bodies'.[26]

Leibniz does not speak of the mind as the idea of the body, but he does say that the mind expresses the body, and in terms of this concept, he puts forward a view which is remarkably similar to Spinoza's. Like Spinoza, Leibniz can be read as holding that, in cases of veridical perception, there is in effect both a direct and indirect object of the perceptual state. In a remarkably Spinozistic passage Leibniz explains to Arnauld that his mental state expresses his body (direct object) better than the satellites of Jupiter and Saturn (indirect object):

> Since we apperceive the other bodies only through the relation which they have to ours, I was quite right in saying that the soul expresses best what belongs to our own body, and that we only know of the satellites of Jupiter and Saturn as a result of a movement taking place in our eyes.[27]

In other words, my mental state encodes complete information about the states of both my body and the satellites, but, given full knowledge of my mental state, a supermind would find it easier to read off the former than the latter.

We can see, then, how Leibniz will handle the standard cases of perception in terms of his theory of expression; he will say, in effect, that there is both a direct and an indirect object that is represented by my perceptual state. But such an analysis still leaves many mental phenomena unaccounted for. It is of course a commonplace fact that many mental states are not cases of perceiving physical objects; more controversially, there appear to be mental states which do not represent anything, real or imaginary. As Malebranche insisted, a pain sensation has no content or object; in the scholastic jargon which Descartes took over, it has no objective reality. Thus Leibniz owes us an account of those mental states which Malebranche calls *sentiments*.

Leibniz invokes his concept of expression to reach anti-Malebranchean conclusions. Leibniz can of course concede that there is a disanalogy between being in pain and perceiving the sun; to that extent he can agree with Malebranche. But, for Leibniz, the difference between the two cases is not a difference between mental

---

[26] *Ethics*, part II, prop. 16, coroll. 2.
[27] Leibniz to Arnauld, 9 Oct. 1687, G ii. 113; L, p. 340. Trans. modified.

phenomena that are representational and those that are not; rather, it is a difference between mental phenomena that are, as it were, singly representational and those that are doubly so. It is true that the pain sensation has no indirect object, at least in the sense of 'indirect' that we have been employing here; none the less, it is certainly the case that there is a direct object. For Leibniz holds that every mental event expresses or represents the body, and he is thus committed to the thesis that even pain states are representational. In the *New Essays* Leibniz draws the conclusion explicitly and consistently:

> It is true that pain does not resemble the movement of a pin; but it might thoroughly resemble the motions which the pin causes in our body, and might represent them in the soul; and I have not the least doubt that it does.[28]

Leibniz's concept of expression allows him to make an additional point against Descartes; the relationship between *qualia* and physical states is not arbitrary, as Descartes supposed, since the *quale* expresses the mental state.

We saw in an earlier chapter that Descartes spoke with an ambiguous voice on the issue of representation. Sometimes Descartes seems to say that only a subset of mental phenomena are representational; these phenomena he calls 'ideas in the strict sense'. At other times, Descartes seems to say that having representational content is of the essence of the mental; he writes as if sensations were to be understood as confused representations of bodily states. Leibniz and Malebranche resolve this ambiguity in opposite ways; in Leibniz's case, as we have seen, the key concept is that of expression. But if on this issue Leibniz deploys this concept against Malebranche, this is not always the case. As we shall see, the notion of expression also plays a role in Leibniz's attempt to accommodate the doctrine of divine illumination.

Divine Illumination

Leibniz was fond of saying that other philosophers were generally right in what they affirmed, and wrong in what they denied.[29] Leibniz's attitude towards Malebranche's doctrine of vision in God

---

[28] *NE* II. viii (A VI. vi; RB, p. 132).
[29] See e.g. Leibniz to Remond, 10 Jan. 1714, G iii. 607.

is fully consistent with his stated belief, for in spite of his disagreements, he is characteristically conciliatory; on a number of occasions he remarks that the doctrine contains at least a kernel of truth. In the *Meditations on Knowledge, Truth and Ideas* he describes it as 'an old opinion which, properly understood, is not entirely to be rejected'.[30] In the *Discourse on Metaphysics* Leibniz goes further; he even follows Malebranche to the extent of associating the theory of divine illumination with the famous opening of St John's Gospel:

It can be said that God alone is our immediate object outside of us and that we see all things through him; for example, when we see the sun and the stars, it is God who has given us and preserves in us the ideas of them and who determines us, through his ordinary concourse, actually to think of them at the moment when our senses are set in a certain manner, in conformity with the laws he has established. God is the sun and the light of souls—*lumen illuminans omnem hominem venientem in hunc mundum.*[31]

There is little, if anything, in this remarkable passage which could not have been written by Malebranche himself.

Leibniz insists, then, that there is much truth in the Augustinian theory of divine illumination, as revived by Malebranche, provided that it is properly interpreted. But it is natural to ask whether, once one adopts a nominalist framework, the Augustinian claims retain any real point. As we have seen, Leibniz is not in a position to interpret divine illumination as Malebranche does; he cannot hold that when I think of a circle, for instance, there is some 'third realm' entity to which my mind is related, and to which all other minds would be related if they had thoughts with the same content as mine. According to Leibniz, there are no such irreducibly abstract objects; on the contrary, in addition to dispositional properties, there are just particular thinkings in particular minds (including the mind of God). It may seem, then, that anything which Leibniz would regard as a proper interpretation of vision in God must simply deprive the doctrine of all real content.

When one examines Leibniz's attempts to interpret the doctrine of divine illumination, one finds that he advances three related claims. In the first place, Leibniz invokes the traditional Christian

---

[30] *Meditations*, G iv. 426; L, p. 294. Cf. Leibniz to Foucher, Sept. 1695, G i. 423; Leibniz to Coste, 16 June 1707, G iii. 392; Leibniz to Remond, 4 Nov. 1715, G iii. 659–60.
[31] *Discourse on Metaphysics*, 28 (G iv. 453; L, p. 321).

doctrine of divine concurrence. God illuminates the mind in the sense that he concurs to it at every moment in its history; in other words, the mind is in a continuous state of ontological dependence on God:

It can be said that because of the divine concourse which continually confers on each creature whatever perfection there is in it, the external object of the soul is God alone, and that in this sense God is to the mind what light is to the eye. This is that divine truth which shines forth in us, about which Augustine says so much and on which Malebranche follows him.[32]

The doctrine of divine concurrence may be familiar in the tradition, but it is not entirely clear how it should be interpreted. It is sometimes tempting to think of divine concurrence in terms of a familiar model; God's conserving activity is a kind of causal background condition like the presence of oxygen in the air in the case of an explosion. It is true that Leibniz seems to hold that, for any occurrent thought, there is a causal division of labour between God and my mind;[33] thus, in addition to my earlier thoughts, God's concurrence is necessary to produce the episode in my mind. But this model is in important respects misleading. For it suggests that God's concurrence—his conserving activity—is a causal factor on a par with the activity of my mind, and this is surely not Leibniz's view. It may be correct to say that divine concurrence is (at least) a causally necessary condition of any event in the created universe, but we must add that it is quite unlike other conditions. Divine concurrence is a special kind of cause.

An illuminating model for understanding divine concurrence has been proposed by Zeno Vendler.[34] Consider the case of an author writing a novel; in plotting the narrative, he has to decide how one of the characters is to die. Let us suppose that he decides in favour of an accidental death for the character: he will be the victim of an appalling fire. Within the narrative there is a complete causal story to be told about the victim's death; its details will include such things as the deplorable state of the wiring in the house. But of course there is also a sense in which the author himself is a cause, for

---

[32] Leibniz to Hansch, 25 July 1707, Dutens ii. 223; L, p. 593.

[33] 'Mais peut estre que la nature de nostre ame, est la cause immediate de nos perceptions des choses materielles, et que Dieu, auteur de tout, est cause de l'accord qu'il y a entre nos pensées et ce qui est hors de nous' (R, p. 74).

[34] Z. Vendler, *The Matter of Minds* (Oxford, 1984), p. 119.

it is he who decided on the causes in the narrative. Yet it would be wrong to suggest that the literary choices of the author are on a par, causally, with such factors as the poor state of the wiring; anyone who confuses them is guilty of a category mistake. The author is a cause, but he is a special kind of cause; in this respect his activity resembles divine concurrence.

Divine concurrence of course is a feature of many metaphysical systems in the Christian tradition; it is not at all distinctively Leibnizian. However, Leibniz's second way of explaining divine illumination involves a strengthening of this familiar thesis into something more distinctive; he claims that God is the only substance which acts causally on the human mind. Leibniz sometimes expresses this point by saying that God is the sole immediate external object of our mind.[35] (Ideas, it should be remembered, are said to be the sole immediate internal objects.) Thus Leibniz brings the pre-established harmony to bear on the doctrine of divine illumination; in Leibniz's system there is no genuine causal interaction between finite substances. It is important to see that this second thesis sets Leibniz apart from Descartes in a way that the first does not. Descartes, like Leibniz, admits the fact of divine concurrence, but unlike Leibniz, he holds that God is not the sole substance which can act causally on created substances; bodies, for instance, causally interact with created minds. Indeed, the stronger thesis places both Malebranche and Leibniz in opposition to Descartes; for in this respect the doctrine of the pre-established harmony agrees with the doctrine of occasionalism.

Lastly, Leibniz attempts to interpret the language of divine illumination in terms of his concept of expression. In the *Discourse on Metaphysics* Leibniz introduces the notion of expression to explain divine illumination in the following way:

It is also only by virtue of the continual action of God upon us that we have in our soul the ideas of all things; that is to say, since every effect expresses its cause, the essence of our soul is a certain expression, imitation or image of the divine essence, thought, and will and of all the ideas which are comprised in God.[36]

A little later in the same work, Leibniz remarks that the human mind 'expresses God, and with him all actual and possible beings as

---

[35] *Discourse on Metaphysics*, 28 (G iv. 453; L, p. 321); and *NE* II. i, A VI. vi; RB, p. 109).
[36] *Discourse on Metaphysics*, 28 (G iv. 453; L, p. 321).

an effect expresses its cause'.[37] As these passages make clear, the claim that the human mind expresses God is not a thesis independent of the other two; on the contrary, it follows from each of them in conjunction with the claim that every effect expresses its cause. For Leibniz, of course, human minds are the effects of God as creator.

In some of his comments on Malebranche, Leibniz seems to regard the claim that the human mind expresses God's mind more as a supplement to the doctrine of vision in God, than as an equivalent of it. This seems to be the way in which the notion of expression is invoked at the end of the *Meditations on Knowledge, Truth and Ideas*:

As to the controversy whether we see all things in God . . . or whether we have some ideas of our own, it must be understood that even if we saw all things in God, it would still be necessary to have our ideas also, not in the sense of some kind of little copies, but as affections or modifications of our mind corresponding to the very object we perceive in God.[38]

It may be questioned whether Leibniz's technical concept of expression can be discerned in this passage. But if Leibniz does mean that our ideas would, in his special sense, express God's ideas, then it leaves the notion of vision in God entirely unexplained; for no attempt is made here to analyse this notion in terms of expression. It is possible that the main thrust of the passage is concessive in spirit; Leibniz may be saying that even if Malebranche were right about the status of God's ideas as irreducibly abstract objects, such ideas could be nothing to us unless we were related to them in thinking. If this is Leibniz's point, then it is not really an objection to Malebranche's position, for, as we have seen, Malebranche should admit that his 'ideas' require acts of thinking if we are to grasp them.

Leibniz's attempts to interpret divine illumination raise an obvious problem. Any worthwhile account of divine illumination must accord a special status to minds; it must show that something important is true of them which is not true of other substances. But one may wonder whether Leibniz is in a position to satisfy this requirement; even his doctrine of expression seems unable to do so. For Leibniz is committed to the quite general thesis that effects express their causes; thus to say that minds express God is to say

---

[37] *Discourse on Metaphysics*, 29 (G iv. 453–4; L, p. 321).
[38] *Meditations*, G iv. 426; L, p. 294.

nothing about them which is not also true of all other created substances. Leibniz could solve the problem by saying that minds express God in some special sense; he could say that, unlike other substances, minds express God by perceiving him, for according to Leibniz, perception is a species of expression. But, in fact, Leibniz tends not to take this line; he simply falls back on the general concept of expression which applies to all substances.

Sometimes Leibniz seems aware of the problem, and he even arouses the suspicion of trying to evade it. On occasion Leibniz appears to try to disguise the general import of his thesis concerning expression; he writes as if, among created substances, only minds express God. In the *Discourse on Metaphysics* Leibniz writes: 'It seems, then, that although every substance expresses the whole universe, other substances express the world rather than God, whereas minds express God rather than the world.'[39] In the *New Essays* Leibniz suggests that even the human soul expresses God by virtue of only a subset of its ideas: 'For the soul is a little world where distinct ideas represent God and confused ones represent the universe.'[40] In passages like these, Leibniz may seem to be trying to salvage the doctrine of divine illumination only by playing down the thesis that all created substances express God.

Leibniz could reply to this objection that he is not being evasive but only elliptical. Leibniz can remind his readers that, on his theory, expression is a continuum concept; one thing may express another more or less well. All created substances express God, since they are all effects of God as creator, but minds do so better than others,[41] and, in the case of minds, distinct ideas express God better than confused ones. In other words, it is easier to read off the attributes of God from distinct ideas than from confused ideas. But even confused ideas express God. In the 'Conversation of Philarete and Ariste', Leibniz gives reasons for thinking that this must be so:

I am convinced that God is the only immediate external object of souls, since there is nothing except him outside of the soul which acts immediately upon it. Our thoughts with all that is in us, insofar as it includes some perfection, are produced without interruption by his continuous operation.[42]

[39] *Discourse on Metaphysics*, 36 (G iv. 461–2; L, p. 327). Trans. modified. Cf. Leibniz to Arnauld, 9 Oct. 1687, G ii. 124; L, p. 346.
[40] *NE* II. i (A VI. vi; RB, p. 109).
[41] *Discourse on Metaphysics*, 35 (G iv. 460; L, p. 326).
[42] *Conversation*, G vi. 593; L, p. 627. Cf. R, p. 207.

Leibniz insists, then, that God is causally responsible for every element of perfection in our thoughts; in other words, he is responsible for every positive element they contain. Where ideas are concerned, their perfections are clarity and distinctness; obscurity and confusion are not perfections—i.e. not positive qualities—but rather the privation of such qualities. On this view, then, God is causally responsible for every element of clarity even in our confused ideas—even confused ideas have some element of perfection—but he is not responsible for the confusion. Thus, God is the cause of our confused ideas, in so far as they include some perfection, but he is not the cause of them *qua* confused. In this way Leibniz can bring his position into line with the Augustinian solution of the problem of evil which he defends in the *Theodicy* and elsewhere.[43]

Leibniz's account of divine illumination in terms of expression is not formally inconsistent with other parts of his system. But in general, Leibniz's attempts to interpret the doctrine tend to arouse misgivings; they prompt one to ask whether they preserve anything of substance or of value from Malebranche and the Augustinian tradition. As we have seen, a prominent feature of Leibniz's accounts of divine illumination is their stress on causality; they all emphasize the mind's causal dependence on God. At first sight, this may seem foreign to the spirit of Malebranche's doctrine, but, strictly speaking, it is not. Malebranche is prepared to attribute causal properties to ideas in God; ideas are said to cause our perceptions by touching our minds. But this is not the happiest of Malebranche's thoughts, and in giving prominence to causality, Leibniz has simply emphasized the least interesting and defensible part of Malebranche's doctrine. By contrast, at the heart of Malebranche's doctrine is a thesis, not about causality, but about the nature of concepts; it is the philosophically controversial thesis that concepts are not mental but abstract objects. But this doctrine, as we have seen, runs counter to Leibniz's nominalist intuitions, and has no place in his philosophy. There is thus something half-hearted about Leibniz's attempts to do justice to divine illumination. It is true that Leibniz often echoes Malebranche, and he even follows him to the extent of quoting the opening of St John's Gospel, but the scriptural phrases have become largely empty formulas. In

---

[43] See e.g. *Theodicy*, I. 30 (G vi. 119–21).

essence, Leibniz preserves the outer shell of the doctrine of divine illumination, but he throws away its philosophical heart.

The Image of God

Leibniz's attempts to do justice to the doctrine of divine illumination are unconvincing, but his philosophy of mind is not without theological advantages of its own; indeed, in at least one respect, Leibniz is in a better position than Malebranche to do justice to Christian teaching. As Edward Craig and others have shown, much of Leibniz's philosophy can be read as a gloss on the doctrine that man is made in the image of God. With quite remarkable frequency, Leibniz insists that human minds are 'images of divinity',[44] and even that they are 'little gods' which 'differ from God only as less from greater'.[45] It is tempting to say that, in returning to this Cartesian theme, Leibniz is simply playing down the opening of St John's gospel in favour of the text from Genesis, but there are hints that Leibniz is doing something rather different; sometimes he seems bent on collapsing the one doctrine into the other. For example, the heading of paragraph 28 of the *Discourse on Metaphysics* prepares us for the theme of divine illumination: 'God alone is the immediate object, existing outside us, of our perceptions, and he alone is our light.'[46] In a sense the expectation is answered, for it is here that Leibniz quotes the opening of St John's Gospel. But in the very same paragraph Leibniz tells us that 'the essence of our soul is a certain expression, imitation or image of the divine essence, thought and will, and of all the ideas that are contained therein'.[47]

Leibniz's theory of ideas is itself an important step in the direction of Genesis; human minds have their own ideas, and these ideas correspond to God's ideas by virtue of expressing them in Leibniz's technical sense. But in order to bring out the importance of the Genesis theme in Leibniz's philosophy, we need to look beyond the theory of ideas. The subject has recently been discussed by Craig,[48] and for this reason we can afford to be brief. It is worth

---

[44] See e.g. Leibniz to Hansch, 25 July 1707, Dutens ii. 222, 225; L, pp. 592, 595; see also *Principles of Nature and of Grace*, 14 (G vi. 604; L, p. 640).
[45] Leibniz to Arnauld, 9 Oct. 1687, G ii. 125; L, p. 346.
[46] *Discourse on Metaphysics*, 28 (G ii. 14; L, p. 321).
[47] Ibid. (G iv. 453; L, p. 321).
[48] E. Craig, *Mind of God and the Works of Man* (Oxford, 1988), 51–64.

emphasizing the theological import of two famous themes from Leibniz's metaphysics.

In the *Principles of Philosophy*, Descartes had defined 'substance' in terms of causal independence, and he had famously recognized that, by this definition, only God is a true substance.[49] It is true that Descartes acknowledged a degree of causal independence in created minds; their existence is at least not causally dependent on the existence of bodies.[50] Moreover, Descartes broke with scholastic tradition by insisting that nothing enters the mind from outside; Cartesian ideas are in this respect radically unlike scholastic sensible species. Yet, at least in his official philosophy, Descartes remains committed to the thesis that there is a class of mental states which are causally dependent on the existence of physical states; sensory ideas may not be literally transmitted into the mind from bodies, but they are none the less caused by bodies. Thus, in Descartes's philosophy, the causal independence of minds is qualified not just by divine concurrence but by the causal role of bodies in sense perception. Leibniz, by contrast, tells a different, more radical story. Like Descartes, as we have seen, Leibniz admits the fact of divine concurrence, but otherwise, he endows minds with an unlimited causal self-sufficiency; for minds get all their states out of themselves. As Leibniz famously puts it, each substance is like a world apart.[51] Thus Descartes had recognized causal independence as a godlike property, and Leibniz goes further than his predecessor in attributing this property to created minds.

Human minds are not only to a large degree self-sufficient; they are also in a sense omniscient. As Craig has stressed, previous philosophers had concentrated on the similarity between human and divine knowledge in its intensive aspect; Leibniz was an innovator in claiming that human knowledge might resemble divine knowledge in its extent.[52] Leibniz feels no shyness about explicitly drawing this moral from his doctrine that each substance is an expression of the universe:

Each substance has something of the infinite in so far as it involves its cause, God; i.e. it has some trace of omniscience and omnipotence. For in the perfect notion of each individual substance there are contained all its

---

[49] *Principles of Philosophy*, 1. 51 (AT viii/A. 24; CSM i. 210).
[50] Ibid. 52 (AT viii/A. 25; CSM i. 210).
[51] *Discourse on Metaphysics*, 14 (G iv. 439; L, p. 312).
[52] Craig, p. 58.

predicates, both necessary and contingent, past, present, and future; indeed, each substance expresses the whole universe according to its position and point of view, in so far as the others are related to it.[53]

Yet there is no need to suggest, as Craig seems to do, that Leibniz sometimes rejects the intensive aspect of the likeness which had impressed Galileo.[54] It is true of course that, though in a sense we are omniscient, most of our knowledge is, unlike God's, very imperfect and confused. But Leibniz can agree with Galileo that, with respect to necessary truths, we are capable of knowing things in much the same way as God.[55]

We can see, then, that Leibniz is remarkably well placed to do justice to the Genesis doctrine that man is made in the image of God. Indeed, he fares far better in this respect than Malebranche. In *The Search after Truth* Malebranche similarly holds that his philosophy can do justice to this doctrine; he claims that it is through the union of our mind with the Word that we are made in God's image and likeness.[56] Yet in Malebranche's philosophy such claims have a rather hollow ring. For Malebranche, it does not even make sense to say that human beings have their own ideas; on the contrary, they are entirely dependent, at least for a priori knowledge, on being appropriately related to the ideas in God's mind. Unless they are illuminated by God, human minds are mired in sensations which have no cognitive value at all; nothing in God of course corresponds to our sensations. There is no real sense, for Malebranche, in which human minds are made in the image of God.

Leibniz is not only well placed to do justice to the teaching of Genesis; by virtue of his nominalism, he is also able to stay clear of a theological trap which almost ensnares Malebranche. As a Platonist, Malebranche is in serious danger of converting God into a merely abstract entity, and this of course would be heresy; Christian teaching requires us to conceive of God as a personal being who is capable of loving and caring for his creatures. There is evidence that Malebranche's contemporaries were worried by his philosophy on precisely this score; some of the charges of atheism and Spinozism which were levelled against Malebranche may have been nourished

---

[53] 'A Specimen of Discoveries', G vii. 311; P, p. 77. On the sense in which the human mind has some trace of divine omnipotence, see Craig, pp. 57–8.

[54] Craig, pp. 58–9.

[55] See e.g. *Principles of Nature and of Grace*, 15 (G vi. 605; L, p. 640).

[56] *Search after Truth*, iii. 2. 6 (OCM i. 446; SAT, 235).

by just such concerns.[57] Of course most Christian philosophers find it hard to escape the tension between the god of the philosophers and the god of Abraham, Isaac, and Jacob, and Leibniz is no exception. But by virtue of his nominalism Leibniz is at least in no danger of making God a purely 'third realm' entity; since ideas are ultimately reducible to mental items, God can be the bearer of appropriately psychological properties.[58] This is an important step in the direction of the God of Christian orthodoxy.

Leibniz's rejection of Malebranche's theory of ideas is thus not all loss from a theological point of view; it includes some positive gains of its own, and there is little doubt that Leibniz was aware of the fact. But theological advantages are not philosophical arguments, and there is no reason to suppose that Leibniz confused the two. Indeed, there is positive reason to suppose that he did not. But it would not be surprising if Leibniz thought that there was a pre-established harmony between truth in philosophy and truth in theology.

[57] It is fair to add, however, that these charges were mainly based on the supposition that Malebranche's doctrine of intelligible extension makes God material. See D. Radner, *Malebranche* (Assen, 1978), 95.

[58] I am indebted here to J. Bennett, 'Locke, Leibniz, and the Third Realm', unpublished paper.

9
Leibniz
The Defence of Innate Ideas

IT was the challenge of Locke's philosophy which called forth
Leibniz's fullest defence of innate ideas. But Locke's challenge did
not find Leibniz unprepared. Nearly twenty years before writing
the *New Essays*, Leibniz had encountered in Malebranche another
philosopher who rejected innate ideas. For many people it will
come as a surprise to find that Locke and Malebranche are agreed in
rejecting this doctrine, for according to tradition, Locke is a
common-sense empiricist, and Malebranche a mystical rationalist. It
is certainly true that they launch their polemics from different
directions, and in some respects it is Malebranche's critique
which cuts deeper; unlike Locke, Malebranche raises fundamental
questions about the ontological status of ideas. None the less, there
is an important degree of overlap in their criticisms of innate ideas;
Locke and Malebranche agree, for instance, in attacking the
dispositional version of the doctrine that Descartes had revived.

It would be foolish to try to pretend that Malebranche is always
Leibniz's primary target in his writings on innate ideas. Obviously,
the arguments of the *New Essays* are powerfully shaped by the
polemical needs of replying to Locke. But it is surely significant that
Leibniz has the resources in his philosophy for answering all
Malebranche's objections, and it is not uncharacteristic of Leibniz
to fight a war on two fronts. Indeed, the fact that Malebranche is a
target can, I believe, throw new light on Leibniz's sometimes
obscure defence of innate ideas; for many features of Leibniz's case
fall into place when they are seen as part of a coherent strategy for
answering Malebranche's objections. In the first part of this chapter
we shall analyse Leibniz's strategy for defending a dispositional
theory of innate ideas against both Locke and Malebranche. In the
last part of the chapter we shall see how Leibniz's defence of innate
knowledge is supported by a psychologistic theory of necessary
truth.

Innatism and Ideas as Dispositions

We saw in the previous chapter how Leibniz responded to Malebranche's theory of ideas; consistently with his nominalism, Leibniz rejects Malebranche's doctrine that ideas are irreducibly abstract objects. We can now see that Leibniz's reductionist approach provides a crucial first step in the defence of innate ideas. Malebranche could object that the whole issue of innate ideas is misconceived since it rests on a conflation of logic and psychology. Leibniz can reply to this charge of conflation that there is no dichotomy between ideas and the mental; ideas are psychological items since they are dispositions to think in certain ways. Thus the doctrine of innate ideas is not the category mistake that Malebranche takes it to be; it is prima facie coherent to ask whether there are any psychological dispositions that we have had since birth. Innate ideas, it would seem, are at least a conceptual possibility.

It is less clear, however, whether Leibniz thinks his theory of ideas as dispositions amounts to more than a first step in the defence of innateness. In the *Discourse on Metaphysics* there is at least a suggestion that Leibniz has something more ambitious in mind; he comes close to implying that the very status of ideas as dispositions provides a quick argument for the conclusion that they are all innate:

Indeed our soul always has in it the disposition to represent to itself any nature or form whatever, when the occasion for thinking of it presents itself. I believe that this disposition of our soul, in so far as it expresses some nature, form or essence, is properly the idea of the thing, which is in us, and is always in us, whether we think of it or not.[1]

With physical examples in mind, we can, of course, concede that dispositions are persistent properties of objects; to say that the glass is fragile is to attribute to it a property that endures through time and which may or may not become manifest. Indeed, that dispositions persist through time may even be a necessary truth about them, and we may be inclined to say that this necessity derives from the fact, which we shall examine later, that they are grounded on the structural characteristics of the objects that instantiate them. But for the present we can establish one clear

---

[1] *Discourse on Metaphysics*, 26 (G iv. 451; L, p. 320). Trans. modified.

consequence of regarding ideas as dispositions: to have an idea is to be in at least a relatively persistent psychological state.

Persistence of course is not permanence, but it is possible to see how one might come to embrace the stronger thesis that dispositions are necessarily permanent properties. Suppose one holds that membership of a natural kind is necessary; something's being salt is a *de re* essential property of that thing. In other words, it could not retain its identity while ceasing to be salt, nor could it have become salt from something else. One might further argue that solubility in water is an essential property of salt; nothing could be salt which did not dissolve when immersed in water. On this basis one might conclude that solubility is an essential and hence permanent property of any substance which is identified as salt.

This of course is a controversial argument, and even in the case of physical dispositions it is open to challenge.[2] But perhaps the most obvious and effective way of challenging it is to appeal to mental dispositions. It is plausible to regard memories as dispositional properties of minds; for we tend to think that in addition to occurrent memories, there are also persistent memory states which can be activated by stimuli. In this way memories resemble such familiar physical dispositions as fragility and solubility. But memories are also paradigmatically the sort of thing that can be acquired and lost; we do not think that a new mind comes into being when a memory is acquired, or that a mind expires when a memory is lost. The mind preserves its identity throughout.

It seems, then, that it would be a mistake to think that dispositions are necessarily permanent properties. Thus the quick argument for innate ideas should be rejected. Fortunately, however, it is not necessary to suppose that Leibniz does endorse this argument. For in the relevant section of the *Discourse on Metaphysics* Leibniz seems to argue for innate ideas from his famous doctrine of expression; all ideas are innate because 'the soul expresses God, the universe and all essences as well as existences'.[3] Of course this argument is not without its own difficulties. For one thing, it is not clear whether it is God or the universe, or both, that is supposed to bear the weight of the argument. It is natural to assume that it is the mind's expressing God that is crucial, for God is the region of all

[2] Cf. D. H. Mellor, 'In Defense of Dispositions', *Philosophical Review*, 83 (1974), 160.

[3] *Discourse on Metaphysics*, 26 (G iv. 451; L, p. 320).

ideas or essences.[4] But if this is Leibniz's meaning, then we may wonder whether the argument is sound. We may grant Leibniz that if the human mind expresses God, then it must have any idea that God has, but it is not clear why this implies that it must have this idea at all times, and hence innately. Perhaps Leibniz has the following argument in mind. Since God has the idea of *x* at all times, then the human mind could not truly express God unless it also has the idea of *x* at all times. The trouble with the argument is that it treats God as a sempiternal being, and we know that Leibniz expressly rejected this way of understanding the eternity of God.[5] But unless Leibniz has some such assumption in mind, it is difficult to see how the argument can go through.

In fact, as the discussion progresses, Leibniz seems to lay weight on another aspect of his theory of expression:

We have all these forms in our own minds, and indeed we have them from all time; for the mind always expresses all its future thoughts, and already thinks confusedly of everything of which it will ever think distinctly.[6]

From this thesis concerning expression it does seem to follow that the mind has a permanent disposition towards its future thoughts, and that this disposition is an innate idea. The problem which the argument now raises is whether there is any good reason to think that its premisses are true.

Leibniz's Reply to Locke

Leibniz may not argue directly for a theory of innateness from the status of ideas as dispositions, but one thing is at least clear. If ideas in general are dispositions to think in certain ways, then innate ideas are innate dispositions to think in certain ways; in other words, they are dispositions which we have had at least since birth. This of course is precisely the version of the doctrine that Leibniz defends against Locke in the *New Essays*: 'this is how ideas and truths are innate in us—as inclinations, dispositions, tendencies or natural

[4] See e.g. 'On the Radical Origination of Things', 23 Nov. 1697, G. vii. 305; L, p. 488.

[5] See e.g. *Ad Christophori Stegmanni Metaphysicam Unitariorum*, printed in N. Jolley, 'An Unpublished Leibniz MS on Metaphysics', *Studia Leibnitiana*, vii (1975), 184.

[6] *Discourse on Metaphysics*, 26 (G iv. 451; L, p. 320). Trans. modified.

virtualities, and not as actions'.[7] But Leibniz must cope with two waves of attack, for both Locke and Malebranche object to the dispositional version of the theory of innate ideas. Thus Leibniz is in effect fighting a war on two fronts.

It is, of course, Locke's objections to the dispositional version which are most familiar. In the *Essay concerning Human Understanding* Locke tries to show at length that any dispositional version of innate ideas is inevitably condemned to triviality; this forms part of a more general, two-pronged attack on the doctrine of innate ideas.[8] According to Locke, to say that the mind has innate ideas or principles in the sense that it has a disposition to acquire them, or come to know them, is merely to say that it is capable of acquiring them, or coming to know them. But in that case all ideas and truths which we acquire or come to know will be innate, and thus the doctrine of innateness is trivialized:

So that if the Capacity of knowing be the natural Impression contended for, all the Truths a Man ever comes to know, will, by this Account, be, every one of them, innate, and this great Point will amount to no more, but only to a very improper way of speaking; which whilst it pretends to assert the contrary, says nothing different from those, who deny innate Principles.[9]

It is not always easy to separate out the various strands in Locke's polemic, but sometimes his argument seems to take a rather different form. When Locke focuses on mathematical ideas and knowledge, for instance, his argument seems to be more of a genuine *reductio*: the protagonists of innate ideas are committed to the absurd consequence that even mathematical theorems are innate:

If they mean that by the *Use of Reason* Men may discover these Principles; and that this is sufficient to prove them innate; their way of arguing will stand thus . . . there will be no difference between the Maxims of the Mathematicians, and Theorems they deduce from them: All must be equally allow'd Innate, they being all Discoveries made by the use of Reason, and Truths that a rational Creature may certainly come to know if he apply his Thoughts rightly that way.[10]

---

[7] *NE*, pref. (A vi. vi, RB, p. 52).

[8] The other prong of the assault is the claim that the doctrine of innate ideas is empirically false. On this issue, see N. Jolley, *Leibniz and Locke: A Study of the New Essays on Human Understanding* (Oxford, 1984), ch. 9.

[9] *Essay*, i. ii. 5.

[10] Ibid. 8.

There is, however, one assumption that is common to both the triviality argument and the *reductio*: if there are any innate ideas and principles, they must be few in number.

As in Locke's polemic, so in Leibniz's defence, it is not always easy to sort out the various strands. But it seems that Leibniz answers each of Locke's two main arguments against the dispositional theory. To Locke's objection that his antagonist must regard even mathematical theorems as innate, Leibniz's reply is somewhat disarming; he seems simply to accept the conclusion of Locke's intended *reductio*. For Leibniz, there is no absurdity in holding that all intellectual ideas and necessary truths are innate:

> I grant you the point, as applied to pure ideas, which I contrast with images of sense, and as applied to necessary truths or truths of reason, which I contrast with truths of fact. On this view, the whole of arithmetic and of geometry should be regarded as innate, and contained within us in a potential way.[11]

To Locke's argument that the dispositional theory trivializes the doctrine of innate ideas, however, Leibniz has a different and more important reply. Leibniz claims that the defender of innate ideas need not be committed to the thesis that all ideas are innate since talk of dispositions is not equivalent to talk of faculties or capacities. As Leibniz puts it, what is in question 'is not a bare faculty, consisting in a mere possibility of understanding these truths; it is rather a disposition, an aptitude, a preformation, which determines our soul and brings it about that they are derivable from it'.[12]

It is easiest to grasp the point of Leibniz's distinction if we focus on the case of physical dispositions. From the fact that an object *x* breaks, we can infer that in a sense *x* had a capacity to break, but a genuine disposition involves more than this. A table may break if hit with a sledge-hammer, but that is not enough to make it fragile. Thus our analysis of the concept of fragility must say something about the nature of the stimulus which will activate the disposition.[13] As we saw in an earlier chapter, we are inclined to say that an object is fragile if and only if it breaks whenever it is dropped.

---

[11] *NE*, I. i (A VI. vi, RB, p. 77).

[12] Ibid. (A VI. vi; RB, 80). Cf. Leibniz's insistence in 'What is an Idea?' that an idea is not a remote, but a proximate, faculty of thinking. G vii. 263; L, p. 207. Cf. Leibniz to Burnett, 3 Dec. 1703, G iii. 291.

[13] I am grateful to Jonathan Bennett for help with this point.

Leibniz can reply to Locke that physical and psychological dispositions run in tandem. The fact that a physical object breaks does not entail that it is fragile; in just the same way, the fact that we have an occurrent thought of *x* does not entail that we have an innate idea of *x*. Thus, to say that we have an innate idea of a triangle, for instance, is to say that at least since birth we possess a disposition to have an occurrent thought of *x* given such and such a stimulus. Here there must be something about the stimulus which prevents a disposition to think of an elephant in the presence of an elephant counting as an innate idea. When Leibniz insists on this constraint, he is in a position to defeat Locke's objection that the dispositional theory trivializes the doctrine of innateness by implying that all ideas are innate.

It may seem surprising that Leibniz should take his stand against Locke on just this ground; for as we have seen, in the *Discourse on Metaphysics* Leibniz had already insisted that all ideas are innate. Consistently with his position in that work, Leibniz could simply reply by rejecting Locke's assumption that if all ideas are innate, then the doctrine is trivialized; Leibniz could insist that, on the contrary, this is a substantive metaphysical truth about the nature of the mind. But perhaps we should see Leibniz as arguing in a concessive vein. For Leibniz, there are metaphysical grounds for holding that all ideas are innate; but these arguments depend on his technical doctrine of expression which would no doubt leave Locke unimpressed. But if Locke would not accept such doctrines, he can at least be brought to see that his argument against the dispositional theory is a bad one; of itself, the theory does not entail that all ideas are innate. Leibniz goes furthest in the *New Essays* towards strong innatism when he accepts the conclusion of Locke's intended *reductio*: all intellectual ideas and necessary truths are innate. But further than this Leibniz is not prepared to go.

Leibniz's Reply to Malebranche

Leibniz's answer to Locke is impressive, but it still leaves Malebranche's objections in the field. Unlike Locke, Malebranche does not think that in order to refute the dispositional theory, it is sufficient to show that it entails that all ideas are innate. On the contrary, it was just such a strong version of the doctrine that

Malebranche examined, and then proceeded to argue against; he must therefore have thought that it needed to be refuted by independent arguments.[14] Malebranche might admit that by distinguishing between capacities and dispositions, Leibniz can avoid the conclusion that Locke thinks must be trivial, but from his point of view such a move is irrelevant. For Malebranche would insist that no such move can meet his worry about explanatory adequacy. Consider again the case of fragility. Not every object which has a capacity to break is fragile, but talk of fragility is no more genuinely explanatory than talk of capacities. For it is simply circular to appeal to fragility when asked to explain the breaking of the glass, when dropped. Thus Leibniz must come up with a new argument in reply to Malebranche.

As is so often the case, Leibniz's reply to Malebranche would be initially conciliatory. Leibniz, as a mechanistic physicist, joins Malebranche in condemning the circular faculty explanations of the scholastics; in the *New Essays* he ridicules those who say that clocks tell the time by virtue of a horological faculty.[15] Indeed, as is well known, Leibniz is so much a child of his time that he has worries about Newton in this respect; he criticizes the Newtonian theory of universal gravitation for reintroducing the occult qualities of the scholastics.[16] But, properly understood, Leibniz's anti-Newtonian strictures provide the key to his defence of dispositions against Malebranche's objections. In the eyes of Leibniz, Newton's cardinal sin lay in (supposedly) postulating gravitational force as a basic property of bodies; he thereby flouted the fundamental principles of the mechanical philosophy, according to which bodies essentially possess only fully actual properties, and their powers derive from these properties.[17] Thus, for Leibniz, it is the mark of a genuine disposition that it is reducible to non-dispositional properties of the object. In what Mates calls the paradigmatic example, the sugar is soluble in virtue of its crystalline structure; the structural description of the sugar, together with an appropriate law of nature,

[14] Malebranche, *Search after Truth*, III. 2. 4 (*OCM* i. 429; *SAT* 226).

[15] *NE*, pref. (A vi. vi; RB, p. 68).

[16] See e.g. *Anti-Barbarus Physicus*, G vii. 342. On this issue see Jolley, *Leibniz and Locke*, ch. 4.

[17] For an illuminating discussion of the principles of the mechanical philosophy, see M. R. Ayers, 'Mechanism, Superaddition and the Proofs of God's Existence in Locke's *Essay*', *Philosophical Review*, 90 (1981), 210–51.

jointly entail that the sugar is soluble under certain conditions.[18] Of course Leibniz need not admit that we always know how the reduction can be brought off, but he will insist that genuine dispositions must be reducible at least in principle. By insisting on this requirement, Leibniz is in a position to meet Malebranche's charge of circularity.

Leibniz's reducibility requirement for dispositions is logically distinct from the restrictions he imposed in reply to Locke. To Locke's charge of triviality, Leibniz replies by insisting that ascriptions of innate ideas discriminate among ideas in the same sort of way that ascriptions of fragility discriminate among bodies which have the power to break; the fact that a table breaks when hit with a sledge-hammer does not mean that it is fragile. But if reducibility is what distinguishes dispositions from 'bare faculties', then it would seem that the capacity to break when hit with a sledge-hammer belongs on the dispositional side of the boundary. There appears to be no reason why this capacity should not be reduced in the same way as fragility or solubility; it can surely be derived from structural descriptions of the table and the sledge-hammer in conjunction with the appropriate laws of nature. Perhaps Leibniz would say that reducibility is a necessary, but not a sufficient, condition of a genuine disposition. This may be so, but Leibniz should have done more to make this point clear.

Malebranche may agree with Leibniz that if dispositions can be grounded in non-dispositional properties, then his worry can be met. But Malebranche would be sceptical as to whether such grounding is possible in the case of psychological dispositions. It is to Leibniz's credit that he seeks to meet this objection head-on. Leibniz does not try to shirk the consequence that the grounding principle applies when we ascribe a dispositional property to the mind; for example, when we say that an infant's mind has an innate idea of a triangle. There is the same basic need for a persistent structural modification, but in this case it must be a purely mental one. Now, as Broad says, it is not entirely clear what is involved in ascribing a persistent structural modification to a Leibnizian mind; it cannot be thought of as a modification in spatial arrangement or motion of particles.[19] Broad's solution to the problem seems just right:

[18] B. Mates, *Philosophy of Leibniz; Metaphysics and Language* (Oxford, 1986), 246.   [19] C. D. Broad, *Leibniz: An Introduction* (Cambridge, 1975), 134.

It seems to me that the view which Leibniz took was that the modification simply is a persistent but unconscious experience. E.g. during intervals when I should ordinarily be said not to be thinking of the fact that $2 \times 2 = 4$ and not to be remembering the late Master of Trinity, I am really continuously thinking of the former and remembering the latter in a perfectly literal non-dispositional sense. But at such times these experiences are unconscious. At times when it would ordinarily be said that the mere cognitive disposition gives rise to an actual experience what really happens is that the cognitive process which has been going on all the time becomes conscious. Thus for Leibniz any evidence for cognitive dispositions would *ipso facto* be evidence for unconscious cognitive experiences.[20]

Thus, for Leibniz, a child's mind possesses an innate disposition to think of a triangle by virtue of a mental modification, and this mental modification is a persistent unconscious perception with triangle content.

This interpretation is strongly supported by the Preface to the *New Essays*, for here Leibniz emphasizes the importance of unconscious perceptions (*petites perceptions*). Indeed, we first hear of unconscious perceptions in connection with the dispositional theory of innate ideas. Having remarked that ideas are innate in us as 'inclinations, dispositions, tendencies or natural virtualities', Leibniz then remarks that 'these virtualities are always accompanied by certain actions, often insensible ones, which correspond to them'.[21] In the following pages Leibniz goes on to insist that 'insensible perceptions are as important in the philosophy of mind as insensible corpuscles are in natural science'.[22] On the present interpretation this is just what we should expect; insensible perceptions are strictly comparable to insensible corpuscles, for they ground ideas in much the same way that the corpuscles ground physical dispositions.

We can now see that Leibniz's defence strategy against Malebranche involves a twofold reduction. Innate ideas are first reduced to innate dispositions to think in certain ways. Innate dispositions to think in certain ways are then in turn reduced to unconscious experiences. In other words, Leibniz holds that from a description of a mind's unconscious experiences, together with the laws of psychology, we could infer that it would have the conscious thought of a triangle under certain specifiable conditions. In this way Leibniz can

[20] C. D. Broad, *Leibniz: An Introduction* (Cambridge, 1975), 134–5.
[21] *NE*, pref. (A vi. vi; RB, p. 52).
[22] Ibid. (A vi. vi; RB, p. 56).

reconcile his commitment to innate ideas with his nominalistic conviction that there are only individual substances and their states.

It should be clear, then, that Leibniz has a powerful strategy for defending the dispositional version of the doctrine of innate ideas against the objections of both Locke and Malebranche. But we have not yet exhausted Malebranche's case against innate ideas, for in *The Search after Truth* Malebranche presents two further objections to the innatist position. We shall see that Leibniz has the resources in his philosophy to answer both of them.

In *The Search after Truth*, III. 2. 4, Malebranche argues that the doctrine of innate ideas is contrary to the simplicity of the divine ways.[23] Here, too, Leibniz must concede that if the objection could be made to stick, it would be grounds for rejecting the doctrine; for according to Leibniz's principle of the best, God shows a preference for the simplest laws consonant with the maximum variety of the phenomena.[24] Thus Leibniz must show that the doctrine of innate ideas is in fact the simplest explanation of the phenomena; it is not the clumsy hypothesis that Malebranche takes it to be.

Leibniz can offer a double-barrelled reply to Malebranche's objection. He can meet the challenge by distinguishing between two levels of analysis. On the one hand, he can answer it at the level of ideas; on the other hand, he can answer it at the level of thoughts or, in his scheme, perceptions.

When Malebranche's objection is interpreted in the former way, Leibniz can turn his opponent's weapons against him. In controversy with Arnauld, Malebranche observes that ideas are not discrete items, but are logically interrelated. For example, the idea of extension, or what Malebranche calls intelligible extension, potentially contains all possible geometrical figures within it. What Malebranche seems to mean by this is that the properties of all possible geometrical figures can be derived from basic geometrical axioms and definitions. Malebranche makes use of an image that Leibniz was to make famous in the *New Essays*:

As in a block of marble all possible figures are potentially contained in it, and can be drawn out of it by the movement or by the action of the chisel, so in the same way all intelligible figures are potentially in intelligible extension and are discovered in it according to the different ways in which this extension is represented to the mind, as a consequence of the general

---

[23] *Search after Truth*, III. 2. 4 (*OCM* i. 431; *SAT* 227).
[24] See e.g. *Discourse on Metaphysics*, 6 (G. iv. 431; L, p. 306).

laws which God has established according to which he continuously acts in us.[25]

Adapting Malebranche's own example, Leibniz could say that God does not have to stock the mind with a series of discrete items; on the contrary, in endowing a mind with an innate idea of extension, he *ipso facto* endows it with innate ideas of all possible geometrical figures. Thus there is no threat to the simplicity of the divine ways. It may be objected that Leibniz is the victim of his reductionism here. From the fact that the idea of x entails the idea of y, it does not follow that John's having the idea of x entails that he has the idea of y; consider the case where y is a very unobvious consequence of x. This objection may be sound, and it may be fatal to attempts to reduce logic to psychology. But it seems that it would leave Leibniz unimpressed, for in the *New Essays* he does appear to hold that a person has at least implicit or potential knowledge of all the logical consequences of his ideas.[26] Indeed, Leibniz surely must say this, given his commitment to analysing talk about ideas in terms of talk about people's psychological dispositions.

When Malebranche's objection is construed in terms of perceptions, however, such a line of defence is no longer available. Although Leibniz reduces logic to psychology, he still allows us to say that ideas are linked by relations of logical entailment. But thoughts and perceptions are clearly not in this category; they are discrete psychological items that occur at particular times. At this level of analysis Malebranche's objection seems to have some bite to it, for Leibniz holds an extremely strong version of the thesis that there are innate perceptions; indeed, it is hard to imagine how it could be stronger than it is. According to Leibniz, it is of the very nature of an individual substance that at every moment it perceives the whole universe according to its point of view; it follows from this that at every moment in its history the mind is in an infinitely complex perceptual state. What generates this complexity is of course the doctrine of unconscious perceptions. Thus Leibniz has metaphysical reasons of his own for holding that a mind has an infinitely large 'magazine' of innate perceptions.

Leibniz answers Malebranche on the principle that attack is the best means of defence. According to Leibniz, it is Malebranche's

[25] *Trois Lettres*, *OCM* vi. 208–9. Cf. *Dialogues on Metaphysics*, 1 (D, pp. 38–9). For a discussion of this issue, see D. Radner, *Malebranche* (Assen, 1978), 92.
[26] *NE* 1. i (A vi. vi; RB, p. 77).

occasionalism that violates the simplicity of the divine ways. However unfairly, Leibniz frequently objects that occasionalism involves a perpetual miracle; it invokes God as a *Deus ex machina* who intervenes constantly to suspend the laws of nature.[27] By contrast, the doctrine of pre-established harmony fares much better; it is an elegant hypothesis which is worthy of the divine wisdom. In creating minds, God endows them with their own laws or programmes, and it is by virtue of the programmes alone that their subsequent states evolve in harmony with those of other substances.[28] God thus has no need to interfere with the laws of nature. The doctrine of pre-established harmony is indeed the simplest of intelligible hypotheses concerning the union of mind and body.

The doctrine of the pre-established harmony also provides the answer to Malebranche's final objection. Malebranche had objected that it is impossible to understand how the mind could make the right selections from its stock of innate ideas. It would seem that it must be a cosmic accident if I regularly perceive the sun as a small round disk when my body is affected in the appropriate way. Leibniz meets this objection by denying the assumption that the mind needs to choose among its innate ideas. At the time of his second reading of *The Search after Truth*, Leibniz had observed that the production of our ideas does not always depend upon our will.[29] In other words, to say that we are the source of our perceptual states does not imply that they depend on our conscious will. The theory of unconscious perceptions explains how this can be so: we have a tendency or 'appetition' to new perceptual states, even though we are not aware of it. Thus according to the doctrine of pre-established harmony the mind is so initially programmed that its perceptions evolve in harmony with those of other substances.

Innate Knowledge and the Eternal Truths

In the *Theodicy*, his reply to Bayle, Leibniz found occasion to congratulate Malebranche for not adopting Descartes's doctrine of the creation of the eternal truths. Bayle had taken the curious

---

[27] See e.g. 'A Specimen of Discoveries', G vii. 313; P, p. 80; and *New System*, G iv. 484; L, p. 457.
[28] 'Specimen', G vii. 313; P, p. 80; and *New System*, G iv. 484; L, p. 457.
[29] R, p. 185.

position of wishing that Malebranche had followed Descartes in this direction, while simultaneously admitting that he could not understand Descartes's doctrine. Leibniz replied with some irony:

Is it possible that the pleasure of doubting can have such power over an able man as to make him wish and make him hope to be able to believe that two contradictories are never found together only because God has forbidden them this, and that he could have given them an order which would have always made them accompany each other? There's a fine paradox. The Reverend Father Malebranche has done very wisely to take other measures.[30]

Leibniz and Malebranche may part company on the issue of innate ideas, but on this matter they are in full agreement; they are at one in rejecting the Cartesian doctrine that the eternal truths depend, not on God's understanding, but on his will.

Leibniz's agreement with Malebranche in rejecting Cartesian voluntarism raises an obvious question. As Loeb noticed, and as we have already remarked, Descartes's advocacy of the creation of the eternal truths is linked to his doctrine of innate knowledge; indeed, Descartes made the connection in his very first pronouncement on innate ideas: 'the eternal truths are all inborn in our minds just as a king would imprint his laws on the hearts of all his subjects if he had enough power to do so'.[31] The connection seems fairly straightforward. The doctrine of the creation of the eternal truths implies that there are absolutely no constraints on what God could have willed to be eternally true. Aside from a special revelation, it is thus difficult to see how we could know what truths he has in fact willed unless they are innate in us, and this condition is satisfied; God has so structured our minds that their propositional contents bear witness to the eternal truths which he has freely ordained. The fact that it is God who has engraven these propositional contents is of course important; it provides them with their epistemic credentials. We can be sure that the propositions we find engraved on our minds are true because God is not a deceiver. We can indeed say if we like that they are necessary truths. But to say this is only to say that we are psychologically compelled to believe them provided we are perceiving clearly and distinctly.

Descartes's doctrine of innate knowledge, as opposed to innate ideas, is thus motivated at least in part by his bizarre teaching

---

[30] *Theodicy*, 185 (G vi. 227).
[31] Descartes to Mersenne, 15 Apr. 1630, AT i. 145; K, p. 11.

concerning the eternal truths. Malebranche himself seems to have been aware of a connection between the two doctrines; as we saw in an earlier chapter, he showed that both doctrines were rooted in the conflation of logic and psychology. In any case, however Malebranche saw the connection, he rejected not merely Descartes's voluntarism but all versions of the doctrine of innate ideas. Leibniz, by contrast, rejects Cartesian voluntarism but agrees with Descartes in insisting that we have not only innate ideas but also innate knowledge. It is natural to ask, then, why Leibniz needs a doctrine of knowledge since he does not have Descartes's special problem on his hands. The answer, I believe, is to be found in the psychologism which sets both Leibniz and Descartes apart from Malebranche.

At first sight it seems easy to see what Leibniz's philosophical reasons are for advancing a doctrine of innate knowledge. As Leibniz insists in the *New Essays*, it is only by means of this doctrine that we can explain how knowledge of necessary truths is possible. Yet, as various writers have pointed out, such a claim is dangerously ambiguous; there are indeed two questions which innateness might be invoked to solve and which need to be carefully distinguished.[32] In the first place, there is a causal question: how do we acquire necessary beliefs, i.e. beliefs to the effect that p is a necessary truth? Secondly, there is the question of justification: what warrant do we have for the claim to know that p is a necessary truth? We must beware of talking loosely about the problem of explaining the possibility of necessary knowledge in a way that masks the ambiguity.

The appeal to innateness is perhaps a plausible answer to the causal question. Leibniz has sometimes been taken to be addressing this question, and to be arguing as follows. We have the belief that necessarily p, and this belief is either innate or it was acquired through the senses. But the belief cannot have been acquired through the senses, for by means of the senses we could never come to believe that necessarily p. The belief must therefore be innate; in other words, our minds are such that they have an innate disposition to believe that necessarily p. If this is Leibniz's position, then it sets him clearly apart from Malebranche, for Malebranche would answer the question by saying that we have the belief—

[32] S. Stich (ed.), *Innate Ideas* (Berkeley and Los Angeles, 1975), Introd., pp. 17–18.

presumably, for him, an occurrent belief—by virtue of being related to ideas and truths in God. But Leibniz does not leave it at that; he seems to hold that by appealing to innateness he can justify claims to necessary knowledge in logic and mathematics. When Leibniz argues to innate knowledge from the insufficiency of the senses, it seems that it is justification that is in question:

It cannot be denied that the senses are inadequate to show [the] necessity [of necessary truths]; and that therefore the mind has a disposition (as much active as passive) to draw them from its own depths; though the senses are necessary to give the mind the opportunity and the attention for this, and to direct it towards certain necessary truths rather than others. The fundamental proof of necessary truths comes from the understanding alone, and other truths come from experience or from observations of senses.[33]

Elsewhere Leibniz writes that necessary truths 'are proved by what lies within and cannot be established by experience as truths of fact are'.[34] But how can we justify our claim to know that p is a necessary truth by citing the fact that it is innate? As Bennett asks, why should not a lie be inscribed on our soul?[35] On this issue Descartes's position is, if not satisfactory, at least relatively clear. We can know that an innate proposition p is true because it has been implanted by God, and God is not a deceiver. As regards the claim that p is a necessary truth, Descartes can say that the necessity is nothing over and above our psychological compulsion to believe it under certain conditions. But unlike Descartes, Leibniz is reluctant to appeal to divine benevolence to solve epistemological problems; he is, for instance, highly critical of Descartes's use of this strategy in order to vindicate our knowledge of the existence of the external world.[36] And unlike Descartes, Leibniz is not in a position to take the easy way with logical necessity; he cannot simply collapse it into facts about human psychology. Moreover, we may feel that Leibniz has a better way of dealing with these issues which has no truck with the notion of innateness. Surely, Leibniz's real position is that claims to necessary knowledge are to be justified by showing that the proposition in question is finitely analytic, i.e. reducible to an identity in a finite number of steps. It thus seems puzzling why

[33] *NE*, pref. (A vi. vi; RB, p. 80).

[34] Ibid. (A vi. vi; RB, p. 79).

[35] J. Bennett, 'Locke, Leibniz, and the Third Realm', unpublished paper, Nov. 1982, 2.

[36] See e.g. *Critical Thoughts on the General Part of Descartes's Principles*, G iv. 366–7; L, pp. 391–2.

Leibniz should look to innateness for any help with the problem of justification.

The first step to a solution of the problem is to see that Leibniz's view of necessary truth seems to be ultimately psychologistic after all. Leibniz cannot say, with Descartes, that logical necessity is nothing over and above what we are psychologically compelled to believe under certain conditions, but, as Bennett has argued, he is under philosophical pressure to say that logical necessity is nothing over and above divine psychology.[37] Such a claim may be greeted with some surprise. In the *New Essays* Leibniz says that God is not merely the region of ideas; he is also the domain of eternal truths.[38] It is not obvious that such claims should be interpreted in psychological terms. But, as we have seen, Leibniz's God cannot be a 'third realm' entity; for Leibniz is committed to the thesis that only individual substances exist, and in his later philosophy at least, he holds that all such substances, including God, are mind-like. Thus Leibniz's remarks to the effect that God is the domain of the eternal truths must be ultimately unpacked in psychological terms; they must be reduced to claims about God's propositional thoughts.

Such an interpretation is confirmed by a subtle difference in emphasis between Leibniz and Malebranche in their criticisms of Cartesian voluntarism. Malebranche, as we have seen, makes many remarks to the effect that Descartes's underlying mistake is the conflation of logic and psychology; this mistake has predisposed him to think that the eternal truths are the sorts of things that must have causes. Leibniz, by contrast, stresses Descartes's confusion, not of logic and psychology, but rather of two faculties of the divine mind; Descartes attributes to God's will what properly belongs to his understanding:

it seems that every act of will implies some reason for willing and that this reason naturally precedes the act of will itself. This is why I find entirely strange, also, the expression of some other philosophers [e.g. Descartes] who say that the eternal truths of metaphysics and geometry, and consequently also the rules of goodness, justice and perfection, are merely the effects of the will of God; while it seems to me that they are rather the

---

[37] Bennett, 'Locke, Leibniz, and the Third Realm', esp. pp. 11–14; and RB (1982), introd., p. xxii. Cf. B. Russell, *A Critical Exposition of the Philosophy of Leibniz* (2nd edn., London, 1937), 178–81.

[38] *NE* IV. xi (A VI. vi; RB, p. 447).

consequences [*suites*] of his understanding, which certainly does not depend upon his will any more than his essence does.[39]

It is natural to read this as saying that the eternal truths are simply those propositional thoughts which God thinks as a result of the structure of his understanding.

Leibniz's attempt to distance himself from Descartes raises some puzzling, but instructive, questions. In Descartes's philosophy, a clear sense can be given to the claim that God could have had a different will; God could have brought it about that two plus three equalled six. For Leibniz, by contrast, the eternal truths depend not on God's will, but on his understanding. Suppose, then, we ask 'Could Leibniz's God have understood that two plus three equalled six?' Clearly, if what is at issue is whether such a state of affairs is logically possible, then the question must be treated with some care; it cannot be interpreted in a way which implies that there is some analysis of logical possibility independent of divine psychology. It is tempting to say that the question must reduce to the issue of whether it is psychologically possible for God to think such a thought. Here too we must be careful, for if what we are asking is whether such a thought is consistent with divine psychology—i.e. with the structure of the divine mind—then again we are in danger of smuggling in some unreduced notion of modality. But however Leibniz interprets the question, it is clear what his answer must be: the structure of God's mind does not allow him to think the thought that two plus three equal six.[40] But in that case we seem to be left with the intuition that it is just a brute fact that the structure of the divine mind is as it is.

Despite the difficulties of the project, Leibniz seems committed to the reduction of logical necessity to divine psychology. But this of course still leaves the role of innate principles unexplained. As Bennett notices, in the *New Essays* Leibniz provides us with at least the materials for a solution to the problem. At one point Leibniz's spokesman, Theophilus, remarks that the divine mind is 'the pattern for the ideas and truths which are engraved in our souls'.[41] Elsewhere Theophilus develops the idea by suggesting that our true beliefs are isomorphic with God's thoughts: 'And when God

---

[39] *Discourse on Metaphysics*, 2 (G iv. 428; L, p. 304).

[40] God can of course think a thought of the form 'John believes that two plus three equal six.'

[41] *NE* iv. xi (A vi. vi; RB, p. 447).

displays a truth to us, we come to possess the truth which is in his understanding, for although his ideas are infinitely more perfect and extensive than ours, they still have the same relationships that ours do.'[42] Bennett glosses this passage by remarking that 'The suggestion seems to be that I can do logic—i.e. divine psychology— by looking at my own mind and assuming that it will be like God's at least in respect of its structural properties, the formal relations among its contents.'[43] But I think that Leibniz would be prepared to say that this is more than an assumption; where innate beliefs are in question, we can *know* that they have the same relations among their contents as God's propositional thoughts. Indeed, this is guaranteed by the fact that the human mind expresses the divine mind.

At first sight it may seem that the doctrine of expression cannot serve Leibniz's purpose here. Leibniz is committed to the thesis that all thoughts, even false ones, are expressions of God; thus from the fact that my beliefs express God, I cannot infer that they are true, let alone necessarily true. But this objection is not compelling; it overlooks the fact that expression can vary in quality, and, given this fact about expression, we can see, at least in broad terms, how Leibniz might argue for the thesis that innate beliefs must be necessarily true. To talk about innate beliefs is to talk about innate mental dispositions to have certain propositional thoughts; in other words, it is to talk about the basic structure of the human mind. And to talk about necessary truths, as we have seen, is to talk about those propositional thoughts which are 'consequences of [God's] understanding', i.e. which God has by virtue of the structure of his mind. It is reasonable to suppose that those structural thoughts of God, as it were, are best expressed, in the realm of created minds, by those beliefs which are built into the structure of the human mind. Thus it seems that Leibniz has the resources for saying that innate beliefs express God's thoughts better than do any other beliefs. Now Leibniz could further claim that innate beliefs express God's thoughts in such a way that, as Bennett says, they must have the same formal relations among their contents. Since the thoughts of God in question are necessary truths, beliefs that are innate in the human mind must also be necessary truths.

---

[42] Ibid. v (A vi. vi; RB, p. 397).
[43] Bennett, 'Locke, Leibniz, and the Third Realm', p. 13.

Leibniz's psychologism about necessary truth thus helps to explain how he can appeal to innateness in connection with the problem of justifying our claims to necessary knowledge; indeed, it explains what would otherwise be very difficult to explain. The psychologism in question is of course different from Descartes's. For Descartes, there are in a sense no necessary truths; at most, necessity is a function of the constitution of the human mind.[44] For Leibniz, by contrast, necessity is a function, not of the human mind, but of the divine mind. Thus the interpretation we have offered has no tendency to eliminate the differences between Leibniz and Descartes with regard to logical necessity. But it certainly suggests that the gap which separates them is less than it has traditionally been supposed to be; it means, for instance, that they are closer to each other than either is to Malebranche. But then, Malebranche rejected the doctrine of innate ideas, whereas both Leibniz and Descartes embraced it.

[44] Cf. M. D. Wilson, *Descartes* (London, 1978), 125.

10

Leibniz
Innate Ideas, Reflection, and Self-Knowledge

THE dispositional theory may be Leibniz's most prominent account of innateness, but it is not the only one, even in the *New Essays*. As is well known, Leibniz attempts to construct a theory of innateness on the basis of Locke's admission of ideas of reflection. Traditionally, Leibniz's claim that ideas of reflection are really innate ideas has been seen as something of an embarrassment.[1] For one thing, it is doubtful whether what we may call the reflection account can really perform the role that Leibniz seems to require of a theory of innateness. Moreover, there are obvious difficulties concerning the relationship of the two accounts which Leibniz seems not to have noticed. It would be foolish to pretend that all these problems can be solved, and no attempt will be made to minimize them in the present chapter. But we can, I think, throw light on the reflection account of innateness if we place it in the wider context of Leibniz's concern with the issue of self-knowledge; as we have seen, this issue became central in philosophy after Descartes. In the first half of this chapter we will explore Leibniz's response to the pessimistic claims about self-knowledge advanced by both Locke and Malebranche. In the second half of the chapter we will seek to tie in Leibniz's reflection account of innateness with the whole issue of self-knowledge.

Background: Self-Knowledge in Malebranche and Locke

Descartes's well-known position on self-knowledge was the subject of two major attacks in later seventeenth-century philosophy: both

---

[1] See e.g. J. L. Mackie, *Problems from Locke* (Oxford, 1976), 213–14. A contrary view is presented by M. Kulstad, 'Leibniz's Theory of Innate Ideas in the *New Essays*', unpublished paper read to the APA Pacific Division, Long Beach, Mar. 1984.

Malebranche and Locke challenged the Cartesian thesis that the mind is better known than body. In direct opposition to his mentor Descartes, Malebranche had argued that body is better known than mind, for we know the nature of body through ideas but we know the mind only through consciousness or internal sensation. Indeed, according to Malebranche, as we have seen, strictly speaking we have no idea of the soul. What Malebranche means by this is that we have no a priori knowledge of the properties of the mind of the sort we possess in geometry and perhaps in physics.

In the *Essay concerning Human Understanding* Locke had also rejected Descartes's claim that mind is better known than body, but he did not simply echo Malebranche's strictures. Malebranche agrees with Descartes that our knowledge of mind and body is asymmetrical, but he disagrees with Descartes about the direction of the asymmetry. Locke, by contrast, holds that there is a parity between the two cases; our ideas of mind and body are equally obscure.

'Tis plain then, that the *Idea* of corporeal *Substance* in Matter is as remote from our conceptions, and Apprehensions, as that of Spiritual *Substance*, or *Spirit*; and therefore from our not having any notion of the *Substance* of Spirit, we can no more conclude its non-Existence, than we can, for the same reason, deny the Existence of Body: It being as rational to affirm, there is no Body, because we have no clear and distinct *Idea* of the *Substance* of Matter; as to say, there is no Spirit, because we have no clear and distinct *Idea* of the *Substance* of a Spirit.[2]

Malebranche remained a Cartesian to the extent of thinking that we do know the essence of matter; he departed from the Cartesians in thinking that we do not know the essence of mind. Locke departs from the Cartesians in holding that the essences of mind and matter are equally unknown to us.

Despite the real differences between their positions, Malebranche and Locke share a pessimistic attitude to the prospects of self-knowledge. And it is just this pessimism which makes the issue of self-knowledge so crucial for Leibniz. For if the nature of the mind is opaque to us, then traditional claims for its freedom, immateriality, and immortality tend to become problematic. It is, of course, true that neither Malebranche nor Locke was blind to such difficulties. In controversy with Arnauld, as we have seen, Malebranche tried to show that traditional claims can be justified

2 *Essay*, II. xxiii. 5.

despite our lack of an idea of the soul. Following Descartes, Malebranche had argued that we are directly aware of the freedom of the will through internal experience; unlike Descartes, he had also argued that our idea of extension is sufficient to provide us with a priori knowledge of the spirituality and immortality of the mind. Locke had similarly addressed himself to the problems posed by his stance on self-knowledge, but he had been perhaps rather more candid about the difficulties. Unlike Malebranche, Locke was prepared to be openly agnostic about the soul's immateriality; for Locke, it is at least epistemically possible that the thinking principle in us is material, although he claims, without real justification, that the soul is probably immaterial. None the less, for Locke, our inevitable agnosticism in this area has no tendency to undermine the doctrine of personal immortality, since

it is evident, that he who made us at first begin to subsist here, sensible intelligent Beings, and for several years continued us in such a state, can and will restore us to the like state of Sensibility in another World, and make us capable there to receive the Retribution he has designed to Men, according to their doings in this Life.[3]

Leibniz could hardly fail to be aware that important issues were at stake in both Malebranche's and Locke's positions on self-knowledge. Locke openly admitted that agnosticism with regard to immateriality was the consequence of our lack of a clear idea of the mind; Malebranche tried to avoid this conclusion, but his attempt to ground a proof of traditional claims in the idea of extension must have appeared to Leibniz as perfunctory at best. It would not be surprising if the issue of self-knowledge became a major concern for Leibniz as a result of Malebranche's and Locke's contributions to the issue, and this is in fact what we find.

Leibniz's Position on Self-Knowledge

In an earlier chapter we sought to define Leibniz's position on the nature of ideas in general in relation to the views of Malebranche and Arnauld. It seems helpful to adopt the same strategy for defining Leibniz's position on self-knowledge. Here again we find that Leibniz makes a number of apparently conflicting statements. Around 1685 Leibniz seems to side with Malebranche against

---

[3] *Ibid.* IV. iii. 6.

Descartes and the Cartesians: 'Father Malebranche has very well brought Cartesianism into line with common opinions by showing . . . that we have no clear idea of our soul'.[4] On other occasions Leibniz seems to say the exact opposite; in a curious passage he endorses Descartes's position on self-knowledge and has to remind himself that Malebranche does not share it:

So I now pass over in silence the fact that the true philosophy by means of certain arguments teaches both the existence of God and the subsistence of the soul; nor is the nature of the soul completely unknown; nor did Malebranche—Descartes, I should say—wrongly say that the knowledge of the soul is more certain than the knowledge of body [*nec inepte Malebranchius, imo jam Cartesius, certiorem animae quam corporis cognitionem dixit*].[5]

And we shall see that in his critical remarks on Locke's own *Examination of Malebranche*, Leibniz firmly ranges himself in opposition to both philosophers.

At first sight it may seem that there is an easy way of reconciling Leibniz's statements on self-knowledge. Indeed, it may even seem that Leibniz is in the position to play the role of mediator between Malebranche and the Cartesian Arnauld. All we need do to make Leibniz consistent with himself is to distinguish between the idea of the soul in general and the idea of an individual soul. Thus Leibniz could agree with Malebranche that we have no idea of an individual soul; according to Leibniz, since every soul is an individual substance, it has a complete concept to which God alone has cognitive access. Thus Malebranche is right that we have no a priori knowledge of our soul, for God alone is in a position to know what is and is not included in our complete concept. But Leibniz could also agree with Arnauld that we do have an idea of the soul in general; in this area, *contra* Malebranche, a priori knowledge is possible for us. We can know a priori that the soul is naturally immortal, just as we can know a priori, for Leibniz, that the Pythagorean theorem is true of Euclidean right-angled triangles.

There is one point in his correspondence with Arnauld where Leibniz may seem to be thinking along these lines. In a well-known passage Leibniz criticizes Arnauld's account of self-knowledge for failing to take note of the difference between ideas of individuals and specific concepts such as occur in geometry:

[4] R, p. 226.   [5] Leibniz to Kestner, 24 Oct. 1709, R, p. 361.

I agree that in order to judge of the notion of an individual substance it is a good thing to consider that which I have of myself, just as it is necessary to consider the specific notion of a sphere in order to judge of its properties. And yet there is a considerable difference; for the notion of *me* and of every other individual substance is infinitely more extended and more difficult to understand than a specific notion like that of a sphere, which is incomplete only. It is not enough that I feel myself a substance which thinks, it would be necessary to conceive distinctly what distinguishes me from all other minds; but of this I have only a confused experience. The result is that, though it is easy to determine that the number of feet in the diameter is not included in the notion of the sphere in general, it is not so easy to determine whether the journey which I intend to make is included in my notion; otherwise it would be as easy for us to be prophets as to be geometers.[6]

In such a passage Leibniz may seem to hint that there is a sense in which Malebranche is right: we have no idea of the soul inasmuch as, unlike God, we have no a priori knowledge of ourselves as individuals. However, we run into difficulties when we try to spell out the sense in which Leibniz would agree with Arnauld. Contrary to what we might expect, Leibniz does not—or, at least does not consistently—hold that we have a clear and distinct idea of the soul in general so that we can have a priori knowledge of its properties. In the following passages, Leibniz writes of thought rather than the mind, but it is clear that he is thinking in general terms; he cannot be read as simply claiming that we have no idea of the individual soul:

Further, I remain in agreement with Father Malebranche that we have no distinct ideas of thought any more than of colour. It is, then, only by confused sensation that we have some notion of it.[7]

I agree that the idea which we have of thought is clear, but not everything that is clear is also distinct. We know thought only through an internal sense as Father Malebranche has already remarked. But through sense we can know only things we have experienced[8]

Thus Leibniz does not seem to mediate between Malebranche and Arnauld in the straightforward way we might suppose.

In fact, Leibniz's view of Malebranche's doctrine of self-knowledge appears to undergo a development in the course of time. Around 1686, the year of the *Discourse on Metaphysics*, Leibniz seems to agree with Malebranche against Descartes and Arnauld: we have no distinct idea of the mind or of thought in general. After

---

[6] Leibniz to Arnauld, May 1686, G ii. 45; P, p. 59.
[7] Leibniz to Arnauld, draft of letter of 9 Oct. 1687, R, p. 238.
[8] Leibniz to Arnauld, 9 Oct. 1687, G ii. 121; L, p. 344.

1700, however, Leibniz takes a more positive view of our knowledge of the mind; it is during this period, for instance, that he sides with the Cartesians against Malebranche and Locke. It is true that even in this later period there are differences of emphasis. In the *New Essays*, for instance, Leibniz takes the position that our knowledge of mind and our knowledge of body run parallel: *petites perceptions* are to pneumatology (the philosophy of mind) as insensible corpuscles are to physics.[9] Thus in both these areas it is reasonable to admit unobservables. On other occasions during these years Leibniz goes even further; as we have seen, he endorses the Cartesian thesis that the nature of mind is better known to us than the nature of body. Despite these differences of emphasis, there seems to be a clear tendency in Leibniz's later remarks; after 1700 he is much less sympathetic to Malebranche's negative claims concerning self-knowledge, and much more ready to identify with the Cartesians.

The change of emphasis in Leibniz's pronouncements on self-knowledge can hardly be denied; relatedly, there is a shift in Leibniz's sense of where his philosophical affinities lie. But does this mean that there is a formal inconsistency between Leibniz's earlier and later positions on self-knowledge? It would be wrong to be too hasty in reaching this conclusion. Consider that when in the later writings Leibniz takes his most optimistic view of self-knowledge, it is a posteriori knowledge that is in question; in other words, Leibniz seems to be emphasizing the adequacy of the knowledge that we can have through reflection or introspection. This appears to be the kind of knowledge that Leibniz has in view when he chastises both Locke and Malebranche for their pessimism.

The Father [Malebranche] had said that we know our soul by an internal sense of consciousness, and that for that reason, the knowledge of our soul is more imperfect that that of the things which we know in God . . . The truth is that we see everything in ourselves and in our soul, and that the knowledge that we have of the soul is very true and very exact [*juste*] provided that we take care about it; that it is by the knowledge we have of the soul that we know being, substance, God himself . . .[10]

---

[9] *NE*, pref. (A vi. vi; RB, p. 56).
[10] G vi. 578. The claim that we know God through the knowledge we have of our soul is yet another remarkable illustration of Leibniz's thesis that the mind is made in the image of God.

Leibniz does not explicitly tell us here that a posteriori knowledge is in question, but there is an unmistakable family resemblance with another passage where he is explicit on this point:

That we are not substances is contrary to experience, since indeed we have no knowledge [*notitia*] of substance except from the intimate experience of ourselves when we perceive the I [*to Ego*], and on that basis we apply the term 'substance' to God himself and other monads.[11]

When, however, Leibniz expressed agreement with Malebranche, a posteriori knowledge through reflection was not the issue; on the contrary, it was a priori knowledge that was in question. As we have seen, Malebranche's central thesis about self-knowledge is that we have no idea of the soul; for Malebranche, this means that we have no a priori knowledge of its properties in the way that we have a priori knowledge of the properties of geometrical figures. Of course, Leibniz might have been unclear about the extent of Malebranche's negative thesis about self-knowledge, but though Leibniz may have later needed to remind himself about it, he seems to have been perfectly clear on the matter around 1686. Consider the interesting analogy that he draws between the idea of the soul and ideas of colour. Our ideas of colours and of the soul are alike indistinct because we are not in a position to analyse them; in other words, in optics as in the philosophy of mind, we lack a priori knowledge. But as the colour analogy shows, this admission is consistent with claiming that we have a posteriori knowledge in these areas through sensation or reflection.

On a fundamental level, then, there is no inconsistency in Leibniz's position. Malebranche is right in denying that we have a priori knowledge of the soul; and the Cartesians are right in the sense that we have a posteriori knowledge of the nature of the soul through reflection or introspection. Indeed, Leibniz comes increasingly to stress the extent of the knowledge that introspection makes possible. In 1687 Leibniz could still write that, lacking a priori knowledge, we must rest content with a confused sensation of our own souls. But in his later writings Leibniz tends to take a more positive view; he stresses that on the basis of internal experience we are justified in believing that the soul—or our own soul at least—is a substance, a unity, and a being. Thus introspection tells us more about the nature of the mind than either Malebranche or Locke supposes.

[11] Gr ii. 558.

Even if we can clear Leibniz of the charge of fundamental inconsistency, we are still left with the fact of a change of emphasis in his discussions of self-knowledge. Leibniz moves from endorsing Malebranche's negative claims to making positive claims for a posteriori self-knowledge; indeed, he also takes a more optimistic view than he had earlier done of the possibilities of self-knowledge through reflection. Commenting on Locke's critique of Malebranche, Leibniz can assert that the knowledge we have of the soul is very true and exact provided we pay attention to it. A possible explanation of this shift is ready to hand. A clue is provided by the fact that Leibniz's most positive statements about self-knowledge all date from the period after his engagement with Locke. Now there is evidence that Leibniz was concerned by what he saw as the materialist tendency of Locke's philosophy,[12] and it would not be surprising if Leibniz became increasingly suspicious of claims about self-knowledge which left the door open to materialism. It is, of course, true that Locke's negative claims in this area had been anticipated by Malebranche, and that at one stage Leibniz had been content to endorse these claims. But Malebranche had at least claimed to provide a proof of the soul's immateriality, whereas Locke was prepared to be openly agnostic on this issue. Thus in response to Locke Leibniz may well have felt the need to stress the positive in his discussion of self-knowledge; indeed, he may even have been led to re-evaluate the extent of the knowledge that we can have through introspection or reflection. And in the course of opposing Locke, Leibniz was also prepared to oppose Malebranche; both Locke and Malebranche are rebuked for failing to see that through reflection we can know that we are substances, unities, and beings. But Leibniz need not be read as withdrawing his earlier assent to Malebranche's thesis that we have no idea of the soul in the peculiar sense that Malebranche gave to that thesis.

Before we conclude this section of the chapter, we should face a possible objection. We have said that—at least around 1686—Leibniz agreed with Malebranche that we have no a priori knowledge of the soul, and we have found no evidence that Leibniz changed his mind on this fundamental issue. Some readers may be inclined to protest here; surely Leibniz must have believed that there were a priori arguments for the immateriality and simplicity of

[12] On this issue, see N. Jolley, *Leibniz and Locke: A Study of the* New Essays *on Human Understanding* (Oxford, 1984), esp. chs. 2, 6.

the mind. There is no need for us to be dogmatic in denying this, but, as various commentators have noticed, it is surprisingly difficult to discover such arguments in the Leibnizian corpus. Indeed, as Margaret Wilson has argued, Leibniz tends to emphasize the a posteriori basis for the truths about the soul he wishes to defend; he writes as if 'we can self-evidently experience ourselves as simple or immaterial entities'.[13] Moreover, readers who believe that Leibniz must have a priori arguments in this area are obliged to give some account of his agreement with Malebranche that we have no distinct idea of the mind. But without claiming to resolve this issue, one thing seems clear; in Leibniz's later writings there is a marked tendency to emphasize the knowledge of mind that we have a posteriori through reflection or introspection.

We must now turn to the account of innateness that Leibniz gives in terms of reflection. As we shall see, there are important links between this account and the claims for self-knowledge that we have examined.

Innate Ideas and Reflection: Problems

Leibniz disapproved strongly of the overall tendency of Locke's philosophy, but in the *New Essays* he characteristically adopts a conciliatory tone; as in the case of his dealings with Malebranche he desires to find common ground wherever possible. The conciliatory tone is perhaps nowhere more evident than in his response to Locke's account of ideas of reflection. Leibniz claims that in admitting that reflection constitutes an independent source of non-sensory ideas, Locke is in effect conceding the case for innate ideas.[14] But as Leibniz makes clear, he is not simply taking over intact Locke's own doctrine of reflection; on the contrary, he thinks that the class of ideas of reflection is larger than Locke supposes:

It is very true that our perceptions of ideas come either from the external senses or from the internal sense, which can be called reflection; but this reflection is not limited to the operations of the mind, as is said [by Locke]; . . . it goes as far as the mind itself, and it is in perceiving the mind that we perceive substance.[15]

---

[13] M. D. Wilson, 'Leibniz and Materialism', *Canadian Journal of Philosophy*, 3 (1974), 508.
[14] *NE*, pref. (A vi. vi; RB, p. 51).
[15] *Échantillon des reflexions sur* l'Essay, A vi. vi. 14.

Thus Leibniz's view seems to be that through reflection we have ideas of the mind and of its most basic affections or properties. We are said to be 'innate to ourselves' in the sense that the mind and its fundamental properties are permanently available to us as potential objects of explicit attention or awareness.[16]

Leibniz's doctrine of ideas of reflection is most fully developed in the *New Essays*, but it is not a mere *ad hoc* response to Locke; it is present, in its essentials, in the *Discourse on Metaphysics*. In this work, for instance, Leibniz had already presented a non-Lockean view of the class of ideas of reflection:

But in whatever way one takes it, it is always false to say that all our notions come from the so-called external senses, for the notion that I have of myself and my thoughts, and consequently of being, substance, action, identity, and many others, come from an internal experience.[17]

It is true in the *Discourse* Leibniz does not explicitly call such ideas innate; that step must wait until the *New Essays*. But even at this date he seems to hold that the existence of such ideas constitutes a refutation of the Aristotelian doctrine of the *tabula rasa*.

Leibniz's attempt to press ideas of reflection into the service of innateness has generally been regarded as an embarrassment, and with good reason; indeed, the full extent of the difficulties it poses has not perhaps been fully appreciated. In the first place, it seems clear that the reflection account is a new theory of innateness; it is not simply a different name for the more familiar and more prominent dispositional theory which we examined in the previous chapter. Consider how the two theories handle the claim that we have an innate idea of substance. According to the one theory, we have an innate disposition to have an occurrent thought of substance under certain specifiable conditions. According to the other theory, we acquire the idea by simply reflecting on the fact that the mind is a substance. It should be obvious that these two claims are not at all equivalent. Yet curiously, Leibniz does very little to signal this fact. Of course, since ideas are dispositions, by acquiring an idea of substance through reflection, we thereby acquire a disposition, and to this exent, as we shall see, even the reflection account contains a dispositional component; but since the disposition is acquired through reflection, it is clear that this is not

---

[16] *NE*, pref. (A vi. vi; RB, p. 51); Leibniz to Bierling, G vii. 488–9. The date, 19 Nov. 1709, is deleted. Cf. *NE* ii. i (A vi. vi; RB, p. 111).

[17] *Discourse on Metaphysics*, 27 (G iv. 452; L, p. 321). Trans. modified.

an innate disposition in the sense of one we have possessed since birth. For this reason it seems appropriate to speak of the reflection account in contrast to the dispositional account.

Indeed, in a number of places Leibniz seems actually to conflate the two accounts. When we examine Leibniz's argument in the Preface to the *New Essays* for the thesis that ideas of reflection are really innate ideas, we find that it appears to depend on a fallacy of equivocation:

> But reflection is nothing but attention to what is within us, and the senses do not give us what we carry with us already. In view of this, can it be denied that there is a great deal that is innate in our minds, since we are innate to ourselves, so to speak, and since we include Being, Unity, Substance, Duration, Change, Action, Perception, Pleasure, and hosts of other objects of our intellectual ideas.[18]

There seems to be a crucial ambiguity in Leibniz's definition of 'reflection' as 'attention to what is within us'. We may be tempted to say initially that the phrase 'what is within us' is ambiguous between mental contents—i.e. ideas—and properties of the mind, and that the argument depends on this equivocation. However, Leibniz might object that this is a false dichotomy, for on his analysis ideas are psychological dispositions, and thus are mental properties. Yet even Leibniz must recognize a difference between dispositional, representational properties of the mind such as ideas and non-dispositional, non-representational properties such as substantiality and unity. But it is just this distinction that Leibniz seems to blur in his account.

Leibniz trades on the same or similar ambiguities in the dialogue of the *New Essays*. To Locke's claim that if any proposition can be in the mind which it has never known, it must be only because it has the faculty or capacity of knowing it, Leibniz replies that there is another possibility:

> Why couldn't it be because of something different, such as that the soul can contain things without one's being aware of them? Since an item of acquired knowledge can be hidden there by the memory, as you admit that it can, why could not nature also hide there an item of unacquired knowledge? Must a self-knowing substance have, straight away, actual knowledge of everything which belongs to its nature? Cannot—and should not—a substance like our soul have various properties and states which could not all be thought about straight away or all at once?[19]

---

[18] *NE*, pref. (A vi. vi; RB, p. 51).   [19] Ibid. i. i (A vi. vi; RB, p. 78).

Here Leibniz seems to slide insensibly from the dispositional account of innate ideas to the reflection account, and the slide is effected by equivocating on the phrase 'everything which belongs to its nature'. Clearly Leibniz is talking about what is essential to the mind, but there is an ambiguity between essential properties—such as unity, identity, substantiality—and essential contents—such as the ideas of unity, identity, and substance. Once again, this distinction needs refining, since, as we have seen, Leibniz holds that ideas are properties of the mind. But there is no doubt that Leibniz can and must find room for a distinction between the idea of substance, for instance, and the property of being a substance. Leibniz may indeed think that it is essential to the mind to have the idea of substance; in this sense the idea belongs to its nature. But this claim is to be spelt out in terms of the mind's having an essential disposition to form certain thoughts under certain conditions. It seems inexcusable that Leibniz should conflate this claim with the very different thesis that substantiality is an essential property of the mind.[20]

There is one final occasion where Leibniz seems to conflate the two accounts of innateness by means of an unnoticed ambiguity. Leibniz claims that 'intellectual ideas, or ideas of reflection, are drawn from our mind [*tirées de notre esprit*]'.[21] Here again Leibniz trades on a treacherous phrase: 'drawn from our mind'. Intellectual ideas might be 'drawn from our mind' in the sense that certain mental dispositions are activated. Or intellectual ideas might be drawn from the mind in the sense that they are framed by our noticing certain properties of the mind; we attend to the fact that we are substances—to the property of substantiality which our mind instantiates—and then form the idea of substance. Since Leibniz is explicitly talking about ideas of reflection, it is the second sense which is relevant, but he seems to be helping himself to the first sense as well. By means of this ambiguity, Leibniz tries to persuade the unwary reader that ideas of reflection are in a real sense innate ideas.

---

[20] It is tempting to bring out the difference by using the idea of God as an example: it may be essential to the mind to have the idea of God, as Leibniz would no doubt argue, but it is hardly essential to the mind to be divine. Yet on reflection, the example may not be apposite, for Leibniz does think that the mind is in a sense divine. See n. 10 above. As we shall see, geometrical ideas provide a better way of making the point.

[21] *NE*, I. i (A VI. vi; RB, p. 85).

Curiously, however, Leibniz's reflection account of innateness also gives rise to an opposite problem. Once we distinguish carefully between the reflection and the dispositional accounts, we can see that they are in tension—even in contradiction—with each other. At least this is the implication of some of Leibniz's more unguarded claims concerning reflection. Leibniz follows up his claim that ideas of reflection are drawn from our mind by issuing a challenge to the reader: 'I would like to know how we could have the idea of being if we did not, as beings ourselves, find being within us.'[22] Taken at his word, Leibniz is claiming that we can have the idea of being only by reflecting on the fact that we are beings. But if this is so, then it cannot also be the case that we have an innate idea of being in the sense of an innate disposition to have the occurrent thought of being under certain conditions; according to this claim, the reflection account and the dispositional account cannot both be true. To the rhetorical challenge that Leibniz issues, we can reply by turning his own weapons against him: we have the idea of being because our minds are such that they possess it as an innate dispositional property.

We have seen, then, that Leibniz does not achieve a coherent view of the relation between the reflection and the dispositional accounts of innateness; either he simply conflates them or he implies that they cannot both be true. Leibniz's reflection account is also subject to a more internal difficulty; it suffers from a crucial explanatory limitation. According to Leibniz, metaphysical concepts, such as being and substance, are not the only innate ideas; all the concepts of mathematics are also supposed to be innate. Now it is just possible to envisage how one might set about explaining the acquisition of arithmetical concepts in terms of the reflection account; unity, after all, is a property of the mind. But the task of explaining geometrical concepts within this framework seems utterly hopeless.[23] We can bring home this point by adapting Theophilus's own rhetorical challenge to Philalethes. Suppose we ask 'How could we have the idea of a triangle, unless as triangles ourselves, we found triangles within us?' The absurdity of the question demonstrates that the reflection account is inherently limited in a way that the dispositional account is not.

---

[22] Ibid. (A VI. vi; RB, pp. 85–6).
[23] This point is acknowledged by Kulstad, p. 7.

Innate Ideas and Self-Knowledge: Two Issues

The reflection theory of innate ideas suffers from a further, more fundamental weakness. The theory is supposed to offer an explanatory account of the origin or acquisition of certain ideas. In other words, I am supposed to turn my mental gaze inwards, and notice that my mind is a substance or a unity; I thereby come to acquire the appropriate idea. But it seems clear that in order to recognize that my mind is a substance, I must already have the idea of substance. Thus the explanation offered by the reflection account is in reality circular; it explains the acquisition of an idea on the assumption that we already have the idea in question.

As an account of idea-acquisition, the reflection theory is fatally flawed. And this may lead us to wonder whether in his discussion of ideas of reflection Leibniz is really after something different. There are indeed indications that Leibniz is less interested in explaining how ideas are acquired than in the question of how claims to self-knowledge can be justified; in particular, he is concerned with justifying the knowledge claim that the mind is a substance. In support of this suggestion, we may note, for instance, that some passages are ambiguous between these two quite different enterprises. In a fragment cited earlier, Leibniz uses the word *notitia*, a word which can mean either 'idea' or 'knowledge', and we get a significantly different result depending on which translation we favour:

That we are not substances is contrary to experience, since indeed we have no *notitia* of substance except from the intimate experience of ourselves when we perceive the I [*to Ego*], and on that basis we apply the term 'substance' to God himself and other monads.[24]

It is possible to read this as saying that we can acquire the idea of substance only by reflecting on the fact that we are substances. But it is also possible to read the fragment as advancing a quite different thesis having to do with justification, not explanation; we can know that our minds are substances simply on the basis of internal experience.

The reflection account may provide a merely circular explanation of how we acquire ideas, but it suffers from no such weakness with regard to the question of justification; it provides at least a coherent

[24] Gr ii. 558.

answer to the question of how claims to self-knowledge can be justified. Consider how Leibniz could appeal to our capacity for reflection in order to justify the knowledge-claim that our mind is a substance. We have the ideas of mind and substance—perhaps as innate mental endowments. We can then notice by reflective attention that our mind is a substance; in other words, we perceive that one and the same thing falls under the concepts of mind and substance. The justification is entirely a posteriori; we verify the claim that our mind is a substance in the same way that we verify the claim that the cow is black, except that the experience to which we appeal is internal, not external. In the fragment above Leibniz seems to have just such an argument in mind.

Leibniz's argument for self-knowledge from reflection provides a valuable resource in his campaign against materialism. Such a claim may be greeted with some scepticism. It may be objected that if Leibniz seeks to refute materialism in this a posteriori fashion, then he needs a stronger thesis concerning the deliverances of internal experience; he must be able to claim that internal experience verifies the thesis not just that our minds are substances, but that they are *simple* substances. So far, however, we have not found that Leibniz advances this stronger claim. But in fact such an objection is misguided, at least with regard to the debate with Locke. Locke's worry is that our minds might simply consist in thought superadded to matter suitably disposed.[25] But in that case our mind would be not a substance but rather a property of a material system. Thus for Leibniz's purpose of answering Locke, it would be sufficient if we could know by reflection that our mind is a substance.

It would of course be foolish to pretend that the argument poses no problems. For one thing, the a posteriori argument from reflection can do no more than ground the claim that my mind is a substance; and this leaves us with the problem of getting from there to the conclusion that all minds are substances. In this respect the a posteriori argument for self-knowledge is subject to a weakness from which the a priori argument is free. But to admit this is simply to acknowledge that the argument is incomplete, not that it is fundamentally flawed. After Kant's paralogisms, we may be tempted to feel that this stronger criticism is justified. But at least we can see that Leibniz's appeal to reflection makes much more

[25] *Essay*, IV. iii. 6.

sense in the context of justification than in the context of explanation.

We are now in a position to pull together the threads of this chapter. I have argued that Leibniz's account of ideas of reflection should be viewed as a contribution to a continuing debate over self-knowledge. We have seen that both Malebranche and Locke had brought this problem to the forefront of philosophical concerns. Locke, in particular, had made the problem an urgent one, for he, unlike Malebranche, had argued that our lack of self-knowledge leaves the door open to materialism. Such a thesis was obviously unacceptable to Leibniz, yet he had committed himself to the extent of endorsing Malebranche's thesis that we have no a priori knowledge—or in Malebranche's terms, no idea—of the mind. The solution to this impasse was to argue that we have a posteriori knowledge of the nature of the mind through reflection or introspection. It is true, as we have seen, that in the process of defending such a claim, Leibniz seems to be guilty of conflation; he appears to conflate questions of explanation and justification. But it is difficult to see how any account of Leibniz's discussion of reflection can avoid the conclusion that he is guilty of some degree of conflation. It is, I believe, a merit of the present interpretation that it explains why Leibniz believed reflection to be so central to his debate with Locke.

11

Some Further Developments

LEIBNIZ'S theory of ideas could have no immediate impact on major philosophers, because the key texts were not available; the *New Essays* did not appear until 1765, and other works were not published until the nineteenth, and even the twentieth century. Yet in one sense Leibniz was eminently successful; in reclaiming ideas for psychology he was at least on the side of the victors. Malebranche's theory of ideas as abstract objects found no major champions in the following century; whatever the influence of occasionalism, the doctrine of vision in God was discredited by its overtones of mysticism. But the fact that Malebranche's theory fell into disfavour does not mean that ideas ceased to be regarded as objects. On the contrary, it is arguable that the object theory of ideas remained the orthodox view until Reid launched his attack on the whole 'way of ideas' tradition. It may have become unfashionable to regard ideas as abstract objects, but the view that ideas are mental objects continued to flourish.

Historians of the 'way of ideas' tradition face a danger of falling into two opposite errors. On the one hand, it is easy to be over-impressed by the fact that Locke, Berkeley, and Malebranche all define ideas in terms of objects of the understanding; as a result one may be tempted to lump them together as champions of a single theory, and ignore the differences between them. To some extent this mistake is made by McRae.[1] On the other hand, philosophers may be over-impressed by the fact that Locke, Berkeley, and Arnauld are all critics of Malebranche's theory of ideas. From this one may be tempted to infer that the theory of ideas as objects of some sort did not have anything like the prominence which it is supposed to have. In particular, the evidence of hostility to Malebranche may serve as a basis for challenging the view that Locke is committed to a representative theory of perception. To some extent this mistake is made by Yolton; Yolton holds that

[1] R. McRae, ' "Idea" as a Philosophical Term in the Seventeenth Century', *Journal of the History of Ideas*, 26 (1965), 175–90.

philosophers have been duped by Reid into ascribing 'the wrong concept of ideas to most of those in the tradition of the way of ideas'.[2] In this concluding chapter I want to steer a middle course between these two errors by examining the reactions of Locke, Berkeley, and Reid to Malebranche's theory of ideas. I shall argue that Locke and Berkeley are critical of Malebranche not because he thought ideas are objects, but because he thought they are not mental objects. We shall also see that in the eyes of Reid this fact about Malebranche's theory of ideas was not a disadvantage but a positive recommendation.

Locke

Locke devoted a separate work to discussing the merits of Malebranche's doctrine of vision in God, and it should not surprise us if Locke was intrigued by the doctrine. There were indeed issues on which the two philosophers were in agreement. Both philosophers were agreed in rejecting the doctrine of innate ideas, and both were concerned to put forward alternative theories. Moreover, as McRae correctly notes, Locke and Malebranche define the term 'idea' in remarkably similar ways. According to Locke, 'idea' is 'that Term, which, I think, serves best to stand for whatsoever is the Object of the Understanding when a Man thinks'.[3] According to Malebranche, 'by the word *Idea*, I mean here nothing other than the immediate object, or the object closest to the mind when it perceives something, i.e., that which affects and modifies the mind with the perception which it has of an object'.[4] But despite the similarities in their definitions, Locke is deeply hostile to Malebranche's theory of ideas; indeed, he dismisses Malebranche's whole doctrine of vision in God as a combination of mysticism and philosophical ineptitude. And this might lead us to suppose that, unlike Malebranche, Locke is not to be taken seriously when he defines ideas as objects of the understanding. Such a conclusion is, however, unwarranted.

Ever since Reid, philosophers have complained that Locke's use of the term 'idea' is ambiguous. The *Examination of Malebranche*,

---

[2] J. W. Yolton, *Perceptual Acquaintance from Descartes to Reid* (Minneapolis, 1984), p. 15.
[3] *Essay*, I. i. 8.
[4] *Search after Truth*, III. 2. 1 (*OCM* i. 414; *SAT* 217).

no less than the *Essay*, furnishes evidence in favour of the charge. At times Locke suggests that 'idea' and 'perception' are interchangeable terms; he seems to count himself among those philosophers for whom ideas are 'nothing but perceptions of the mind . . .'.[5] Such a claim might suggest that Locke is in fact committed to a theory of ideas as mental acts or events, rather than objects. Yet even in the *Examination* Locke reveals some sympathy with the theory that ideas are objects. Consider, for instance, how Locke reacts to Malebranche's distinction between ideas and *sentiments*. We shall see later that Locke has difficulty in grasping this distinction; for the moment let us notice that he entertains, but ultimately dismisses, the possibility that what Malebranche has in mind is the distinction between the act and object of perception:

If by 'sentiment', which is the word he uses in French, he means the act of sensation, or the operation of the soul in perceiving; and by 'pure idea', the immediate object of that perception, which is the definition of ideas he gives us here in the first chapter; there is some foundation for it, taking ideas for real beings or substances.[6]

Locke stops short of endorsing this distinction, and throughout the *Examination* he is reluctant to state his own positive views. But such a passage hardly suggests that Locke was hostile to a theory of ideas as objects as such. And when we remember Locke's official definition of idea in the *Essay*, it is difficult indeed to believe that this was the basis of his opposition to Malebranche.

Why, then, is Locke so critical of Malebranche's theory of ideas? The answer is surely that though Malebranche's ideas are objects of the understanding, from Locke's perspective, they are objects of the wrong sort; they are not mind-dependent entities in the way that Locke takes them to be. But to say that Locke sees that Malebranche's ideas are extra-mental entities is not to say that he really understands Malebranche's motivation for putting ideas in God. Locke's critique of Malebranche has won him few admirers, and we shall see that in a number of places Locke reveals not merely hostility to, but misunderstanding of, Malebranche's theory of ideas.

One part of Malebranche's doctrine which gave Locke trouble was the thesis that God is the place of spirits. Predictably perhaps, Locke found this claim unintelligible: 'there is not, I confess, one

---

[5] Locke, *Works*, ix. 218.   [6] Ibid. 232–3.

word that I can understand'.[7] If Malebranche's claim is taken
literally, it is false and indeed absurd; if it is taken metaphorically, it
is meaningless. Leibniz takes Locke to task for his complacent
admission that he does not understand what Malebranche is talking
about; surely, Leibniz remarks, Locke can at least understand that
the following analogy is being drawn:

> Space,   place,   body
>
> God,   place,   spirit[8]

Indeed, given Malebranche's theory of ideas as abstract entities, the
claim can be demystified; God is the locus of ideas or concepts, and
concepts are objects to which minds or spirits are related in thinking
and perceiving. So understood, Malebranche's claim has affinities
with Frege's talk of the 'third realm' and Wittgenstein's talk of
'logical space'; indeed, Wittgenstein resembles Malebranche to the
extent of employing the same spatial metaphor.

Perhaps one of Locke's strangest critical comments was excited
by Malebranche's claim that the ideas of things are unchangeable:

> In his Eclaircissements on the Nature of Ideas . . . he says, that 'he is certain
> that the ideas of things are unchangeable.' This I cannot comprehend, for
> how can I know that the picture of any thing is like that thing, when I never
> see that which it represents? For if these words do not mean that ideas are
> true unchangeable representations of things, I know not to what purpose
> they are.[9]

Locke's response here has been regarded as philosophically important,
at least for the interpretation of his own philosophy; it has been
taken by Woozley as decisive evidence that Locke himself does not
hold a representative theory of perception.[10] Yet in context Locke's
comment makes little sense. For Malebranche's point is surely clear;
ideas are unchangeable inasmuch as they are concepts which have
timeless logical implications. The idea of a triangle is unchangeable
in the sense that it is eternally and necessarily true that (*inter alia*) its
internal angles equal two right angles. Once we are clear that
Malebranche's ideas are concepts, there can be no mystery about his
meaning. It is difficult indeed to see how Locke's criticism is even
relevant. It is true that within Malebranche's philosophy a sense

---

[7] Locke, *Works*, ix. 223.   [8] G vi. 576.

[9] Locke, *Works*, ix. 250.

[10] J. Locke, *An Essay Concerning Human Understanding* (1690), ed. A. D. Woozley
(London, 1964), editor's introd., 26–7.

can be given to the claim that ideas are true unchangeable representations of things. The idea of a circle is a true representation of a circular body in the sense that a circular body, *qua* circular, necessarily has the properties contained in the idea of a circle. We can know this to be true because for a body to be circular just is for it to instantiate the idea of a circle. But this does not of course mean that there is any body which remains unchangeably circular. At the root of Locke's criticism seems to be a serious misunderstanding of Malebranche's theory of ideas.

Perhaps Locke's major failure to come to terms with Malebranche's theory of ideas emerges in his reaction to Malebranche's distinction between ideas and *sentiments*. As we have seen, Locke is aware that he does not understand the distinction; he realizes that it does not coincide with the distinction between the object and act of perception. But Locke adds that if this is not Malebranche's point, then he does not know what it is. A philosopher who introduces a distinction where none has been recognized before must 'show some ground of the distinction',[11] but Locke can find no basis for the idea/*sentiment* distinction which is consistent with Malebranche's text and produces the results that Malebranche wants.

Locke's misunderstanding of Malebranche's distinction between ideas and *sentiments* is at least twofold. In the first place, Locke supposes Malebranche to be saying that it is only in the case of *sentiments* that the mind undergoes any kind of modification; Malebranche's ideas, Locke supposes, are perceived without any kind of corresponding change of mental state. But Locke insists that my mind is surely just as much modified in perceiving a triangle as in sensing a colour:

For the question here is . . . whether the soul be capable of perceiving, or having the idea of figure, without a modification of itself, and not capable of having the idea [*sic*] of colour without a modification of itself. I think now of the figure, colour, and hardness of a diamond that I saw some time since: in this case I desire to be informed how my mind knows that the thinking on, or the idea of the figure, is not a modification of the mind; but the thinking on, or having an idea of the colour or hardness, is a modification of the mind? . . . For when he says seeing a colour, and hearing a sound, is a modification of the mind, what does it signify but the alteration of the mind from not perceiving to perceiving that sound or colour? And so when the mind sees a triangle, which it did not see before, what is this but the

---

[11] Locke, *Works*, ix. 236.

alteration of the mind from not seeing to seeing, whether that figure be seen in God or no? And why is not this alteration of the mind to be called a modification, as well as the other?[12]

This is a misunderstanding, but it is a pardonable misunderstanding; indeed, the same mistake is committed by Leibniz. Malebranche does not mean to deny that my mind undergoes a modification when it perceives an idea, and when he is being careful, he makes this explicit; his point is rather that in the case of *sentiments*, there is nothing—i.e. no object—over and above the modification of the mind.[13] But Locke's other misunderstanding is much more puzzling. Locke is confessedly looking for a ground for Malebranche's distinction between ideas and *sentiments*, but he fails to look in the most obvious place; he does not explicitly connect this distinction with his own distinction between primary and secondary qualities. He sees that, for Malebranche, we perceive figures through ideas and colours through *sentiments*, but he makes nothing of it. This is very surprising, for unlike Berkeley, Locke regarded the primary/secondary quality distinction as a paradigm example of a well-grounded distinction. One would thus naturally expect him to develop the hint that Malebranche provides.

Locke's reticence on this issue is puzzling, but it is possible to see the direction in which his thought was moving. In the first place, we should note that Locke does not draw the primary/secondary quality distinction in the same terms as Malebranche, and for this reason the connection between the two distinctions is not so close for Locke as it is for Malebranche. For Malebranche, secondary qualities are simply sensations (*sentiments*) in the mind, but for Locke they are not mind-dependent in this strong sense at all; they are genuine properties of bodies, albeit relational and dispositional ones. And this fact about the status of secondary qualities for Locke suggests the form that his reply might have taken. Locke could insist that he does indeed recognize a distinction between primary and secondary qualities, but he would also insist that it is basically a distinction between two kinds of physical property; it is not a distinction between two kinds of perception, sensation, or experience. Phenomenologically, Locke might insist, our perceptions of primary and secondary qualities are on a par. In particular, our perceptions of secondary qualities are no less intentional than

---

[12] Ibid. 247.

[13] Cf. C. J. McCracken, *Malebranche and British Philosophy* (Oxford, 1983), 145.

our perceptions of primary qualities; we have sensations of red patches just as surely as we have perceptions of triangular figures. Locke would surely resist Malebranche's attempt to assimilate secondary qualities to pains by giving an adverbial analysis of both.

Locke may be right to insist that our perceptions of primary and secondary qualities are equally intentional. But it is difficult to believe that Locke would really want to hold that there is no experiential difference between primary and secondary qualities, for in that case he would be vulnerable to an obvious objection. For one thing, philosophers beginning with Aristotle have noticed that we can perceive what came to be called primary qualities through more than one sense. Not merely can I see the shape of the glass but I can also feel it with my hands, but if I am blind, I am denied all experience of colours. As Bennett has argued, there is no clear analogy between colour-blindness and size-blindness.[14] We cannot suppose that a person is size-blind without also supposing that he suffers from 'a fantastically complicated distortion of his perceptions as compared with those of other people'.[15]

But the fundamental reason for Locke's failure to come to terms with the idea/*sentiment* distinction seems to lie elsewhere. As we saw in an earlier chapter, in order to make sense of Malebranche's doctrine of vision in God, we need a Cartesian premiss to the effect that there is an irreducible intellectual element in visual perception; as Descartes puts it, bodies are perceived through the intellect, not through the senses. Despite some suggestive remarks about the role of judgement in visual perception, Locke does not hold the Cartesian thesis; he certainly does not agree with Descartes and Malebranche that, strictly speaking, only light and colour are sensed in visual perception. But secondly, even if Locke came so far, he would still be at a loss to understand why, in the case of primary qualities, the immediate objects of perception should be said to be extra-mental entities in God. The answer that must be given on Malebranche's behalf is clear. To say that there is an intellectual element in perception is to say that the mind must be related to concepts, and concepts are irreducibly abstract entities whose locus is God. Locke sees that Malebranche's ideas are extra-mental entities in God, and he is aware that Malebranche is in the Platonic tradition, but it is doubtful if he understood Malebranche's

---

[14] J. Bennett, *Locke, Berkeley, Hume: Central Themes* (Oxford, 1971), 96–100.
[15] J. L. Mackie, *Problems from Locke* (Oxford, 1976), 33.

philosophical motivation for placing ideas in God; he is one of the first to popularize the view that the theory is simply gratuitously visionary and mystical. But without a firm grasp of the basic theory of ideas, it is impossible to understand Malebranche's doctrine of visual perception and the distinction between ideas and *sentiments* which it involves.

Berkeley

In the second of the *Three Dialogues* Philonous indignantly rejects the charge that he advocates Malebranche's doctrine of vision in God:

Few men think, yet all will have opinions. Hence men's opinions are superficial and confused. It is nothing strange that tenets, which in themselves are ever so different, should nonetheless be confounded with each other by those who do not consider them attentively. I shall not therefore be surprised, if some men imagine that I run into the enthusiasm of Malebranche, though in truth I am very remote from it. He builds on the most abstract general ideas, which I entirely disclaim. He asserts an absolute external world, which I deny. He maintains that we are deceived by our senses, and know not the real natures or the true forms and figures of extended beings; of all which I hold the direct contrary. So that upon the whole there are no principles more fundamentally opposite than his and mine.[16]

Berkeley's hostility to Malebranche's doctrine of vision in God may be more surprising that Locke's. For not merely is Berkeley's own metaphysics theocentric, but as is now well known, his philosophical development was powerfully influenced by his exposure to Malebranche. Of course it is possible to argue that Berkeley simply protests too much because the accusation that his philosophy is derivative touches a raw nerve. But we should resist this suggestion if we can; it is best to begin by assuming that Berkeley was justified in disclaiming any real similarity between his idealism and the doctrine of vision in God.

It is true of course that, for Berkeley, ideas are objects of the understanding; indeed, following Malebranche rather than Locke, he tends to speak of ideas as *immediate* objects of the understanding. Berkeley claims no originality here; he is explicit

---

[16] *Three Dialogues between Hylas and Philonous*, 2, in G. Berkeley, *Philosophical Works*, ed. M. R. Ayers (London, 1975), 169–70.

that he is simply employing the term 'idea' as it is 'now commonly used by philosophers'.[17] Clearly, Berkeley needs ideas to be objects if they are to bear the full weight which his idealist metaphysics demands of them. Indeed, in one sense Berkeley may be said to be taking the thesis that ideas are objects more seriously than any of his predecessors. That Berkeley himself sees his strategy in these terms is suggested by Philonous' remark that 'I am not for changing things into ideas, but rather ideas into things'.[18] But in spite of the fact that Berkeley follows Malebranche in taking ideas to be the immediate objects of perception, their theories of ideas are really very different.

One writer who has studied the relationship between the two philosophers on this issue is McCracken. McCracken begins by admitting the considerable differences between the two theories of ideas, but he claims that none the less Malebranche's notion of ideas was instructive to Berkeley. For one thing, Berkeley follows Malebranche's lead in insisting that ideas, as objects, are not modes or modifications of the mind. But McCracken also suggests that Berkeley's ideas have some of the characteristics of Malebranche's *sentiments*; in particular, Berkeley claims in the *Principles* that ideas are 'fleeting'.[19] McCracken concludes that Berkeley's ideas have an anomalous character which may be explained in part by saying that they are a compound of Malebranche's ideas and *sentiments*.

Berkeley's ideas do indeed have a somewhat anomalous character, and Berkeley has to tread carefully in order to accommodate consistently all the things he wants to say of them. On the one hand, ideas for Berkeley are mind-dependent; they are even said to be in the mind as in a substratum. On the other hand, they are not properties or modifications of the mind. Thus in the case of minds or spirits, Berkeley notoriously invokes the notion of substratum which he had dismissed as unintelligible in the case of matter. Berkeley's defence of his consistency here is, of course, that in the case of spirit the metaphor of the substratum is innocuous because it can be unpacked in terms of perception:

And that the objects immediately perceived are ideas, is on all hands agreed. And that sensible qualities are objects immediately perceived, no one can deny. It is therefore evident there can be no substratum of those qualities

---

[17] *Three Dialogues*, 3 (*Philosophical Works*, p. 186).
[18] Ibid. (*Philosophical Works*, p. 193).
[19] *Principles of Human Knowledge*, 1. 89 (*Philosophical Works*, p. 104).

but spirit, in which they exist, not by way of mode or property, but as a thing in that which perceives it.[20]

Thus Berkeley's ideas are certainly very different from Descartes's ideas$_m$ for these are modes of thinking, i.e. modes of the mind; but it is rash to conclude from this that the influence of Malebranche must be at work. In fact, if we are to find a predecessor for Berkeley's theory of ideas in the seventeenth century, we need look no further than Descartes himself, for, as we have seen, Descartes advanced more than one theory of ideas; in important respects, Berkeley's ideas resemble Descartes's ideas$_o$. Here too the fit is not exact, for the paradigm examples of Descartes's ideas$_o$ are intellectual rather than sensory. But at least with regard to their ontological status, Descartes's ideas$_o$ are indeed on the same footing as Berkeley's ideas in that while they are mind-dependent, they are not modifications of the mind. By contrast, Malebranche's ideas are ontologically completely distinct from the mind; their *esse* is not *percipi* or even *posse percipi*.

Did Berkeley in fact understand Malebranche's theory of ideas? In the *Principles* Berkeley admits that the doctrine of vision in God is to him unintelligible, and Philonous' remarks in the *Dialogues* raise doubts as to whether he understood the theory any better than Locke himself. Consider, for instance, Philonous' claim that Malebranche builds upon 'the most abstract general ideas'. In one sense, the characterization is accurate; Malebranche's ideas are, typically at least, universals—especially geometrical universals such as the concept of a triangle. Yet in another way Berkeley's characterization is profoundly misleading. For in Berkeley's terminology, to speak of ideas as abstract might suggest that they are formed as a result of a process of abstraction; it is this sense of 'abstract idea' which underlies Berkeley's polemic against Locke. What Berkeley attacked in Locke was a certain theory of how the mind came to form general ideas, such as the idea of a triangle. But Malebranche's ideas are not in the least like Lockean abstract ideas in this respect, for they are not the products of any mental process. Indeed, as Malebranche insists against Descartes, it makes no sense to suppose that ideas are caused at all.

---

[20] *Three Dialogues*, 3 (*Philosophical Works*, p. 188).

Reid

Locke may have had a 'personal kindness' for Malebranche,[21] and Berkeley was certainly influenced by him, but it is Reid who publicly expresses the most favourable estimate of his philosophy:

Malebranche, with a very penetrating genius, entered into a more minute examination of the powers of the human mind than anyone before him. He had the advantage of the discoveries made by Descartes, whom he followed without slavish attachment.[22]

Indeed, Reid even wrote sympathetically of Malebranche's doctrine of vision in God:

However visionary this system may appear on a superficial view, yet when we consider that he agreed with the whole tribe of philosophers in conceiving ideas to be the immediate objects of perception, and that he found insuperable difficulties, and even absurdities, in every other hypothesis concerning them, it will not appear so wonderful that a man of very great genius should fall into this; and probably it pleased so devout a man the more, that it sets in the most striking light our dependence upon God and his continual presence with us.[23]

Reid's relatively favourable verdict on Malebranche may seem surprising. Reid is famous for his assault on the representative theory of perception, and Malebranche is in a sense the representationalist *par excellence*. Yet in another way Reid's attitude is not so strange. As McCracken observes and as the above quotation bears out, Reid appreciates Malebranche for demonstrating the difficulties attending the thesis that the immediate objects of perception are mental entities.[24] But we can perhaps go further than this. Malebranche took ideas out of the mind in order to put them in God, and though Reid could not of course endorse the doctrine of vision in God, we can see why the doctrine might appear to him to have advantages over other versions of the representative theory of perception. In the first place, Malebranche's ideas are not private to the mind which perceives them; there is a quite literal sense in which you and I can perceive numerically the same idea or immediate object of perception. Secondly, Malebranche's ideas exist before and

---

[21] Locke to Molyneux, 26 Apr. 1695, *Correspondence of John Locke*, ed. E. S. de Beer, v (Oxford, 1979), 353.
[22] T. Reid, *Essays on the Intellectual Powers of Man*, ed. A. D. Woozley (London, 1941), I. 7, p. 87.
[23] Ibid. 89.   [24] McCracken, pp. 292–3.

after the mental acts by which they are apprehended; unlike Berkeley, Malebranche does not have to struggle with the objection that on his theory the objects of perception are 'every moment annihilated and created anew'.[25] In both these ways Malebranche's doctrine of vision in God agrees with Reid's direct realism, and departs from Berkeley's idealism and from versions of the representative theory of perception which treat ideas as mental objects. The extent of the agreement between Malebranche and Reid must not be exaggerated. For Malebranche, the immediate objects of perception are eternal; for Reid, by contrast, they are physical objects in space and time. But the two philosophers can at least agree on the important fact that what we directly perceive is neither fleeting nor private.

Reid, then, may not just have approved of Malebranche for taking the objects of perception out of the mind; he may even have seen some of the advantages of putting them in God. But it is doubtful if Reid fully appreciated what was involved in Malebranche's doctrine of ideas. Certainly, he shows no signs of grasping that Malebranche's ideas are concepts construed as abstract, logical entities. The limitations of Reid's insight into Malebranche's theory may reflect the fact that he is preoccupied with the problem of perception, and he takes it for granted that so is Malebranche. Now, *The Search after Truth* may do much to encourage such an interpretation, but it is unfaithful to Malebranche's mature views. In fact, the doctrine of vision in God, construed narrowly as a theory of visual perception, is only a specific application of a much more general theory. Moreover, even if Reid understood Malebranche's basic theory of ideas, it is doubtful whether he would have understood its relevance for the theory of perception. For like Locke, Reid does not seem to appreciate that Malebranche must be committed to the Cartesian thesis that there is an intellectual element in our perception of bodies. Thus Reid is in no better position than Locke to see how ideas as abstract entities can be brought to bear on vision in God in this narrow sense.

Reid may have denounced the 'way of ideas' tradition, but it was of course Kant who finally laid the whole tradition to rest. Kant argued that the 'way of ideas' was based on a profound error which had ensnared philosophers of seemingly opposite camps;

---

[25] Berkeley, *Principles of Human Knowledge*, 1. 45 (*Philosophical Works*, p. 90).

rationalists and empiricists alike had failed to recognize that understanding and sensibility are separate sources of representation. In Kant's famous words, 'Leibniz *intellectualized* appearances just as Locke *sensualized* all concepts of the understanding.'[26] Yet if Kant hammered away at the distinction between understanding and sensibility, he was, by contrast, not much concerned with the quite different distinction between logic and psychology. Thus Kant is a curiously marginal figure with respect to the debate which has formed the focus of the present study. It was not until the time of Frege and Husserl that the debate returned to the centre of the philosophical stage. By that time, of course, the issues could be discussed without the theological trappings which have so effectively concealed the seventeenth-century debate from the view of contemporary philosophers.

[26] *Critique of Pure Reason*, trans. N. Kemp Smith (London, 1929), A, p. 271, B, p. 327.

Bibliography

Note: works cited in the Abbreviations list are not included.

ADAMS, R. M., 'Where Do our Ideas Come from?', in S. Stich (ed.), *Innate Ideas*, (Berkeley and Los Angeles, 1975), 71–87.

—— 'Phenomenalism and Corporeal Substance in Leibniz', in P. A. French, T. E. Uehling, and H. K. Wettstein (eds.), *Contemporary Perspectives on the History of Philosophy* (Midwest Studies in Philosophy, 8; 1983), 217–57.

ANSCOMBE, G. E. M., 'Times, Beginnings, and Causes', in Kenny (ed.), *Rationalism, Empiricism, and Idealism*, pp. 86–103.

ARNAULD, A., *Des vraies et des fausses idées*, in *Œuvres de Messire Antoine Arnauld*, xxxviii (Paris, 1780; repr. Brussels, 1967).

AYERS, M. R., 'Mechanism, Superaddition and the Proofs of God's Existence in Locke's *Essay*', *Philosophical Review*, 90 (1981), 210–51.

BENNETT, J., *Locke, Berkeley, Hume: Central Themes* (Oxford, 1971).

—— 'Locke, Leibniz, and the Third Realm', unpublished paper read to a conference on Locke and Leibniz, Rice University, Nov. 1982.

—— *A Study of Spinoza's* Ethics (Cambridge, 1984).

BERKELEY, G., *Philosophical Writings*, ed. D. M. Armstrong (New York and London, 1965).

—— *Philosophical Works*, ed. M. R. Ayers (London, 1975).

BRÉHIER, E., 'The Creation of the Eternal Truths in Descartes's System', in Doney (ed.), *Descartes: A Collection of Critical Essays*, pp. 192–208.

BROAD, C. D., *Leibniz: An Introduction* (Cambridge, 1975).

BUTLER, R. J. (ed.), *Cartesian Studies* (New York, 1972).

CHAPPELL, V., 'The Theory of Ideas', in Rorty (ed.), *Essays on Descartes's* Meditations, pp. 177–98.

CHURCH, R. W., *A Study in the Philosophy of Malebranche* (London, 1931).

COOK, M., 'Arnauld's Alleged Representationalism', *Journal of the History of Philosophy*, 12 (1974), 53–62.

COTTINGHAM, J., *Descartes* (Oxford, 1986).

CRAIG, E., *The Mind of God and the Works of Man* (Oxford, 1988).

CRANSTON, M., *John Locke: A Biography* (London, 1957).

CURLEY, E. M., 'Descartes on the Creation of the Eternal Truths', *Philosophical Review*, 93 (1984), 569–97.

DAVIDSON, D., *Essays on Actions and Events* (Oxford, 1980).

DONEY, W. (ed.), *Descartes: A Collection of Critical Essays* (London, 1967).

—— 'Malebranche', in Edwards (ed.), *Encyclopaedia of Philosophy*, v, 140–3.

—— 'Rationalism', in H. Robinson (ed.), *The Rationalist Conception of Consciousness, Southern Journal of Philosophy*, 21, suppl. (1983), 1–14.

EDWARDS, P. (ed.), *The Encyclopedia of Philosophy* (8 vols., New York, 1967).

FOUCHER, S., *Critique* de la recherche de la vérité (Paris, 1675).

FRANKFURT, H., 'Descartes on the Creation of the Eternal Truths', *Philosophical Review*, 86 (1977), 36–57.

GOUHIER, H., *La Philosophie de Malebranche et son expérience religieuse* (Paris, 1948).

GUEROULT, M., *Malebranche* (3 vols., Paris, 1955–9).

HACKING, I., *Why Does Language Matter to Philosophy?* (Cambridge, 1975).

—— 'Leibniz and Descartes: Proof and Eternal Truths', in Kenny (ed.), *Rationalism, Empiricism, and Idealism*, pp. 47–60.

HATFIELD, G., and EPSTEIN, W., 'The Sensory Core and the Medieval Foundations of Early Modern Perceptual Theory', *Isis*, 70 (1979), 363–84.

HOBBES, T., *Leviathan* (1651), ed. C. B. MacPherson (Harmondsworth, 1968).

HUME, D., *A Treatise of Human Nature* (1739–40), ed. L. A. Selby-Bigge (Oxford, 1960).

JOLLEY, N., 'An Unpublished Leibniz MS on Metaphysics', *Studia Leibnitiana*, 7 (1975), 161–89.

—— *Leibniz and Locke: A Study of the* New *Essays on Human Understanding* (Oxford, 1984).

—— 'Leibniz and Malebranche on Innate Ideas', *Philosophical Review*, 97 (1988), 71–91.

KANT, I., *Kritik der reinen Vernunft* (1781), *Critique of Pure Reason*, trans. N. Kemp Smith (London, 1929).

KENNY, A., *Descartes: A Study of his Philosophy* (New York, 1968).

—— (ed.), *Rationalism, Empiricism, and Idealism* (Oxford, 1986).

KULSTAD, M., 'Leibniz's Conception of Expression', *Studia Leibnitiana*, 9 (1977), 55–76.

—— 'Leibniz's Theory of Innate Ideas in the *New Essays*', unpublished paper read to the APA Pacific Division, Long Beach, Mar. 1984.

LOCKE, J., *Works* (10 vols., London, 1823; repr. Scientia Verlag Aalen, 1963).

—— *An Essay concerning Human Understanding* (1690), ed. A. D. Woozley (London, 1964).

—— *Correspondence of John Locke*, ed. E. S. de Beer, vols. iv and v (Oxford, 1979).

LOEB, L. E., *From Descartes to Hume: Continental Metaphysics and the Development of Modern Philosophy* (Ithaca and London, 1981).

LOVEJOY, A. O., ' "Representative Ideas" in Malebranche and Arnauld', *Mind*, 32 (1923), 449–61.

MCCRACKEN, C. J., *Malebranche and British Philosophy* (Oxford, 1983).

MACKIE, J. L., *Problems from Locke* (Oxford, 1976).

MCRAE, R., ' "Idea" as a Philosophical Term in the Seventeenth Century', *Journal of the History of Ideas*, 26 (1965), 175–90.

—— 'Innate Ideas', in R. J. Butler (ed.), *Cartesian Studies* (New York, 1972).

—— *Leibniz: Perception, Apperception, and Thought* (Toronto, 1976).

MATES, B., *The Philosophy of Leibniz: Metaphysics and Language* (Oxford, 1986).

MATTHEWS, E., 'Locke, Malebranche and the Representative Theory', in I. Tipton (ed.), *Locke on Human Understanding* (Oxford, 1977), 55–61.

MELLOR, D. H., 'In Defense of Dispositions', *Philosophical Review*, 83 (1974), 157–81.

NADLER, S., *Arnauld and the Cartesian Philosophy of Ideas*, Princeton, 1989.

RADNER, D., 'Spinoza's Theory of Ideas', *Philosophical Review*, 80 (1971), 338–59.

—— 'Representationalism in Arnauld's Act Theory of Perception', *Journal of the History of Philosophy*, 14 (1976), 96–8.

—— *Malebranche* (Assen, 1978).

RÉE, J., *Descartes* (London, 1974).

REID, T., *Essays on the Intellectual Powers of Man* (1785), ed. A. D. Woozley (London, 1941).

RICHARDSON, R. C., 'The "Scandal" of Cartesian Interactionism', *Mind*, 91 (1982), 20–37.

RORTY, A. (ed.), *Essays on Descartes's Meditations* (Berkeley and Los Angeles, 1986).

RORTY, R., *Philosophy and the Mirror of Nature* (Princeton, 1979).

RUSSELL, B., *A Critical Exposition of the Philosophy of Leibniz*, (2nd edn., London, 1937).

RYLE, G., *The Concept of Mind* (London, 1949).

SPINOZA, B., *Ethica* (1677), *The Ethics and Selected Letters*, trans. S. Shirley, ed. S. Feldman (Indianapolis, 1982).

STICH, S. (ed.), *Innate Ideas* (Berkeley and Los Angeles, 1975).

VENDLER, Z., *The Matter of Minds* (Oxford, 1984).

WARNOCK, G. J., *Berkeley* (Harmondsworth, 1953).

WATSON, R. A., *The Downfall of Cartesianism 1673–1712* (The Hague, 1966).

WILLIAMS, B., *Descartes: The Project of Pure Enquiry* (Hassocks, 1978).

WILSON, M. D., 'Leibniz and Materialism', *Canadian Journal of Philosophy*, 3 (1974), 495–513.

—— *Descartes* (London, 1978).

—— 'Skepticism without Indubitability', *Journal of Philosophy*, 81 (1984), 537–44.

WOOLHOUSE, R. S., 'Leibniz's Reaction to Cartesian Interactionism', *Proceedings of the Aristotelian Society*, 86 (1985–6), 69–82.

YOLTON, J. W., *Perceptual Acquaintance from Descartes to Reid* (Minneapolis, 1984).

Index

Adams, R. M. 40–1, 139
Anscombe, G. E. M. 78
Aquinas, St Thomas 29
Aristotle 28, 48
Arnauld, A. 4–5, 6, 14, 16, 17, 57–9, 86,
   106, 114–15, 119, 124–30, 133,
   134–5, 138, 176–8
Augustine, St 7, 8, 92–8, 144

Bayle, P. 165–6
Bennett, J. 74, 77, 88, 97, 134, 135, 168,
   170, 171, 195
Berkeley, G. 18, 83, 189, 196–8
Broad, C. D. 161–2

causality 40–3, 100–3, 104
   see also occasionalism
causal likeness principle 41–2
Chappell, V. 17, 18–19, 20, 21
circle, Cartesian 62
complete concepts 119, 120
Cottingham, J. 28
Craig, E. 8–9, 149–51

Davidson, D. 78
Descartes, R.
   and image of God doctrine 9, 24–31
   and occasionalism 42
   and wax meditation 89–90
   dualism of 3, 79
   on causality 40–3
   on eternal truths 11, 32, 49–54, 65–7,
      165–7
   on innate ideas 20, 32–54, 68, 70–1, 73
   on intentionality 4, 22–4, 60, 142
   on perception 39–44, 85, 88, 90–2
   on self-knowledge 115–17
   on true and immutable natures 19, 50,
      51, 64
   psychologism of 53, 61, 65–6
   theory of ideas of 6–7, 12–31, 56–7,
      58–60
divine illumination 7, 10, 81–2, 93, 98,
   132, 142–9
   see also vision in God

Epstein, W. 90–1
essences 16–17, 49, 50, 51, 74, 119

eternal truths 11, 32, 49–54, 65–7,
   165–72
   creation of 11, 32, 49–52, 65, 165–6
   innateness of 50–1, 53, 166
expression 5, 24, 136–8, 141, 145–7, 171

Foucher, S. 78, 86
freedom 128–30, 175
Frege, G. 192, 201

Galileo Galilei 9, 151
Gassendi, P. 116
Genesis 8–9, 149, 151
God
   as abstract entity 79, 151
   as cause 38–9, 76, 102, 144–6
   as necessary being 74
   as person 79, 151
   as substance 26, 150
   benevolence of 31, 52, 67–8, 168
   concurrence of 143–5
   idea of 25, 38
   ideas in 13, 55–6, 62–4, 74, 76, 78–80,
      87, 96, 118–19, 120–1, 135, 137–8,
      146, 148, 155–6, 170–1
   immutability of 66–7, 82, 93, 94, 95
   intellect of 27, 169–70
   will of 67, 102, 166, 169–70
Gueroult, M. 75–6, 80, 97

Hatfield, G. 90–1
Hobbes, T. 128–9
Hume, D. 43, 100, 101, 103
Husserl, E. 201
Hyperaspistes 25

ideas
   adventitious 33, 39–41, 42, 44
   as abstract entities 18–19, 63, 74, 79,
      87, 88, 119, 133, 135–6, 189, 192,
      200
   as acts 6, 17, 19
   as dispositions 6, 19–21, 34, 132–9,
      154–5, 182
   as divine archetypes 12, 62–3, 64, 119
   as forms 13, 14, 15, 16–17, 133, 134
   as ideas$_m$ 17, 18, 19, 22, 23, 56, 198
   as ideas$_o$ 17, 18, 19, 21–2, 56, 198

ideas (*cont.*):
  as objects 6, 17, 19, 56, 85, 86, 133–4,
    189, 190, 196–7
  causal properties of 76–8, 111, 148
  clear 118, 126
  eternity of 64, 74, 75, 95, 96
  factitious 33, 42
  formal reality of 13–14
  immutability of 64, 74, 75, 95, 96,
    192–3
  infinity of 75–6
  innate, *see* innate ideas and knowledge
  intellectual 2, 23, 44–9, 184
  necessity of 74, 75
  objective reality of 13–14, 15–16, 17
  sensory 29, 40, 41–2, 43
image of God doctrine 8–9, 24–31,
    149–52
innate ideas and knowledge 10, 20,
    32–54, 67–74, 153–72, 173, 181–8
  as occurrent 47–8
  dispositional account 20, 33–9, 70–2,
    154–63, 164, 171, 182–6
  reflection account 173, 181–6
intentionality 4–5, 22–4, 24, 60, 139–42

John, St 7, 8, 143, 149

Kant, I. 200–1
Kenny, A. 12, 13, 15, 19, 21, 33, 34, 35,
    47–8
knowledge
  actual 48
  a posteriori 120, 178–9, 187
  a priori 119, 120, 121–2, 176–7, 179,
    180–1
  by acquaintance 118
  by description 118
  explicit 48
  implicit 48, 164
  potential 48, 164
  through consciousness 118, 174, 178
  through ideas 118–24, 174

laws
  of communication of movements 101,
    104
  of nature 101–2, 103, 123, 124, 160
  of union of mind and body 104, 107,
    108, 109, 112, 113
Leibniz, G. W.
  and materialism 180, 187
  nominalism of 5, 132, 135–6, 151–2

on complete concepts 119, 120
on divine illumination 10, 142–9
on eternal truths 165–72
on expression 5, 24, 136–8, 141,
    145–7, 171
on innate ideas 32, 153–72, 173, 181–8
on intentionality 5, 139–42
on *petites perceptions* 162, 178
on pre-established harmony 106, 145,
    165
on self-knowledge 172, 174, 158–81,
    186–8
psychologism of 167, 169–72
theory of ideas of 6, 132–9, 154–5
Lennon, T. 89
Locke, J. 1–2, 3, 4, 6, 28, 32, 79, 81, 83,
    84, 86, 87, 128–9, 130, 153, 156–9,
    173, 174–5, 180, 181, 183, 187, 188,
    189, 190–6
Loeb, L. 33, 43, 49–51, 104–6

McCracken, C. J. 119, 121, 122, 130,
    197, 199
McRae, R. 6, 19, 21, 189
Malebranche, N.
  and Augustine 7, 8, 92–8, 144
  and Cartesian theory of mind 2–4, 13,
    24, 80, 115–18, 130–1
  anti-psychologism of 56, 61–2, 64,
    65–6
  anti-scepticism of 61–4
  anti-voluntarism of 65–7
  controversy with Arnauld 4–5, 57–9,
    114–15, 124–30, 133, 134–5
  occasionalism of 3, 42–3, 99–108, 113,
    164–5
  on freedom 128–30, 175
  on immortality 128–30
  on innate ideas 32, 54, 67–74, 159–61,
    162–5
  on intentionality 4, 60, 140
  on *sentiments* 60, 73, 109–10, 140,
    141, 193–4, 195, 197
  on vision in God 55–6, 81–98,
    99–100, 108–13, 142–3, 189, 190,
    196, 199
  representative theory of perception
    of, 85–8, 95–6
  theory of ideas of 4, 6, 55–80, 85–7,
    133–4, 189–91, 199–200
  trialism of 4, 79–80
materialism 180, 187
Mates, B. 5, 135

mind
    as substance 24–5, 182, 184, 186–7
    idea of 118–20, 121–2, 123, 125, 126,
        130, 174–5, 176–7, 178
    immateriality of 130, 174, 175, 180–1
    immortality of 128–30, 174–5
    knowledge of, *see* self-knowledge
    simplicity of 180–1
    union with body 28, 104, 107, 108,
        109, 110, 112
    union with God 100, 108, 109
Molyneux, W. 81

necessary truths 51, 53, 102, 120, 122,
    167–9, 171–2
Newton, Sir I. 160
nominalism 5, 132,135–6, 143, 148,
    151–2

occasionalism 3, 42–3, 84–5, 99–108,
    113, 145, 164–5

Paul, St 8
perception
    Aristotelian theory of 41
    direct vs indirect 85, 86–7, 95–6
    representative theory of 85–8, 95–6,
        199–200
    see also ideas
petites perceptions 162, 178
Plato 50, 111, 133
Platonism 7, 8, 11, 135
pre-established harmony 106, 145, 165
psychologism 56, 61, 64, 65–6, 118–19,
    167, 169–72
psycho-physical laws, *see* laws, of union
    of mind and body

qualities, primary and secondary 46,
    82 5, 92, 94, 194–5

Radner, D. 78, 92
reflection 2, 173, 178–9, 180, 181–8
Reid, T. 87, 190, 199–200
representationalism, *see* perception,
    representative theory of
representation, *see* intentionality
Rorty, R. 2, 4, 22, 23, 60
Russell, B. 118

scepticism 11, 52, 55, 61–4, 67–8
scholasticism 15, 25, 26, 27, 40, 192–3
self-knowledge 10, 114–31, 172–81,
    186–8
sentiments 60, 73, 109–10, 140, 141,
    193–4, 195, 197
soul, *see* mind
Spinoza, B. 5, 75, 77, 102, 107–8, 140–1
substance 25–6, 150, 174, 182, 184, 186,
    187

tabula rasa 28, 182
true and immutable natures 19, 50, 51,
    64

Vendler, Z. 144–5
vision in God 55–6, 81–98, 99–100,
    108–13, 142–3, 146, 189, 190, 196,
    199
    see also divine illumination

wax meditation 89–90
Williams, B. 89–90
Wilson, M. D. 48, 115
Wittgenstein, L. 3, 192
Woolhouse, R. S. 106, 107–8
Woozley, A. D. 192

Yolton, J. W. 189–90